ALSO BY JOSEPH J. ELLIS

JOSEPH J. ELLIS

REVOLUTIONARY SUMMER

Joseph Ellis is the Pulitzer Prize–winning author of *Founding Brothers*. His portrait of Thomas Jefferson, *American Sphinx*, won the National Book Award. He is the Ford Foundation Professor of History Emeritus at Mount Holyoke College. He lives in Amherst, Massachusetts, with his wife and their youngest son.

www.josephellishistorian.com

REVOLUTIONARY SUMMER

REVOLUTIONARY

✦ ✦ ✦ SUMMER ✦ ✦ ✦

The Birth of American
Independence

JOSEPH J. ELLIS

VINTAGE BOOKS
A Division of Random House LLC
New York

FIRST VINTAGE BOOKS EDITION, JUNE 2014

The Library of Congress has cataloged the Knopf edition as follows:
Ellis, Joseph J.
Revolutionary summer : the birth of American independence /
by Joseph J. Ellis.—1st ed.
pages cm
Includes bibliographical references and index.
1. United States—History—Revolution, 1775–1783. I. Title.
E208.E48 2013
973.3—dc23 2012026140

Vintage Trade Paperback ISBN: 978-0-307-94637-9
eBook ISBN: 978-0-385-34962-8

Author photograph © Erik Jacobs
Book design by Cassandra J. Pappas
Maps by Jeffrey L. Ward

Printed in the United States of America

10 9 8 7 6 5 4

In memory of

ASHBEL GREEN

CONTENTS

PREFACE

If you will grant a somewhat expansive definition of summer, then the summer of 1776 was the crescendo moment in American history. During the five months between May and October, a consensus for American independence emerged and was officially declared, the outlines for an American republic were first proposed, the problems that would shape its future were faced and finessed, and the largest armada ever to cross the Atlantic arrived to kill the American rebellion in the cradle, which it then very nearly did.

There are two intertwined strands to this story that are customarily told as stand-alone accounts in their own right. The first is the political tale of how thirteen colonies came together and agreed on the decision to secede from the British Empire. Here the center point is the Continental Congress, and the leading players, at least in my version, are John Adams, John Dickinson, Thomas Jefferson, and Benjamin Franklin.

The second is the military narrative of the battles on Long Island and Manhattan, where the British army and navy delivered a series of devastating defeats to an American army of amateurs, but missed whatever chance existed to end it all. The focal point of this story is the Continental Army, and the major actors are George Washington, Nathanael Greene, and the British brothers Richard and William Howe.

My contention in the pages that follow is that the political and military experiences were two sides of a single story, which are incomprehensible unless told together. They were both happening at the same time, events on one front influenced outcomes on the other, and what most modern scholarship treats separately was experienced by the participants as one.

More specifically, the political consensus that formed around American independence in June and July was driven by a widespread loathing of the looming British invasion at New York. And the commanders of both the British and the American armies made battlefield decisions on multiple occasions based on their perceived political impact on public opinion. The battles on Long Island and Manhattan were political contests for hearts and minds more than military maneuvers for territory.

Knowing the outcome of the American Revolution has also blinded us to the problematic character of this intense moment, when everything was in the balance, history was happening at an accelerating pace, and both sides—especially the Americans—were improvising on the edge of catastrophe. The delegates in the Continental Congress and the officers in the Continental Army were forced to make highly consequential decisions without knowing what the consequences would be. In this compressed moment, they were living, as Adams put it, "in the midst of a Revolution," which almost by definition meant that they were making it up as they went along.

Two articles of faith were also colliding. The first was that the British army and navy were invincible, which turned out to be true. The second was that the cause of American independence, often referred to in semi-sacred incantations as "The Cause," was inevitable, which turned out to be truer. Recovering this supercharged moment as a historian necessarily entails seeing the choices as they were perceived by the participants at the time, on both the American and the British sides. But how we assess those choices is inescapably a function of our privileged perch in the twenty-first century.

For example, the Continental Congress made a deliberate decision to avoid any consideration of the slavery question, even though most delegates were fully aware that it violated the principles they claimed to be fighting for. Adams is most revealing on this score because, more than anyone else, he articulated the need to defer the full promise of the American Revolution in order to assure a robust consensus on the independence question. Whether this was an admirably realistic decision in the Burkean tradition or a moral failure in the "justice delayed is justice denied" mode is a question we cannot avoid asking, knowing as we do how the next century of American history would play out.[1]

To take another example, our recent experiences in Southeast Asia and the Middle East have prepared us to understand the dilemmas confronting armies of occupation in a distant land, facing an indigenous enemy with a revolutionary agenda. The Howe brothers had the misfortune to encounter those conditions for the first time in modern history, so they confidently assumed that their military superiority would prove decisive because they had no reason to believe otherwise. And from a conventional military point of view, at least tactically, their conduct of the New York campaign was a textbook example of a coordinated naval and ground operation. But our perspective as a somewhat chastened imperialistic power changes the core question. It was not "How could the British possibly lose?" but rather "Was there any realistic chance for them to win?"[2]

If such a chance ever did exist, it occurred in the summer of 1776, when the Howe brothers missed several opportunities to destroy the Continental Army on Long Island and Manhattan. Chance, luck, and even the vagaries of the weather played crucial roles, as did the strategic and tactical decisions of the Howes, which came under considerable criticism after the war, when hindsight revealed that their more measured and limited goals were rooted in a fundamental misreading of the challenges they were facing. There was disagreement within the American camp at the time about the fate of the rebellion if the Continental Army ceased to exist. We can never know, because it did not happen, though it was a very close call. Hindsight does allow us to know that once the Howes missed the opportunity to destroy the Continental Army early in the war, it would never come again.

So this is the story of the birth of the American Revolution, the pains and tribulations that accompanied that process, and the large and small decisions in both the political and the military arenas that shaped the outcome. It is told as a story, which means that narrative is presumed to be the highest form of analysis, and recovering the way it looked to the participants must precede any imposition of our superior wisdom in the present.

Before we begin our trek back to the past, two oddly shaped features of the terrain merit mention, chiefly because they do not align themselves with the expectations we carry in our heads and therefore need to be marked on the map beforehand.

The first is a distinctive sense of honor, a lingering vestige of the medieval world that was still alive and pervasive, especially within the military culture of the eighteenth century. The core concept in this quasi-chivalric code was character, the notion that a clearly defined set of principles governed a gentleman's behavior at all times, most especially in highly stressful or life-threatening situations. Men driven by this aristocratic sense of honor would tend to behave in ways we consider strange, like standing at attention in the face of a salvo of gunfire rather than lying down or seeking cover. Generals would discuss strategic and tactical options on the battlefield in similarly peculiar ways, because they regarded retreat as dishonorable and harmful to their reputations. Washington is the most conspicuously honor-driven character in our story, and his conduct throughout the Battle of New York is inexplicable unless viewed from this eighteenth-century perspective.

The second place we need to mark on the map is actually an empty space. Because we know that the American Revolution eventually led to the creation of a consolidated nation-state and subsequent world power, it is nearly irresistible to read these future developments back into the story. But in truth, no shared sense of American nationhood existed in 1776, even though the Continental Congress and the Continental Army can be regarded as embryonic versions of such. All alliances among the colonies, and then the states, were presumed to be provisional and temporary arrangements. Allegiances within the far-flung American population remained local, or at most regional, in scope. To presume otherwise is to impose a level of political coherence on a much messier reality and to underestimate the dilemma that American leaders in the congress and the army were truly facing. They were attempting to orchestrate a collective response to multiple political and military challenges on behalf of an American population that had yet to become the American people. In that sense, the very term *American* Revolution is misleading.

   With these cautionary signs in place, let us return to the late spring of 1776. An undeclared war has been raging for over a year, and a huge British fleet is preparing to sail across the Atlantic to deliver a decisive blow that will crush the American rebellion at its moment of birth. Meanwhile, the Continental Congress has not declared American independence because moderate delegates regard war with Great Britain as suicidal, and it is not clear where the loyalties of most American colonists lie. The proverbial arrow is in the air, and it is clearly going to land at New York, the obvious target for the British invasion. Whether there is a consensus on American independence is much less clear, though John Adams claims to know where history is headed.

REVOLUTIONARY SUMMER

Prudence Dictates

Is it not a saying of Moses, "Who am I, that I should go in and out before this great People?" When I consider the great events which are passed, and those greater which are rapidly advancing, and that I may have been instrumental in touching some Springs, and turning some small Wheels, which have had and will have such Effects, I feel an Awe upon my Mind, which is not easily described.

—JOHN ADAMS TO ABIGAIL ADAMS, May 17, 1776

B y the spring of 1776, British and American troops had been killing each other at a robust rate for a full year. While the engagements at Lexington and Concord had been mere skirmishes, the battle at Bunker Hill had been a bloodbath, especially for the British, who lost more than 1,000 men, nearly half their attack force. The American dead numbered in the hundreds, a figure inflated by the fact that all the wounded left on the field were dispatched with bayonets by British execution squads enraged at the loss of so many of their comrades. Back in London, one retired officer was heard to say that with a few more victories like this, the British Army would be annihilated.

Then, for the next nine months, a congregation of militia

units totaling 20,000 troops under the command of General George Washington bottled up a British garrison of 7,000 troops under General William Howe in a marathon staring match called the Boston Siege. The standoff ended in March 1776, when Washington achieved tactical supremacy by placing artillery on Dorchester Heights, forcing Howe to evacuate the city. Abigail Adams watched the British sail away from nearby Penn's Hill. "You may count upwards of 100 & 70 sail," she reported. "They look like a forrest." By then the motley crew of militia was being referred to as the Continental Army, and Washington had become a bona fide war hero.[1]

In addition to these major engagements, the British navy had made several raids on the coastal towns of New England, and an ill-fated expedition of 1,000 American troops led by Benedict Arnold, after hacking its way through the Maine wilderness in the dead of winter, suffered a crushing defeat in the attempt to capture the British stronghold at Quebec. Though most of the military action was restricted to New England and Canada, no reasonable witness could possibly deny that the war for American independence, not yet called the American Revolution, had begun.

But if you widen the lens to include the Continental Congress in Philadelphia, the picture becomes quite blurry and downright strange. For despite the mounting carnage, the official position of the congress remained abiding loyalty to the British Crown. The delegates did not go so far as to deny that the war was happening, but they did embrace the curious claim that George III did not know about it. Those British soldiers sailing away from Boston were not His Majesty's troops but "ministerial troops," meaning agents of the British ministry acting without the knowledge of the king.[2]

While everyone in the Continental Congress knew this was

a fanciful fabrication, it was an utterly essential fiction that preserved the link between the colonies and the crown and thereby held open the possibility of reconciliation. Thomas Jefferson undoubtedly had these motives in mind when he crafted the following words a few months later: "Prudence, indeed, will dictate that governments long established should not be changed for light and transient causes; and accordingly all experience hath shown, that mankind are more disposed to suffer, while evils are sufferable, than to right themselves by abolishing the forms to which they are accustomed."[3]

One might argue that those wounded American boys who were bayoneted to death on Bunker Hill amounted to something more than light and transient reasons. Washington himself, once he learned of those atrocities, let it be known that he had lost all patience with the moderates in the congress who were—it became one of his favorite phrases—"still feeding themselves on the dainty food of reconciliation." Though he made a point of reminding all his subordinates that the army took its orders from the Continental Congress—civilian control was one of those articles of faith that required no discussion—Washington did not believe he could send brave young men to their deaths for any cause less than American independence. That was what "The Cause" had come to mean for him and for the army. His civilian superiors down in Philadelphia were straggling behind him on the patriotic path, but Washington simply presumed that, sooner or later, they would catch up.[4]

In the meantime, however, during the final months of 1775, the military and political sides of the American Revolution were not aligned. There were, in effect, two embodiments of American resistance to British imperialism, two epicenters representing the American response to Parliament's presumption of sovereignty. The Continental Army, under Washington's command, regarded American independence as a foregone conclusion, indeed the only justification for its existence. The Continental Congress regarded American independence as a last resort, and moderate members under the leadership of John Dickinson from Pennsylvania continued to describe it as a suicidal act to be avoided at almost any cost.

It was clear at the time, and became only clearer in retrospect, that the obvious strategy of the British government should have been to exploit the gap between these two positions by proposing some reconfiguration of the British Empire that gave the American colonists a measure of control over their domestic affairs in return for a renewed expression of American loyalty to the king. Two years later, the British ministry actually proposed just such an arrangement, but by then it was too late. Too many men had died or been maimed for life, too many women had been raped, too many lives had been altered forever. Nothing less than complete American independence would do.

. . .

HOW HAD IT COME to this? A comprehensive historical account would need to spend many pages reviewing the constitutional arguments over the preceding decade that began with the passage of the Stamp Act in 1765. A more succinct distillation of political history would cast the core of the constitutional argument as a conflict over the question of sovereignty. The seminal argument on the British side was most clearly and forcefully made by the great British jurist William Blackstone, who, in his *Commentaries on the Laws of England* (1765), insisted in his most authoritative tone that there must in every state reside "a supreme, irresistible, absolute, uncontrolled authority, in which the *jura summi imperii;* or the rights of sovereignty reside." In the British Empire, that supreme authority was Parliament. Once you accepted this argument, it followed logically and necessarily that Parliament possessed the authority to levy taxes and make laws for the American colonies.[5]

The colonists had resisted that constitutional interpretation, resting their case on the semi-sacred Whig principle that no British citizen could be taxed or required to obey any law that was passed without his consent. And since the American colonists were not represented in Parliament, the statutes passed by that body were not binding on them, who needed to obey only the laws passed by their own colonial legislatures.

By the early 1770s, then, the argument had reached a logical and legal impasse in which two conflicting views of the British Empire were forced to coexist: the resoundingly imperial view, in which sovereignty resided in Parliament; and the American view, in which consent was the ultimate priority and sovereignty resided in multiple locations, the only common American allegiance being to the king. The British model took its inspiration from European empires of the past, chiefly the Roman Empire. The American model had no precedents in the past, but foreshadowed what, a century later, became the British Commonwealth.

In 1774 the British government decided that this impasse was intolerable, and in response to a wanton act of destruction in Boston Harbor called the Tea Party, it decided to impose martial law on Massachusetts. In retrospect, this was the crucial decision, for it transformed a constitutional argument into a military conflict. And it raised to relief the competing visions of a British Empire based on either coercion or consensus.

But at the time—that is, early in 1775—voices on both sides

of the Atlantic urged caution, fully aware that they had more
to lose than to gain by a war and wholly committed to avoid it
at all costs.

On the British side, the arguments to change course came
from two of the most prominent members of Parliament. In
the House of Lords, no less a leader than William Pitt, Earl of
Chatham, the acknowledged architect of the British victory in
the French and Indian War, rose to condemn the decision to
militarize the conflict. He recommended the withdrawal from
Boston of all British troops, who could only serve as incendiar-
ies for a provocative incident that triggered a war. The British government should then negotiate a political settlement in
which "the sacredness of their property remain[s] inviolate and
subject to their own consent." Pitt was arguing that the American colonies were too valuable to lose, and that the British government would be well advised to give them everything they
were asking for.[6]

Edmund Burke rose in the House of Commons to make
many of the same points, though Burke's emphasis was on the
Whig values that the American colonists embraced and on the
more menacingly coercive values that the British ministry was
advocating. As Burke saw it, the Americans had the better part
of the argument, and if a war should ensue, they were likely to
win. So the essence of political wisdom was to avoid such a war
and the painful consequences it would entail.[7]

Pitt and Burke were two of the most eloquent and respected
members of Parliament, and taken together, by early 1775, they
were warning the British ministry that it was headed toward a
war that was unwise, unnecessary, and probably unwinnable.

Voices on the other side of the Atlantic also counseled caution and compromise. Within the Continental Congress, most
of the moderate delegates came from the middle colonies,

chiefly Pennsylvania and New York. For at least two reasons this made excellent sense: first, the full wrath of British policy had been directed at Massachusetts, and while the residents of Philadelphia and New York felt obliged to make common cause with their brethren in Boston, that feeling did not translate into a willingness to be carried over the abyss into some brave new world of American independence; second, the population of the middle colonies was more diverse ethnically, politically, and religiously than New England's, more a demographic stew in which Germans, Scotch-Irish, and French Huguenots coexisted alongside a Quaker elite to create a social chemistry that put a premium on live-and-let-live toleration.[8]

As a result, the political as well as the seasonal climate was milder southwest of the Hudson. If the lingering vestiges of Calvinism gave New Englanders like John Adams a sharp edge, prominent leaders in the middle colonies tended to resemble smooth stones that skipped across the surface of troubled waters. It was no accident that Benjamin Franklin would become the self-invented paragon of benevolent equanimity only after moving from Boston to Philadelphia.

The epitome of this moderate mentality in the Continental Congress was John Dickinson. Physically as well as psychologically, Dickinson was the opposite of Adams: tall and gaunt, with a somewhat ashen complexion and a deliberate demeanor that conveyed the confidence of his social standing in the Quaker elite and his legal training at the Inns of Court in London. His early exposure to the cosmopolitan world of British society had convinced him that the British Empire was a transatlantic family bound together by mutual interests and mutual affections. Unlike Adams, who regarded Parliament's efforts to impose taxes on the colonies as a systematic plot to enslave them, Dickinson believed these impositions were temporary aberrations, merely another family quarrel, waves that would pass under the ship.[9]

During the early years of the imperial crisis, Dickinson was perhaps the most prominent advocate for colonial rights within the empire, chiefly because of a series of pamphlets titled *Letters from a Pennsylvania Farmer* (1768), which argued that Parliament not only lacked the authority to tax the colonists but also could not regulate trade for the purpose of raising revenue. Alongside Adams, he was generally regarded as the most impressive constitutional thinker on the American side, and his selection as a delegate to the Continental Congress in 1774 was a foregone conclusion.

But whereas Adams believed that the denial of Parliament's authority must inevitably lead to American withdrawal from the British Empire, Dickinson clung to the conviction that there must be some middle course that preserved colonial rights but averted American independence, which he regarded as an extremely dangerous course. The British were certainly not going to permit the colonists to go in peace, which meant a war that the Americans could not hope to win:

> We have not yet tasted deeply the bitter Cup called Fortune of War . . . A bloody battle lost . . . Disease breaking out among our troops unaccustomed to the Confinement of Encampment . . . The Danger of Insurrection by Negroes in the Southern Colonies . . . Incidental Proposals to disunite . . . False hopes and selfish Designs may all operate hereafter to our Disadvantage.[10]

This was not an unrealistic vision. (Indeed, everything that Dickinson foresaw came to pass.) There was every reason, then, to find a way out of the impasse short of independence.

And so, while Dickinson was resolute in his support of the beleaguered citizens of Massachusetts, to include the raising of money and men for a Continental Army, his fondest hope was for the appointment of a peace commission that would travel to London and negotiate some kind of sensible compromise.

Though such a commission was never appointed, the outline of a Dickinsonian compromise was reasonably clear. The British ministry would recognize the sovereignty of the colonial legislatures over all questions of taxation and legislation. The colonists would voluntarily consent to Parliament's regulation of trade, not for the purpose of raising a revenue but to ensure a privileged commercial relationship between the colonies and Great Britain. The colonists would also profess their loyalty to the king and their desire to remain within the protective canopy of his paternal affection. It was, in effect, a return to the status quo ante that existed in 1763, before the British ministry had attempted to impose its misguided imperial reforms.[11]

As long as the imperial crisis remained a constitutional conflict, the Dickinsonian compromise provided an eminently viable solution, indeed the obvious answer that British statesmen like Burke and Pitt were prepared to embrace. But once the fighting started in April 1775, and even more so after Bunker Hill, the shift from a constitutional to a military conflict altered the political chemistry forever. Moderates on both sides of the Atlantic were swept to the sidelines, and the obvious compromise became a casualty of war.[12]

Adams found Dickinson's insistence on reconciliation in this new context both misguided and irritating. "A certain great Fortune and peddling Genius whose Fame has been trumpeted so loudly, has given a silly cast to our whole Doings," he scoffed in a private letter to a friend. When the British intercepted the letter and then saw to its publication,

Adams was embarrassed, though he insisted to friends that the controversy only exposed the futility of Dickinson's vanishing hopes. For Dickinson's moderate solution depended entirely on a conciliatory king, and the events of late 1775 and early 1776 had shown conclusively that George III had no interest in playing that role.[13]

. . .

MANY YEARS LATER, when John Adams was asked who deserved the lion's share of the credit for advancing the agenda toward independence in the Continental Congress, most of the questioners assumed that Adams would make a gesture of modesty, then claim the honor for himself. But he relished surprising them by bestowing the prize on George III. He was undoubtedly referring to the royal proclamation issued in August 1775 and the king's address to both houses of Parliament the following October.[14]

Apparently, George III was much shaken by the after-action reports on what was called "the ruinous victory" at Bunker Hill, which convinced him that events in the American colonies had moved past the point where any political settlement short of war was possible. And so he proclaimed the colonists to be in a state of rebellion and no longer under his protection. Then he froze all American assets in Great Britain, closed all British ports to American ships, and urged approval of a massive task force to crush the incipient rebellion with one decisive blow. In addition to 20,000 British regulars, he ordered the recruitment of another 10,000 mercenaries either from Russia or from those German principalities with professional soldiers trained in the highly disciplined tradition of Frederick the Great. When news of this last initiative reached America, Adams could not resist commenting on it with his customary irreverence. "By Intelligence hourly arriving from abroad," he wrote one friend, "we are more and more confirmed that a Kind of Confederation will be formed among the Crowned Skulls, and Numbskulls of Europe, against Human Nature."[15]

By the start of the new year, then, George III had single-handedly undermined the reconciliation agenda of the moderate faction in the congress. For the moderates had invested all their hopes in a wise and loving monarch whose paternal affection for his American subjects would eventually bring the warmongers in the ministry and Parliament to their senses. Now George III had demonstrated that he was perhaps the most ardent advocate for war in the British government. The king had seized the initiative himself, and his advisers promptly lined up behind their sovereign. While the moderates were busy blocking any declaration of American independence from the British Empire, George III had in effect issued his own declaration of independence from them.

The final blow to the prospect of a political accommodation— almost a coup de grâce, given the recent news from London— came in the form of a fifty-page pamphlet by an anonymous author titled *Common Sense,* which appeared in January 1776. Both the style and the substance of *Common Sense* were true to its title, since it was written in an idiom that was both accessible and electric, replicating the vocabulary of conversations by ordinary American in taverns and coffeehouses, where intricate constitutional arguments were replaced with straightforward assertions that "an island cannot rule a continent." *Common Sense* was also a frontal attack on monarchy itself, poking fun at the ludicrous claim that the king spoke directly to God, describing the royal lineage as a criminal lineup of *banditti,* dismissing the notion that George III cared a whit about his American subjects as a fairy tale, or perhaps as a sentimental dream from which all responsible citizens needed to awake. The timing of *Common Sense* was perfect, for it provided a blanket indictment of British royalty in general and George III in particular just as the news of his plan to launch an enormous invasion began circulating in the American press. The pamphlet's style, message, and timing combined to make it a sensation that sold 150,000 copies within three months.[16]

The author, it turned out, was a thirty-nine-year-old Englishman named Thomas Paine, who had taken up residence in Philadelphia only two years earlier. Nothing in Paine's background marked him as a candidate for greatness. He had failed as a shopkeeper, husband, and corset maker in Lewes and London, though he had internalized a keen sense of British injustice based on his experience as a member of London's impoverished working class. As for his dazzling prose style, it was like a beautiful woman's beauty, a God-given gift that was simply there. Since no one had ever heard of Paine, and since John Adams was the most visible and outspoken advocate for American independence, Adams was initially identified as the author of *Common Sense*. "I am innocent of it as a Babe," Adams retorted. "I could not reach the Strength and Brevity of his style. Nor his elegant Simplicity nor his piercing Pathos."[17]

There were some features of *Common Sense* that Adams found troubling, chiefly Paine's prescription of a large, single-house legislature as the proper form of government once the colonies had thrown off British rule. Paine struck Adams as "better at tearing down than building up." But since the colonies were still in the "tearing down" phase of their relationship with George III and the British Empire, *Common Sense* was a highly visible and valuable contribution to "The Cause." In part because of its influence, by the spring of 1776 support for an American declaration of independence had moved from a minority to a majority position in the congress. What remained unclear was the political opinion in the middle colonies, especially in the loyalist and moderate strongholds of New York and Pennsylvania.[18]

. . .

THE MAN WHO, more than anyone else, would shape the answer to that question was John Adams, who had emerged as the leader of the radical faction in the Continental Congress. He did not look the part. By the time he turned forty-one in 1776, he was already losing his teeth and what remained of his hair. At five foot six he was shorter than most males of his time, with a torso that his enemies compared to a cannonball and that eventually led to the label "His Rotundity." As a young man fresh out of Harvard, he began keeping a diary that made frequent references to the "raging bulls" he felt galloping through his soul. These interior surges periodically took the form of dramatic mood swings that declined but never wholly disappeared after his marriage to Abigail Smith in 1764, leaving an impression among friends and foes alike that he was, on occasion, slightly out of control. It was no accident that the beau ideal of his political philosophy was balance, since he projected onto the world the conflicting passions he felt inside himself and regarded government as the balancing mechanism that prevented those factions and furies from spinning out of control.[19]

Adams entered the Continental Congress in 1774 already convinced that Great Britain's imperial agenda left little room for negotiation or accommodation. The passage of the Coercive Acts (1774), which imposed martial law on Massachusetts, had pushed him over the line toward independence, and once beyond that formidable barrier, he never looked back. "I had passed the Rubicon," he recalled. "Swim or sink, live or die, survive or perish with my country was my unalterable determination."[20]

Adams was early to "The Cause" at least in part because he was looking for it. This, after all, was a young man who stood before mirrors practicing Cicero's oration against Catiline, perfecting his body language and facial expressions to achieve the most dramatic effect. The constitutional crisis with Great Britain represented a providential opportunity to lash his enormous ambitions to a cause larger than himself and to a calling that would catapult him beyond the provincial horizons of a Boston lawyer to heights that were truly historic. He had been auditioning for the role of American Cicero in the privacy of his own mind for nearly a decade. Now a handful of incompetents in the British ministry, with an able assist from George III, had handed him a script eventually to be titled "The American Revolution." He was poised to play a starring role.[21]

From the very start, he alienated his moderate colleagues in the Continental Congress by telling them that the centerpiece of their strategy toward Great Britain—reconciliation on the basis of some kind of shared power with Parliament or some benevolent intervention by the king—was an illusion: "I have reasoned, I have ridiculed, I have fretted and declaimed against this fatal Delusion," he lamented. "But a Torrent is not to be impeded by Reasoning, nor a Storm allayed by Ridicule." For the moderates, who in 1774 and 1775 were a substantial majority in the congress, independence meant war with the greatest military power on the planet, which was unthinkable. On the contrary, Adams replied; whatever the consequences might be, independence was inevitable. "We shall be convinced eventually that the cancer is too deeply rooted," he predicted, "and too far spread to be cured by anything short of cutting it out entirely." As he put it to Abigail, "We are waiting for a Messiah . . . who will never come."[22]

Adams acknowledged that he had made himself obnoxious to many of his colleagues, who regarded him as a one-man bonfire of the vanities. This never troubled Adams, who in his more contrarian moods claimed that his unpopularity provided clinching evidence that his position was principled, because it was obvious that he was not courting popular opinion. His alienation, therefore, was a measure of his integrity. Most frustrating to his opponents, events kept aligning themselves in accord with his predictions—this was why he gave George III so much credit as an indispensable ally—thereby reinforcing his claim to know where history was headed.

Ironically, by the early spring of 1776, when events came his way in waves (i.e., George III's rejection of political reconciliation in favor of war, the sensational impact of *Common Sense*), Adams had begun to sound a more cautious note. Despite his bravado in denouncing popularity and his ridicule of moderate delegates as hopelessly naïve, he worried that the accelerating pace of the movement for American independence had gotten too far ahead of popular opinion. Paine's pamphlet had certainly helped "The Cause" on this score, but it was not at all clear that the majority of Americans, especially in the middle colonies, were ready for a break with the crown. The former firebrand became the prudent manager of revolutionary energies, dedicated not to speeding up the political process but to slowing it down. The American colonies were "advancing by slow but sure steps, to that mighty Revolution"—on that crucial point he remained confident—but "forced Attempts to accellerate their Motions would be attended with Discontent and perhaps Convulsions."[23]

Despite his well-earned reputation as a flaming radical, Adams now showed his true colors as that rarest of beasts, a conservative revolutionary. While completely committed to secession from the British Empire, he thought there had to be a conspicuous consensus within the American citizenry for the revolution to succeed. And popular opinion needed to "ripen on the vine" before that consensus became convincingly clear. Moreover, the transition from British colonies to American states must occur seamlessly rather than traumatically. "I have ever Thought it the most difficult and dangerous Part of the Business," he warned, "to contrive some Method for the colonies to glide insensibly from under the old Government, into a peaceable and contented Submission to new ones." He wanted to orchestrate, if you will, an evolutionary revolution, to control the explosion. His voracious reading of history was not much help, since it showed that no one else who had tried to do this had ever succeeded.[24]

. . .

ADAMS SAW HIMSELF as the responsible revolutionary who would defy that historical pattern. In the current context, that meant establishing a new political framework for the American colonies *before* independence was officially declared. Abigail had already anticipated the problem with a series of pointed questions: "If we separate from Great Britain, what code of laws will be established? How shall we be governed so as to retain our liberties? Can any government be free which is not administered by general laws? Who shall frame these laws? Who will give them force and energy?" For unless new political institutions were already in place, Americans ran the risk of escaping the tyranny of the British Empire for a home-grown version of anarchy.[25]

Throughout the spring of 1776, as he allowed the idea of independence to "ripen," Adams focused his fullest energies on devising the framework of an American government after independence. A proper sequence of events that he saw in his mind's eye would ensure a seamless transition from British rule to a stable American republic. "The colonies should all assume the Powers of Government in all its Branches first"; then, after they had revised their own constitutions along republican lines, "they should confederate with each other, and define the Powers of Congress next." Only after each of these steps had been completed should a public declaration of independence be made. Events were about to make a mockery of this orderly scheme, but it accurately reflected Adams's deep desire to control the explosive energies released by the repudiation of British authority. Before they leaped, the colonies needed to know where they would land.[26]

The first task, then, was for each colony to revise its own government in accord with republican principles. Because he was regarded as one of the leading constitutional thinkers in the congress, Adams was asked by delegates from three colonies—North Carolina, Pennsylvania, and New Jersey—to provide his wisdom. Adams drafted three memoranda for that purpose in late March and early April. He then decided to write a fourth draft for publication in order to make his advice available to all the colonies. Titled *Thoughts on Government,* it appeared in the *Pennsylvania Packet* on April 22.[27]

Though Adams later dismissed *Thoughts* as "a mere sketch" that was "done in haste," it represented his attempt to propose a thoroughly republicanized version of the English "mixed Constitution." Each state government should be comprised of three parts, on the English model of executive, bicameral legislature, and judiciary. But instead of a hereditary monarch, it would have an elected governor, and instead of a hereditary House of Lords, it would have an elected upper house or senate—a clear statement that political power flowed upward from its primal source in "the people" rather than downward from the king.

He was especially eager to oppose Thomas Paine's prescription in *Common Sense* for a huge single-house legislature that purportedly embodied the will of "the people" in its purest form. For Adams, "the people" was a more complicated, multivoiced, hydra-headed thing that had to be enclosed within different chambers. He regarded Paine's belief in a harmonious and homogeneous popular collective just as delusional as the belief in a divinely inspired monarch. Lurking within the Adams formulation was an early version of two overlapping principles—checks and balances and separation of powers—that would become core features of the federal Constitution eleven years later.[28]

There were many possible models for a republic, Adams was quick to observe, and the version he proposed in *Thoughts* ought not to be regarded as cast in stone. Different colonies had different histories and different traditions. Each ought to take from *Thoughts* what best fit its own political experience, whenever possible producing a republicanized adaptation of the old constitution in order to minimize the sense of change and maximize continuity.

A formal resolution by the congress to implement the Adams proposal for new state constitutions to replace the colonial constitutions sanctioned under the authority of the British

Crown was approved on May 12. Adams described it as "the most important resolution that was ever taken in America." Three days later he added a preface that, in both form and content, made the resolution a giant step toward independence.[29]

The preface began with a list of grievances against the king, emphasizing his rejection of the colonists' petitions for redress of grievances, then his decision to assemble "the whole force of that kingdom, aided by foreign mercenaries, to be exerted for the destruction of the good People of these Colonies." (This was the first time that an official document of the congress had implicated the king as an accomplice in the conflict.) It then followed that all British laws "and every kind of authority under the said crown should be totally suppressed," and that the people of the United Colonies should fill the void with governments of their own making, "exerted under the authority of the people of the colonies for the preservation of internal peace, virtue and good order; as well as for the defence of their lives, liberties, and properties against the hostile invasions and cruel depredations of their enemies."[30]

Adams immediately sensed that something truly historic had just happened. Two days later, on May 17, he wrote Abigail, brimming over with pride that he had just assured himself a page in the history books:

> Is it not a saying of Moses, "Who am I, that I should go in and out before this great People?" When I consider the great events which are passed, and those greater which are rapidly advancing, and that I may have been instrumental in touching some Springs, and turning some small Wheels, which have had and will have such Effects, I feel an Awe upon my Mind, which is not easily described.[31]

Over the ensuing years, Adams liked to claim that the resolution of May 15 was the *real* declaration of independence, and that Jefferson's more famous declaration six weeks later was a merely ceremonial afterthought. In effect, the lightning had already struck in May, and the July document was only a thunderous epilogue. This argument over authorship, over who deserved the credit for carrying the colonies "across the Rubicon," distorts the complicated context of the political situation that existed in the late spring of 1776. Adams was certainly correct that the resolution of May 15 was a major step toward independence, and the fierce debate in the Continental Congress preceding the vote makes it clear that the delegates understood that, with passage of this resolution, there would be no turning back. Negative votes by the delegates from New York and Pennsylvania also showed that independence remained controversial within the congress.

If only in retrospect, the political crisis had reached the point of no return. For ten years (1765–75) the American colonists had engaged in a constitutional duel over the powers of Parliament, initially rejecting its authority to tax them, eventually opposing its authority to legislate for them at all. The outbreak of hostilities in the spring of 1775 had altered the political chemistry of the constitutional debate, leaving the connection with the king the last remaining link to the British Empire. Now George III's hostile and aggressive actions severed that last link, effectively ending any realistic prospect of a negotiated political settlement. Both the resolution of May and the more famous declaration of July, then, were rhetorical responses to a nonnegotiable political crisis that had already moved from the diplomatic desks of London and Philadelphia to the battlefield, which turned out to be New York. In April, Washington had moved the Continental Army to that location on the presumption, correct as it turned out, that the British invasion would happen there. Military events were dictating political decisions.[32]

That said, the resolution of May 15 was distinctive, and different from Jefferson's later manifesto, in one significant sense. For it was not just a rejection of British authority but also an assertion of the need to create state governments to replace discredited British rule. In that sense, it was an invitation to declare what an independent American republic, or confederation of republics, should look like. Adams was reasonably confident that the former colonies would unite behind the call to independence and draft new state constitutions along the lines he had suggested. Beyond that, however, he was worried that he had lifted the lid of Pandora's box and that the most ardent advocates of independence would attempt to implement a truly revolutionary agenda. He could only hold his breath and wait, but he had reason to fear that the war for independence would actually become the American Revolution.[33]

. . .

THAT FEAR WAS well-founded, indeed rooted in the very logic of the constitutional arguments that Adams and his fellow patriots had been hurling at Parliament for more than a decade. For at its core, the colonists' argument insisted that all political power was arbitrary and illegitimate unless it enjoyed the consent of the governed. And once consent was established as the nonnegotiable essence of any republic worthy of the name, lights began to go on up and down the line, illuminating several dark corners of American society inhabited by groups that could claim, with considerable plausibility, that they were being denied their rights without their consent.

Slavery was the most blatant contradiction of everything the budding American Revolution claimed to stand for. It required herculean feats of denial not to notice that 20 percent of the American population, about 500,000 souls, were African Americans, and that fully 90 percent of them were slaves, the vast majority residing south of the Potomac. Adams received several requests to place this glaring anomaly on the agenda of the Continental Congress from petitioners who claimed that failure to address this issue would expose the entire case against British tyranny as fraudulent and hypocritical.

An anonymous petitioner from Virginia put the problem most succinctly: "Is it not incompatible with the glorious Struggle America is making for her own Liberty, to hold in absolute Slavery a Number of Wretches, who will be urged . . . to become the most inveterate Enemies of their present Masters?" Adams received perhaps the most poignant plea from a barely literate Pennsylvanian who styled himself "Humanity": "What has the negros the afracons don to us that we shud tak them from thar own land and mak them sarve us to the da of thar death . . . ? God forbit that it shud be so anay longer."[34]

An even larger disenfranchised group, the entire female population, could neither vote nor own property if they were married. And the chief petitioner for women's rights was none other than the ever saucy Abigail Adams. On March 31, 1776, in the midst of a newsy letter that touched on several different topics—the effects of the smallpox epidemic in Boston, the crops she intended to plant in their garden—Abigail unburdened herself in what became one of the most famous "by the ways" in American letters:

And, by the way, in the New Code of Laws which I suppose it will be necessary for you to make, I desire you would

Remember the Ladies, and be more generous and favourable to them than your ancestors. . . . Remember all Men would be tyrants if they could. If particular care and attention is not paid to the Ladies we are determined to foment a Rebellion, and will not hold ourselves bound by any Laws in which we have no Voice, or Representation.[35]

This was a petition that Adams could not afford to ignore. He responded in a jocular tone, suggesting that Abigail's proposal was intended as a playful piece of mischief. "We know better than to repeal our Masculine systems," he joked, "which would completely subject Us to the Despotism of the Petticoat." Several volleys went back and forth between Braintree and Philadelphia, in which Abigail acknowledged that she was being playful but was also deadly serious in her insistence that the very arguments her husband was deploying against the arbitrary power of Parliament had profound implications for the status of women in an independent American republic. "But you must remember," she concluded in her final volley, "that arbitrary Power is like most things that are very hard . . . and notwithstanding all your wise laws and maxims, we have in our Power, not only to free ourselves, but to subdue our Masters, and without violence, throw your natural and legal authority at your feet."[36]

Just two weeks before Abigail launched her broadside on behalf of women's rights, an editorial appeared in the *Pennsylvania Evening Post* in which yet another disenfranchised group, the working-class artisans and mechanics of Philadelphia, describing themselves as "men who wear LEATHER APRONS," protested the long-standing property requirement to vote: "Do not mechanics and farmers constitute ninety-nine out of a hundred people of America? If these, by their occupations are to be excluded from having any share in the choice of their rulers or forms of government, would it not be best to acknowledge the jurisdiction of the British Parliament?"[37]

For the past two years, a large number of working-class residents of Philadelphia had become actively involved in the various revolutionary organizations and committees that seized control of the city government. Not so incidentally, the arrival of Thomas Paine gave this group an eloquent new voice, which took as its clarion call the obvious injustice of the property requirement to vote. For them, citizenship was not a privilege to be enjoyed only by those with landed wealth, but a right of every adult male, vested in his person rather than in his property.

In April 1776 Adams received a letter from James Sullivan, a prominent New Hampshire patriot, who was having similar thoughts. Sullivan claimed to be surprised at the conclusion he had reached, but the logic of the American argument against British imperialism carried him to a place that only a few years earlier he would have considered alien territory: "Laws and Government are founded on the Consent of the People. . . . Why a man is supposed to consent to the acts of a Society of which in this respect he is an absolute Excommunicate, none but a lawyer well Labeled in the feudal Sistem can tell."[38]

Already reeling from Abigail's salvo on behalf of women, Adams could only caution Sullivan that his case for broadening the electorate would have catastrophic consequences. "There will be no end to it," Adams warned, "and every Man, who has not a Farthing, will demand an equal Voice with any other in all Acts of State." Sullivan could only reply that, yes, it was a strange new world we were creating, but it followed naturally and inevitably from the republican principles that Americans claimed to stand for.[39]

Hindsight allows us to see that in the space of a very few months, the entire liberal agenda for the next century was inserted into the political conversation. It was, in effect, a preview of coming attractions. But for Adams, the most prominent presence in this superheated moment, the all-important item on the current American agenda, was independence from Great Britain. And if that failed, all the other political goals became meaningless pipe dreams.

Obsessed as he was with controlling the pace of the movement for independence, Adams now feared that the debates about to occur in the separate colonies-cum-states as they drafted new constitutions would get sidetracked by a more far-reaching political agenda that would make consensus on the core question of independence impossible. The chief threat on this score was slavery, since once it entered the discussion, every state south of the Potomac would have second thoughts about independence. Adams believed that the debate about the kind of republic America wished to become must be postponed until *after* the war for independence had succeeded. Raising such controversial issues now was like stopping your racehorse a few yards from the finish line in order to engage in a debate about the size of the winner's purse.

But the very resolution of May 15 that made Adams so proud essentially required each of the thirteen colonies to conduct a debate on independence that could easily fall victim to different notions about the future character of an independent American republic. And there was really nothing that Adams could do about it. For in the end, an aspiring republic had only one way to resolve such weighty questions, and that was to surrender control to the people out there in all those towns, villages, and farms. This was not easy for Adams, who harbored no illusions about the preternatural wisdom of the common man. But he really had no choice. The British government had made a top-down decision in the monarchical way to smash the American rebellion with an overwhelming display of military power, currently poised to cross the Atlantic and deliver the decisive blow. The Continental Congress had made a bottom-up decision in the republican way to conduct an open-ended referendum on American independence and what it meant. It was a much messier way of proceeding, but it was also true to the principles the colonists claimed to stand for.

And so, as summer approached, all the revolutionary ingredients, like pieces of a puzzle, were falling into place. George Washington had just moved the Continental Army down from Boston to New York, where the British task force was expected to strike. The largest fleet ever to cross the Atlantic was assembling in several British ports under the command of Admiral Richard Howe, older brother of William Howe, who himself was coming down from Halifax with the seven regiments that Abigail Adams had watched sail out of Boston Harbor three months earlier. The legislatures of all the colonies were gathering to revise their constitutions and register their opinions on independence.

Only John Adams was not in motion, though his thoughts and emotions were racing inside him as he watched the gathering storm from his post in Philadelphia. On May 14 he was joined by a somewhat obscure delegate from Virginia named Thomas Jefferson, reporting for duty again after tending to his ailing wife at his hilltop estate in the foothills of the Blue Ridge Mountains. Though Jefferson did not know it at the time— nor, for that matter, did anyone else—he was the final piece of the puzzle.

2

Of Arms and Men

I have often thought how much happier I should have been if, instead of accepting a command under such Circumstances, I should have taken my musket upon my Shoulder & entered the Ranks or . . . had retir'd to the back country & lived in a Wig-wam.

—GEORGE WASHINGTON TO JOSEPH REED,

January 14, 1776

Although American independence was still not officially declared by the late spring of 1776, it already had a martyr and a hero. The martyr was Joseph Warren, a local physician who was marked as a rising star in Boston politics and who also just happened to be the doctor for the Adams family. Warren had bravely stood his ground at Bunker Hill until the redcoats overwhelmed his redoubt; he had been shot in the back of the head as he turned to escape, and then his dead body had been bayoneted by several British soldiers caught up in the heat of the battle. The next day, an execution squad that was finishing off the American wounded made a point of desecrating Warren's body, thereby ensuring his martyrdom.[1]

The hero was George Washington, the commander in chief of the haphazard collection of militia units now being referred to as the Continental Army. Over six feet tall and just over two hundred pounds, Washington was a physical specimen produced by some eighteenth-century version of central casting. (There is an ongoing scholarly debate about Washington's height. In his instructions to his tailor, he described himself as six feet tall. Fellow officers in the French and Indian War described him as six foot two. Measurements of his corpse for his coffin list him at six foot three and a half.) Adams had been the one to nominate him as American military commander in June 1775, later explaining that he was the obvious choice, in part because he was a Virginian and Virginia's support for the still-undeclared war was critical, and in part because he was a full head taller than anyone else in the room.[2]

Although the Boston Siege was really less a battle than a prolonged tactical minuet in which the Americans enjoyed a three-to-one superiority in manpower, the fact that the British Army eventually sailed away to fight another day was regarded in the American press as a major victory. And the obvious symbol of this triumph was Washington. Not only did Harvard grant him an honorary degree, but the Massachusetts General Court issued a statement predicting that monuments would be constructed in his name. And the Continental Congress ordered a gold medal cast to commemorate his triumph. John Hancock, the president of the congress, explained what the medal was intended to celebrate: "Those Pages in the Annals of America, will record your Title to a conspicuous Place in the Temple of Fame, which shall inform Posterity that under your Directions, an undisciplined Band of Husband men, in the Course of a few Months, became Soldiers [and then defeated] an Army of Veterans, commanded by the most experienced Generals."[3]

So there it was. The widespread apprehension that the British Army was invincible had just been disproved. Not only was the British fleet sailing away in defeat and disgrace, but the formula for American military success had now been discovered. Rank amateurs who believed in the cause they were fighting for could defeat British veterans who were fighting for pay— that is, if the Americans were commanded by a natural leader who proved himself capable of tapping the bottomless well of patriotism in his citizen-soldiers. Washington was obviously that man, now the one-man embodiment of "The Cause."

As he headed south from Boston with slightly less than 10,000 troops to oppose the presumed British attack at New York, Washington was greeted with parades, multiple toasts to "His Excellency," and the kind of spontaneous public adulation that would become commonplace throughout the rest of his life. If all successful revolutions require heroes, and they do, the American Revolution had discovered its larger-than-life personality around whom to rally.

Washington not only fit the bill physically, he was also almost perfect psychologically, so comfortable with his superiority that he felt no need to explain himself. (As a young man during the French and Indian War, he had been more outspoken, but he learned from experience to allow his sheer presence to speak for itself.) While less confident men blathered on, he remained silent, thereby making himself a vessel into which admirers poured their fondest convictions, becoming a kind of receptacle for diverse aspirations that magically came together in one man. All arguments about what independence stood for ceased in his presence. As the toasts to Washington put it, he "unites all hearts."[4]

Beneath this magisterial veneer, however, Washington himself harbored serious doubts about the assumptions underlying Hancock's uplifting assessment, chiefly his confidence in the military prowess of an army of amateurs. During the Boston

Siege, he had unburdened himself on several occasions on this very point. "To expect then the same Service from Raw, and undisciplined Recruits as from Veteran Soldiers," he warned, "is to expect what never did, and perhaps never will happen." Patriotism was an indispensable ingredient, no question, but it was not an adequate substitute for military discipline and experience. What no one seemed to notice was that the triumph at the Boston Siege had been achieved without a major battle. In that sense, the Continental Army was still untested. And Washington was uncertain that it would perform with equivalent success when confronted by the full power of the British Army in New York. If he had known what the British intended to throw at him there, he would have been more skeptical.[5]

Here, for the first time, an underlying contradiction that in fact was never wholly resolved began to take shape. (In Washington's mind, it was the shape of a satanic specter.) Namely, the very values that the American patriots claimed to be fighting for were incompatible with the disciplined culture required in a professional army. Republics were committed to a core principle of consent, while armies were the institutional embodiments of unthinking obedience and routinized coercion. The very idea of a "standing army" struck most members of the Continental Congress and the state legislatures as a highly dangerous threat to republican principles. And yet, at least as Washington saw it, only a professional army in the British mode could win a war that then permitted those republican principles to endure. At least logically, this dilemma was insoluble, an ends-means problem of the most dramatic kind. Even at the rhetorical level, it was never really resolved so much as obscured beneath the glittering gloss of the Washington mystique. Because he was the universally recognized symbol of all the American cause claimed to stand for, any army that he commanded was, by definition, republican in character. Thomas Jefferson was about to declare some rather significant self-evident truths of his own, but for now, and in fact for the entire war, Washington was the towering self-evident truth on horseback, indispensable because he rendered all argument unnecessary.

．　．　．

WHAT WASHINGTON KNEW, having learned it over and over again during the nine-month-long Boston Siege, was that the Continental Army he was leading down the coast through Rhode Island and Connecticut to New York was neither continental in character nor an army in anything like the professional sense of the term.[6]

On the first score, over 90 percent of his troops were New Englanders. This made perfect sense, given that the initial military actions had all occurred in and around Boston; the militia units that rallied to "The Cause" were overwhelmingly volunteers from Massachusetts, New Hampshire, and Connecticut. Moreover, if patriotism had a temperature, the hottest region in the American colonies was New England, where political indifference in many towns and villages was stigmatized as treasonable behavior. Outright expressions of loyalty to the crown were severely punished with tar and feathers in the town square, mobs that tore down and burned your house, and public notices of your imminent demise. Not for nothing did the British ministry regard New England as the cradle of the rebellion.[7]

But if the army was the clearest expression of American resistance and patriotism, the hegemonic presence of New

Englanders raised serious questions about the level of political commitment in the middle and southern colonies. Washington was acting on the presumption that he was leading a consolidated American effort to withdraw from the British Empire, but no political statement to that effect had yet been sanctioned by the Continental Congress. Despite the confidence that Washington projected as he rode through Providence, New London, and New Haven, it was still unclear whether the colonies south and west of the Hudson would rally to "The Cause" in the manner of the New Englanders.

The army marching behind Washington might charitably have been called a work in progress. It represented the enduring remnant of the militia units that had formed around Boston the preceding summer and then become incorporated into what was now being called the Continental Army. In fact, most of the men with farms and families, the prototypical yeomen farmers, had gone home to till their fields and resume their role as state militia. The troops who stayed represented the bottom rung of the social ladder—former indentured servants; recent Irish immigrants; unemployed artisans, blacksmiths, and carpenters—who stayed because they had nowhere else to go. What Washington called "the soldiery" of the Continental Army was a motley crew of marginal men and misfits, most wearing hunting shirts instead of uniforms, spitting tobacco every ten paces, all defiantly confident that they had just humiliated the flower of the British Army at Boston and would soon do the same at New York. Free-spirited, rough-hewn, and full of youthful vigor, they were not the kind of men you wanted living in your neighborhood.

They had driven Washington to the edge of exasperation for the past nine months, resisting most forms of military discipline, relieving themselves wherever and whenever the spirit moved them, and mocking their junior officers, whom in many cases they had elected and regarded as their representatives rather than their superiors. "I have often thought," Washington confessed to a trusted aide, "how much happier I should have been if, instead of accepting a command under such Circumstances, I should have taken my musket upon my Shoulder & entered the Ranks or . . . had retir'd to the back country & lived in a Wig-wam."[8]

On several occasions, when Washington had recommended an assault on the British defenses in Boston, all the general officers, meeting in councils of war, had convinced him that the troops lacked the discipline and unit cohesion to conduct an offensive operation. They were simply too inexperienced. (The average length of service in the Continental Army was less than six months. In the British Army it was seven years.) Washington eventually, if reluctantly, accepted the limitations imposed by the kind of troops he was commanding and adjusted his tactics accordingly: "Place them behind a Parapet—a Breast Work—Stone Wall . . . and they will give a good Acct. . . . But they will not March boldly up to a work—or stand exposed on a Plain." The paradigm was Bunker Hill. Occupy a strong defensive position, then invite the British to attack, and the men would fight like demons. That was the picture and tactical vision that Washington was carrying in his mind on the road to New York.[9]

.   .   .

THEIR COMPENSATING ASSET, intangible but essential, was that they were all volunteers fighting for a cause they believed in passionately. On several occasions outside Boston, Washington had brandished this asset before them. "Whilst we have men who in every way are superior to mercenary troops," he urged, "why cannot we in appearance also be superior to them, when we fight for Life, Liberty, Property and our Country?" But the question made no sense to the bulk of the troops, who regarded instinctive obedience to orders and ready acceptance of subordination within a military hierarchy as infringements on the very liberty they were fighting for. They saw themselves as invincible, not because they were disciplined soldiers like the redcoats but because they were patriotic, liberty-loving men willing to risk their lives for their convictions.[10]

In that sense they embodied what came to be called "the spirit of '76," also known at the time as *rage militaire.*" This was the heartfelt but romantic notion that the moral supremacy of the American quest for independence was an indefatigable and undefeatable force—picture Joseph Warren going down in glory at Bunker Hill. Neither Washington, who was too much of a realist to embrace this attitude, nor the troops themselves knew it at the time—there was no way they could—but the so-called spirit of '76 was dying even before the year itself ended and, most ironically, even before the Continental Congress got around to making American independence official. What one historian has called "the Norman Rockwell moments of the war" were over. The military struggle was not going to be a short conflict won by a burst of American patriotism that convinced the British that the game was not worth the candle. It was going to be a protracted war in which the capacity to endure would count more than the purity of "The Cause." For that kind of conflict, and Washington knew this, the Continental Army as currently constituted was woefully inadequate, indeed no match for their disciplined British opponents.[11]

For once you got past the patriotic rhetoric and the romantic glorification of amateur status, the simple fact was that the so-called Continental Army was less than a year old. For over a century, the British Army had been building up an institution with rules and procedures that were now established. The Continental Army had to start from scratch, improvising on the run to create a centralized commissary system for providing food, a quartermaster corps to deliver equipment and clothing, and rules for hygiene and medical care, right down to the elemental matters of latrines and waste disposal.

Nor was that all. Questions of pay rates for officers, procedures for courts-martial, and uniform regulations for marching and drill all had to be invented and then standardized. And because enlistments for the vast majority of the troops lasted only a year, the Continental Army would become a permanent turnstile, different soldiers always coming and going, so that by the time they had learned the rudiments of military life, they were replaced by inexperienced recruits. Washington kept pressing his civilian superiors in the congress for mandatory troop allotments from each state and inducements for those willing to serve for three years or, better yet, "for the duration." But the response from the congress was stunned silence, since what Washington was requesting sounded very much like a permanent standing army, the epitome of everything Americans were rebelling against.

Moreover, allegiances were still provincial rather than national, meaning circumscribed by local and at most state loyalties, so all the political incentives favored service in the state militia, and in most states the pay rates were higher as well, making the Continental Army the choice of last resort.

Creating an officers' corps de novo, especially at the senior level, also presented a unique set of problems. In the British

Army, senior officers were the product of privilege and merit. The privilege came from being born into the aristocracy, the merit from undergoing about twenty years of experience as a proven leader on the battlefield. Since America had no such thing as a titled aristocracy and the only military theater in which soldiers could have acquired experience was the French and Indian War, the pool of candidates was quite small, though large enough to include Washington and a few others like Charles Lee, the most experienced and colorful general in the Continental Army. Lee's many eccentricities included an ever-present pack of dogs that accompanied him into battle and the nickname "Boiling Water," given him by the Mohawk tribe for his unpredictable volatility.[12]

But Washington and Lee, in different ways that would eventually collide, were singular figures. More typical, and more illustrative of the leadership problem facing the fledging Continental Army, were two men who, over the long course of the war, turned out to be examples of Washington's excellent eye for talent.

One was Nathanael Greene, a Rhode Island Quaker who was cast out of the Society of Friends because of his support for the war. In 1775 Greene was a private in a Rhode Island militia unit called the Kentish Guards. A year later he was a brigadier general, plucked from the ranks outside Boston on the basis of his conspicuous intelligence and dedication.[13]

The other was Henry Knox, one of the fattest men in the Continental Army at well over three hundred pounds, whose only experience of war had been acquired through books, which he devoured feverishly in his own Boston bookstore. Impressed with Knox's resourcefulness in transporting the British cannons captured at Ticonderoga on forty sleds over the ice and snow, the near-impossible logistical feat that had provided the firepower on Dorchester Heights so crucial in forcing the British withdrawal from Boston, Washington appointed Knox to head the artillery regiment in the Continental Army.[14]

The appointment of Greene and Knox as senior officers is usually cited as an example of Washington's uncanny judgment about latent ability. And this is unquestionably correct, as their performance over the next seven years would confirm. But in the moment, which is to say in the spring of 1776, Greene and Knox represented the unprecedented level of military inexperience leading the Continental Army. In any European context, or from the perspective of the officer class of the British Army, they were preposterously unimaginable. To be sure, America was already renowned as the land of opportunity, where credentials mattered less than demonstrated ability. But Greene and Knox, neither of whom had ever before heard a shot fired in anger, were measures of Washington's desperation and the novice status of the Continental Army. No one wanted to say it outright, but the looming battle in New York represented their opportunity to acquire on-the-job training.

Finally, there was the problematic character of New York itself as the site for a stand. Unquestionably, New York enjoyed enormous strategic significance. As Adams had already apprised Washington, it was "the nexus of the Northern and Southern colonies . . . the key to the whole Continent, as it is a Passage to Canada, to the Great Lakes, and to all the Indian Nations." Sent south to reconnoiter the terrain because of his experienced eye, Charles Lee confirmed Adams's assessment, agreeing that "the consequences of the Enemy's possessing themselves of New York have appeard'd to us so terrible that I have scarce been able to speak." But Lee then went on to conclude that New York was indefensible. "What to do with this city, I own puzzles me," Lee wrote, "it is so encircled with deep navigable water, that whoever commands the sea commands the town."[15]

There was no question as to who commanded the sea. The Royal Navy ruled the waves like no other navy in modern history. And one look at a map confirmed that the city of New York consisted of three islands—Staten Island, Long Island, and Manhattan—and that the shorelines of all were accessible to amphibious landings in multiple locations via Long Island Sound and the Hudson and East rivers. There was no such thing as a Continental navy, only a small flotilla of privateers capable of harassing smaller British vessels off the New England coast. Total naval supremacy gave the British Army floating platforms of artillery at any point of attack and the tactical agility to move troops wherever and whenever they wished. This was not to mention that New York contained the highest percentage of loyalists of any colony in North America.[16]

And so, as the spring flowers bloomed and the grasses greened along the road to New York, the honeymoon phase of the American Revolution was coming to an end. The victorious insurgency was about to become a full-scale war. The multiple toasts to Washington in the towns and villages through which he and the army passed echoed the patriotic chords of a hymn to "The Cause," which was simultaneously glorious and invincible. A more detached assessment would have produced a more ominous tune, with lyrics about a quasi-army of marginal misfits, led by a team of overconfident amateurs, marching to defend a strategically significant city that, truth be known, was indefensible.

· · ·

AS THE MAKESHIFT AMERICAN ARMY trudged south and the Continental Congress waited for popular opinion on independence to congeal, the British war machine was gearing up at lightning speed. In a nearly miraculous burst of logistical energy, Great Britain assembled a fleet of 427 ships equipped with 1,200 cannons to transport 32,000 soldiers and 10,000 sailors across the Atlantic. It was the largest amphibious operation ever attempted by any European power, with an attack force larger than the population of Philadelphia, the biggest city in America. Having concluded that nothing less was at stake than retention of all its American colonies, the top echelon of the government at Whitehall had decided to show the imperious face of the British Empire.[17]

The man most responsible for this logistical legerdemain was Lord George Germain, whose appointment as secretary of state for the American colonies signaled the commitment of the British ministry to an aggressive policy designed to smash the American rebellion with one massive blow. Germain had made his own convictions clear soon after the stunning report of the bloodletting at Bunker Hill reached London. "As there is no common sense in protracting a war of this sort," Lord George wrote, apparently unaware of his echo of Thomas Paine's pamphlet, "I should be for exerting the utmost force of this Kingdom to finish the rebellion in one campaign." The enormous armada assembling at several English ports—nearly half the British fleet—plus the 18,000 mercenaries eventually recruited from several German principalities at considerable cost, all represented Germain's commitment to the projection of Britain's full military might in order to ensure a decisive outcome.[18]

All historical assessments of Germain are clouded by the

vilification that befell him in the wake of the eventual American victory, when he was described as "probably the most incompetent official that ever held an important post at a critical moment." This retrospective description made perfect sense, since the loss of its entire North American empire was beyond much doubt the biggest blunder in the history of British statecraft, and Germain more than anyone else shaped the ill-fated British policy. And once this interpretive angle was established, Germain's belligerent tendencies fell into line as the inevitable excesses of a man whose military reputation had been tarnished by accusations of cowardice and incompetence at the Battle of Minden (1759), which he then spent the rest of his career trying to redeem with conspicuously aggressive policies.[19]

But in this case, hindsight tends to obscure rather than clarify our understanding of a highly dramatic and consequential historical moment. For Germain grasped instinctively the seriousness and depth of the threat represented by the American rebellion. He dismissed as blatant idiocy the condescending confidence of several retired British generals, one of whom claimed that he could march across the American colonies with 5,000 men and subdue the rebellion in a month. Germain knew that he was up against a formidable force that defied conventional measures of military effectiveness, and he worried that in a protracted war, space and time would be on the side of the rebels. The vast size of the American theater, plus the latent energies of a proud people, numerous and armed, would gradually wear down the British resolve unless the rebellion was quashed before these larger forces could be brought to bear.

Moreover, Germain had a military strategy that reflected his keen sense of political urgency. For all the reasons John Adams had listed, New York was the preferred target. But then, once subdued and occupied as the base of operations for the British army and navy, Germain envisioned mounting a campaign up the Hudson corridor that would meet a British army coming down from Canada, thereby sealing New England off from the middle and southern colonies. Once joined, these two British armies would march through western New England toward Boston, destroying the cradle of the American rebellion as they went, while the British navy wreaked havoc on all the coastal cities and towns.

Even in retrospect, it was an extremely sophisticated strategy that might well have worked if it had been implemented early in the war. It showed that Germain recognized from the start the great danger hovering over any military campaign against the Americans: namely, that the British Army—no matter how large and experienced—would dissipate its strength marching hither and yon across the vast American landscape in search of a strategic center of the rebellion that in fact did not exist. (This is eventually what happened.) Germain's plan avoided that ill-fated prospect by insisting on a concentrated display of British military supremacy against a focused objective, an isolated New England, which he identified as the wellspring and soul of the American insurgency.[20]

Finally, Germain handpicked the Howe brothers to lead the British naval and ground forces. Admiral Lord Richard Howe, nicknamed "Black Dick" for his congenital gravity, was at forty-nine near the peak of his powers as the ablest seaman in the greatest navy in the world. Like William, his younger brother, Lord Richard was connected by blood to the royal family, albeit in an awkward fashion: their grandmother had been the favorite mistress of George I. Both had attended Eton, the preferred gateway for the most privileged members of the British aristocracy, and both occupied secure seats in Parliament, where as good Whigs they had originally favored a diplomatic resolution of the Anglo-American conflict, at least in part because of their mutual affection for the citizenry of Massachusetts, who had raised 250 pounds for a monument in honor of their older brother, George Augustus Howe, killed at Ticonderoga in 1758. By 1776, however, both men had concluded that the ongoing war could be ended only by delivering a decisive blow that would bring their American cousins to their senses. Both relished the opportunity to deliver such a blow but relished even more the opportunity to then negotiate a peace that would end this misguided and unfortunate conflict promptly.[21]

General William Howe, the younger but taller brother at forty-five and nearly six feet, had the more glamorous military record. And because his decisions during the battle for New York proved so consequential, his career merits a more extended pause.

Much in the manner of Washington, the foundation of Howe's military education was laid during the French and Indian War. And again like Washington, he had survived several actions without a scratch when all around him went down in heaps of blood and gore. As a young officer, Howe had led the "forlorn hope" assault (i.e., suicide mission) on the Plains of Abraham at Quebec, which proved to be the decisive action in the culminating battle of the war. In the middle years of his career, he developed a reputation for mastery of light infantry tactics that put a premium on speed of maneuver. After his conspicuous display of tactical agility at the Battle of Havana, he was generally regarded as the most brilliant regimental commander in the British Army.

Howe's role at Bunker Hill reinforced his reputation for personal courage but also added a new dimension of fatalism to his military mentality. He had led the first wave, accompanied by his staff and a servant carrying a silver tray with a decanter of wine. Obviously unimpressed with the fighting prowess of the militia, Howe had presumed the assault would be a waltz. But his entire staff, including the servant, was wiped out that day, along with nearly half the attacking force, more than 1,000 men. Howe never fully recovered from the trauma of the experience and internalized both a newfound respect for the fighting spirit of American troops and a nearly obsessive aversion to frontal assaults against entrenched positions.

Something snapped in Howe after Bunker Hill. In one sense, his aristocratic style became even more flamboyant. While holed up in Boston, he spent more time at the card tables and consumed almost obscene amounts of food and drink. He threw caution to the wind and developed an openly scandalous relationship with Elizabeth Loring, the blond and beautiful twenty-four-year-old wife of a Boston loyalist, who acquiesced to the liaison, correctly presuming that Howe would reward him for his broad-mindedness. The Lorings accompanied Howe in the retreat to Halifax, where Mrs. Loring resumed her role as Cleopatra to Howe's Marc Antony. While gaming by day and enjoying the company of Mrs. Loring at night, Howe received word of his appointment as commander of His Majesty's ground forces in North America, as well as Germain's orders to prepare for a campaign against New York.[22]

Howe's response to Germain conveyed a combination of weariness and wariness about his new mission. "The scene here at present wears a lowering aspect," he confided to Germain, "there not being the least prospect of conciliating the continent unless its armies are roughly dealt with, and I confess my apprehension that such an event will readily be brought about." In effect, Howe concurred with Germain's strategic analysis that a decisive blow had to be delivered, and that any effort at reconciliation could only come *after* a military campaign of overwhelming force had shocked the rebels into recognizing the futility of their cause.

While Howe harbored no doubts that a British army of the size Germain proposed could deliver such a blow, he worried that the Americans would refuse to cooperate by attempting to defend New York. "Knowing their advantages in having the whole country, as it were, at their disposal," Howe predicted, "they will not readily be brought into a situation where the King's troops can meet with them on equal terms." The rebel army was likely to withdraw inland, away from the coast, where the British navy gave its army such a tactical and logistical advantage. "Their armies retiring a few miles back from the navigable rivers," Howe concluded, "ours cannot follow them from the difficulties I expect to meet with in procuring land carriage." Howe was already anticipating the kind of problems generals John Burgoyne and Charles Cornwallis would encounter once marooned inland without the protection of the British fleet. But his major point was that he seriously doubted the Americans would be so foolish as to fight a conventional battle against a numerically and professionally superior British force. And the last place they would choose to do so was New York, which he fully expected they would abandon and probably burn to the ground.[23]

. . .

THE CONTINENTAL ARMY, in fact, did not have a comprehensive strategy for the conduct of the war. During the Boston Siege, several of Washington's senior officers, chiefly Charles Lee and Horatio Gates—both not so incidentally veterans of the British Army—had argued for a defensive strategy along just the lines that Howe had anticipated. Gates had even suggested taking the army west of the Alleghenies and daring the British Army to pursue them, while Lee seemed to favor a "war of posts" in which the Continental Army avoided any full-scale engagements except on the most favorable terms. On occasion Lee suggested dividing the army into several smaller units, then conducting quasi-guerrilla operations designed to harass and frustrate the British Army.[24]

But these were merely conversations during councils of war outside Boston. Devising a comprehensive strategy for the conduct of the war required an established government with clearly delineated powers and designated decision makers charged with coordinating the quite monumental civil and military considerations. Both the Continental Congress and the Continental Army were still provisional improvisations, managing the imperial crisis as best they could, one step at a time. Indeed, at the moment, the question of military strategy had to be deferred until the all-important question of independence was resolved. A decisive presence like Lord Germain was unimaginable in an American context, because no political infrastructure or lines of authority had yet been devised, and until independence was decided, it was unclear that any would be needed.

And so, when Washington arrived in New York on April 13, the question of whether New York should be defended had never even been raised. "The designs of the Enemy are too much behind the Curtain for me to form any accurate opinion of their Plan of operations," Washington confided to Hancock, adding that "we are left to wander in the field of conjecture." All such wanderings, however, led to the conclusion that "no place—all of its consequences considered—seemed of more

Importance in execution of their Grand Plan than possessing themselves of Hudson's River."[25]

Since no American version of a "Grand Plan" was in place to guide a decision, Washington was implicitly acknowledging that British strategy would dictate American strategy. In practice, this meant that wherever Howe (or Germain) chose to attack, Washington felt obliged to defend. Everyone on both sides seemed to agree that New York was the obvious target, which was why Washington was setting up his new headquarters in Manhattan by mid-April. The fact that Lee's earlier reconnaissance of the terrain had concluded that New York was inherently indefensible had at least temporarily dropped out of the strategic equation.

It dropped back in over the ensuing month as Washington's own eyes surveyed the same terrain, now dotted with multiple forts, redoubts, trenches, and barricades, all being constructed by a small army of day laborers, soldiers, and slaves according to an engineering scheme Lee had devised to transform a vulnerable archipelago into something resembling an armed camp. Lee's primary purpose had been to restrict British naval mobility at the entrances to the Hudson and East rivers and then to construct a series of defensive positions on Manhattan Island that would permit American troops to inflict heavy casualties on the British, then fall back to the next line. It was not so much a recipe for American victory as an attempt to create a series of Bunker Hills in which the probable British victory would come at a very high cost.[26]

As this grim scenario began to settle in his mind, Washington decided that the best way to bolster his waning confidence was to redouble the forts and entrenchments on Manhattan and Long Island. He enlisted one of his brigadiers who had been born and raised in New York, General William Alexander, to oversee two full regiments, who proceeded to dig and build ten hours a day. (Alexander claimed descent from Scottish royalty, and though the House of Lords rejected his claim, he insisted on being called Lord Stirling, and everyone, including Washington, somewhat strangely complied.) As Long Island loomed larger in Washington's mind as a likely invasion route, he assigned the construction of its defenses to Nathanael Greene, who, true to form, began to turn Brooklyn Heights into a honeycomb of connected forts, redoubts, and trenches, a kind of Bunker Hill on steroids.[27]

But as the weather warmed, it became quite clear that New York resisted all comparisons with Boston. "The Fortifications in and about this City are exceedingly strong, and strengthening everyday," Greene wrote his brother. "But the New England Colonies without the least fortification [are] easier defended than this Colony . . . owing to the different dispositions of the People. Tories here are as plenty as Whigs with you."[28]

Indeed, reports had it that most of the farmers on Long Island were loyalists, or at least British sympathizers, and that they were organizing a militia unit to join the British Army once it arrived in force. The governor of the colony, the mayor of New York City, and the majority of the wealthiest residents were all loyal to the crown and thereby lent considerable credibility to the British claim that any invasion and occupation of New York was less a hostile act than a much-welcomed liberation. And so, while the water-laced geography of New York made it strategically indefensible, probably the worst spot on the Atlantic Coast for the Americans to make a stand, the political architecture of the city and surrounding countryside made it the most hostile environment in all the American colonies to defend, because so many of the residents did not wish to be defended.

As these depressing realizations continued to mount, Washington tried to take solace from all those new forts and artillery emplacements—defense mechanisms against his own growing skepticism as much as against the looming British leviathan. He also issued orders on an almost daily basis designed to project the impression that the Continental Army was a welcomed guest in the city and must conduct itself according to the highest standards of civility and manners. "The General flatters himself," read one typical General Order, "that he shall hear no Complaints from the Citizens, of abuse, or ill treatment, in any respect whatsoever; but that every Officer, and Soldier, of every Rank and Denomination will pride themselves (as Men contending in the glorious Cause of Liberty ought to do) in an orderly, decent, and regular deportment."[29]

The less patriotic and more prosaic reality was that relations between the troops and the residents were tense, often violent and abusive, much in the manner of an unwelcome occupying army. The toxic social chemistry was rendered more poisonous by the presence of the largest brothel in North America, in a neighborhood sardonically named the Holy Ground, populated by a veritable army of prostitutes eager to share their charms and venereal diseases with virile young men lacking families or futures. Most of the prostitutes were tough-minded loyalists, and when two soldiers were murdered and castrated, then stuffed in a barrel, their regiment retaliated the next day by pulling down two houses of ill repute where the suspected killers plied their trade. Washington condemned the regiment's behavior as a conspicuous violation of regulations, ignoring the real source of the problem.[30]

Finally, to make matters worse, the Continental Congress ordered Washington to release six of his regiments to bolster an ill-conceived campaign to capture Quebec, part of a bold initiative that Washington had earlier endorsed to deny Great Britain a safe base from which to spread mischief among the Six Nations, the Native American confederation already leaning toward an alliance with the redcoats. Washington somewhat reluctantly agreed, apprising Hancock that although New York had become "the Grand Magazine of America," at this rate there would be no one left to oppose the imminent British invasion.[31]

Assurances from the congress took the form of guarantees that militia units from New York, Connecticut, New Hampshire, and New Jersey were already placed on alert and poised to move as soon as the British fleet was sighted on the horizon, adding about 15,000 troops to Washington's New York garrison. From a patriotic perspective, this was splendid news, confirmation that America's minutemen were ready to live up to their name. From a more professional perspective, however, this arrangement had an almost comical character, since none of the militia units had been given designated areas of responsibility on either Manhattan or Long Island, had not been integrated into the regimen of the Continental Army, and were presumably expected to make a difference just by showing up.

By late May, Washington had seen enough to recognize the strategic and political precariousness of his position and had begun to adopt a fatalistic posture toward the looming calamity. "We expect a very bloody Summer of it at New York," he wrote his brother, "as it is here I expect the grand efforts of the Enemy will be aim'd; and I am sorry to say that we are not either in Men, or Arms, prepared for it." But for several unspoken reasons—all that work on all those forts, the sense that he had bested Howe before and could do it again, and the near unanimity of his civilian superiors in the congress that New York must not be abandoned—he never gave serious consideration to doing what Howe presumed he would do and abandon New York for more defensible terrain inland. Since all the tangible signs were bad, he took final refuge in the intangible potency of "The Cause" itself: "If our cause is just, as I do most religiously believe it to be, the same Providence which has in so many Instances appeared for us, will still go on to afford its aid." He was counting on a miracle.[32]

·   ·   ·

THE LAST OPPORTUNITY to rethink the New York commitment occurred in late May and early June, when Washington was called to Philadelphia to confer with the delegates of the Continental Congress about overall American strategy. It was the first such session ever, but for several reasons the gravity of the military situation in New York never received the concerted attention it deserved. Washington brought along his wife, Martha, so that she might undergo inoculation, and given the risky character of the procedure, a part of Washington's mind was preoccupied with her recovery. News of the complete debacle suffered by American troops at Quebec also arrived during this time, casting a pall over the deliberations because it was the first unmitigated American defeat in the war and was wholly unexpected, but it was explained away on the grounds—not wholly unfounded—that the American troops were riddled with smallpox. A delegation of Native American chiefs being cultivated as prospective allies added to the confusion by insisting that they would remain in attendance only if assured that they would be provided with sufficient amounts of alcohol during the negotiations.[33]

But the big distraction came in the form of a resolution passed on May 15 by the Virginia legislature that arrived in

Philadelphia just before Washington and his entourage. For obvious reasons, it immediately dominated the agenda of the Continental Congress because it proposed "that these United Colonies are, and of right ought to be, free and independent States." In effect, the summit on military strategy was coinciding with the climactic political moment when the long-delayed discussion on American independence finally came before the congress. Richard Henry Lee of Virginia moved the resolution on June 7, and the congress immediately appointed a five-member committee to draft a document implementing Lee's resolution. The crucial military and political decisions were cresting simultaneously.[34]

Washington kept an elaborate account of all his expenses for the trip to and residence in Philadelphia but made no record of the all-important deliberations about the defense of New York. Part of his own attention was diverted by the looming vote on independence, which he was not sure would carry because of the lingering reluctance of moderate delegates like John Dickinson to face the inevitable. "Members of Congress, in short, the representation of whole Provinces," he wrote his brother, "are still feeding themselves on the dainty food of reconciliation." The recent arrival of news from London that the British ministry was sending peace commissioners to negotiate a political solution to the conflict struck Washington as an obvious ploy designed to enhance the futile hopes of the moderate faction in the congress, a tactic he could only deplore as blatant manipulation.[35]

Though no record of the committee's deliberations was kept, correspondence over the ensuing weeks and subsequent reports of the congress made it clear that the committee made two decisions. First, it created a new Board of War and Ordnance to coordinate all military strategy and to be chaired by

John Adams, making him the de facto secretary of war. Adams accepted the new post reluctantly, echoing Washington's statement, almost exactly a year earlier, that he was unqualified for the job. "It is a great Mortification to me I confess," he confided to Greene, "and I fear it will too often be a Misfortune to our Country, that I am called to the Discharge of a Trust to which I feel myself so unequal, and in the Execution of which I can derive no assistance from my Education or former Course of Life." He began asking friends in Boston to scour the Harvard library for books on how to run an army. An array of amateur soldiers and officers was now to be supervised by a civilian with no military experience whatsoever.[36]

Second, the question of New York's defense received extended attention, but the focus was on the additional resources Washington believed he needed to stop the looming invasion, not on whether New York should be defended at all. The latter, of course, was the most crucial and consequential consideration, the most elemental strategic issue of all, but it was never faced or even raised. Though it is always intellectually awkward to explain a nonevent, in this case the effort seems justified, knowing as we do that the entire cascade of battlefield horrors about to befall Washington and his inexperienced troops followed inevitably from this basic strategic blunder.

Context helps explain what is otherwise bafflingly inexplicable. It helps to recall the relentless outpouring of praise for Washington and his troops in the wake of the British evacuation of Boston. As noted earlier, though there was never a real battle, the British retreat was portrayed as a monumental victory for the Continental Army. Most if not all the delegates in the Continental Congress, Adams included, harbored an inflated opinion of the military prowess of Washington's raw recruits, as well as an ill-informed and wholly unrealistic estimate of the militia as a dependable fighting force. Greene once tried, albeit gently and diplomatically, to disabuse Adams about all this. "You think the present army assisted by the militia is sufficient to oppose the force of Great Britain," he warned. "I can assure you it is necessary to make great allowances in the calculation of our strength . . . or else you'll be greatly deceived." Adams was, in fact, convinced that Washington would repeat in New York the same splendid outcome over Howe's army that he had delivered in Boston.[37]

Washington himself knew better, but he found it impossible to tell his civilian superior that the florid praise they were passing out so freely was misplaced and that the confidence in both him and his army was equally excessive. He appeared to take refuge in the quasi-spiritual power of "The Cause" and in the possibility of multiple repetitions of the Bunker Hill carnage on Long Island and Manhattan. "If our troops will behave well," he confided to Hancock, Howe's troops "will have to wade through much blood & Slaughter before they can carry any part of our Works, If they carry 'em at all. . . . May the sacredness of our cause Inspire our Soldiery with sentiments of Heroism, and lead 'em to the performance of noblest exploits."[38]

It also made a difference that Howe's army was likely to arrive at the same moment that the question of American independence would be decided. How would it look if just as the political climax to years of debate finally occurred, the military embodiment of that glorious cause fled New York for the security of the Connecticut hills and allowed Howe to occupy the city without a fight? The mounting political momentum for independence also buoyed confidence in the military commitment to defend New York. The Americans had profound political reasons to avoid appearing militarily weak and vulnerable at this propitious moment when, at last, independence was about to be declared.

Of course, someone could have asked how it would look if precisely when the celebrations of American independence were ringing in the air, news arrived from New York that the Continental Army had just been annihilated. Even to pose such a question seemed almost unpatriotic in this overheated moment, and no one did.

While in Philadelphia, Washington was promised a major injection of new militia from New Jersey, Delaware, and Maryland, raising his troop strength to slightly over 25,000, more than half of whom were militia. He was authorized to round up and arrest the known loyalists on Long Island, thus ending the pretense that they could not be touched until a formal declaration of independence had been made. He was directed to construct "as many fire rafts, row gallies, armed boats, and floating batteries as may be necessary," a final gesture at impeding British naval access up the Hudson and East rivers.[39]

On the day Washington arrived back in New York, his aides apprised him that many of the incoming militia lacked muskets. The next day, headquarters issued an order that these men be equipped with spears. This was an ominous sign.[40]

3

Dogs That Did Not Bark

We are in the very midst of a Revolution, the most compleat, unexpected, and remarkable of any in the History of Nations.

—JOHN ADAMS TO WILLIAM CUSHING, June 9, 1776

The British invasion was choreographed by Lord Germain and his minions at Whitehall much like a transatlantic race. First off in early June were General William Howe and his 9,000 veterans of the Boston Siege, sailing out of Halifax, Betsy Loring's blond hair blowing in the wind alongside the dapper if paunchy Howe, whose only worry was that Washington would refuse to make a stand in New York. Coming up from the South Carolina coast was a smaller fleet with 2,900 troops under the command of General Henry Clinton, who had just failed to capture Charlestown and was eager to avenge that setback in New York, where he had been born and raised as the son of the royal governor.[1]

Last off the mark was Admiral Richard Howe with by far the largest fleet, more than 150 ships with 20,000 troops and a six-month supply of food and munitions, by itself the largest armada to cross the Atlantic before the American Expeditionary Force in World War I. Lacking any semblance of modern communications technology, Germain had somehow managed to defy the insuperable obstacles of space and distance to coordinate this three-pronged assault so that it converged on Staten Island, if not simultaneously, at least within a matter of weeks. No transatlantic military operation of this scale and scope had ever been tried before, and the deftness with which it was carried off was eloquent testimony to the matchless prowess of the Royal Navy.

. . .

AS BRITISH MILITARY POWER WAS converging, American political power was spreading out. The resolution passed by the Continental Congress on May 15 was a clarion call to force an up-or-down vote in the colonial legislatures on the question of independence. Several colonies insisted that the question be forwarded to local governments at the county or town level, thereby extending the debate beyond the colonial capitals to the countryside. Massachusetts, for example, requested and received fifty-eight responses from towns and counties in late May and June, all answering the question whether "said Inhabitants . . . solemnly engage with their Lives and Fortunes to Support the [Continental] Congress in the Measure."[2]

In British history there had been several occasions when Parliament had issued petitions or declarations designed to limit or terminate monarchical power, most famously during the English Civil War and the Glorious Revolution. So the legal precedent for disposing of kings who had allegedly violated the covenant with their subjects was well established. Indeed, if you were a king and were shown a document that began with the word "Whereas," you should expect a list of grievances to follow and realize that your reign was likely to be of short duration. But there was no precedent for the extensive and far-reaching mandate that the Continental Congress was now requesting, which had the appearance of a full-scale popular referendum, something resembling the approach of an unbridled democracy.[3]

The British ministry and the Continental Congress were, in fact, looking at the crisis from different ends of the same telescope in ways that accurately reflected their contrasting political assumptions. The British approach was decisively imperial, top down from George III, through Lord Germain, to all those converging ships and men. The American approach was decidedly republican, bottom up, dependent upon broad-based popular consent from that enigmatic entity called "the people." To repeat, nothing so sweepingly democratic had ever been attempted before, for the quite sound reason that a poll of the people was almost assured to produce a muffled or divided response or, worse, a chaotic cacophony.

What seems most historically significant, at least in retrospect, is how true each side was to the core values it claimed to be fighting for. It was the coercive power of an empire against the consensual potency of a fledgling republic. History seldom provides pure embodiments of such contrasting political alternatives, but in the summer of 1776 they were both on display, and the military projections of both perspectives were committed to a collision at the mouth of the Hudson.

. . .

IF THE CONTINENTAL CONGRESS WAS asking for a referendum on American independence, and it was, the answer came back in the form of a landslide. Massachusetts lived up to its reputation as the cradle of the rebellion by delivering a nearly unanimous verdict. The town of Ashby put it most suc-

cinctly: "That should the honorable Congress, for the safety of
the Colonies, declare them independent of *Great Britain,* the
inhabitants of *Ashby* will solemnly engage with their lives and
fortunes to support them in the measure."[4]

Massachusetts had experienced the brunt of British military harassment over the past year and had also enjoyed the
most long-standing tradition of robust participation at the
town level, so it was not surprising that the turnout in the Bay
Colony proved so huge and the verdict so resounding. Nevertheless, there is something almost elegiac about the picture of
ordinary farmers, most accustomed to meeting for discussions
about local property lines or regulations against roaming cows
or pigs, gathering in the meetinghouse to debate the fate of
America's role in the British Empire.[5]

The residents of Topsfield, for example, observed that it
was "the greatest and most important question that ever came
before this town." They went on to explain that only a few
years earlier "such a question would have put us into surprise,
and we apprehend, would have been treated with the utmost
contempt." But now the political landscape had changed dramatically: "She who was without any just cause, or injury
done by these Colonies, has become their greatest Enemy. The
unprovoked injuries these Colonies have received; the unjusti-
fiable claims that have been made on the Colonies by the Court
of *Great Britain,* to force us, and take away our substance from
us, without our consent . . . have been cruel and unjust to the
highest degree."[6]

Topsfield, in fact, was in tune with multiple resolutions
throughout the colonies in describing their embrace of independence as a recent and reluctant development forced upon
them by the policies of George III and his ministers over the
past year. "The time was, sir," said the good people of Mal-

den, Massachusetts, "when we loved the King and the people of *Great Britain* with an affection truly filial . . . but our sentiments are now altered forever." Boston, predictably, weighed in with the most defiant response, describing any thought of reconciliation "to be as dangerous as it is absurd," and "loyalty to the worst of tyrants as treason to our country." Elaborate constitutional arguments were laid aside in favor of more elemental pronouncements of lost affection for a father figure who was sending the flower of the British army and navy, along with a hired team of Germanic mercenaries, to murder them in cold blood.[7]

This response validated the Adams strategy of delay while the fruits of independence ripened on the imperial vine. It was the accumulation of evidence about the belligerent intentions of George III and the British ministry that wore down old allegiances and made the decisive difference among ordinary Americans. The recruitment of foreign mercenaries was frequently mentioned as the ultimate stab in the back. Reading the resolutions that poured into the colonial legislatures and then the Continental Congress was like harvesting a political crop that had been planted and nourished by the king himself. A year earlier, independence had seemed some combination of impossible and improbable. Now it seemed inevitable.

The returns from Virginia were just as resolute as those from New England, though the voices beyond Williamsburg came from counties rather than towns because of the different demographics. The Virginia Convention, in fact, was the first off the mark, delivering its decisive commitment to independence even before receiving the request to do so by the Continental Congress. Again, like most of their fellow colonists, the Virginians cataloged the list of oppressive policies imposed by George III and his ministers in recent months, culminating in the dispatch of "Fleets and Armies . . . and the aid of foreign troops engaged to assist these destructive purposes."

Virginia cited one grievance unique to its situation, which somewhat awkwardly raised the forbidden subject of slavery: "The King's representative in this colony [Lord Dunmore] hath not only withheld all the powers of Government for operating for our safety, but having returned on board an armed ship, is carrying on a piratical and savage war against us, tempting our slaves by every artifice to resort to him, and training and employing them against their masters." Dunmore had in fact issued a blanket offer of emancipation to all Virginia slaves who joined him, simultaneously igniting a primal fear of slave insurrection harbored by the planter class, while also exposing the moral contradiction south of the Potomac of slave owners wrapping themselves in the rhetoric of liberty.[8]

The resolutions from the Virginia Convention and the instructions from four Virginia counties were all pro-independence and anti-reconciliation, like those of their compatriots in New England, but they were also more philosophical and expansive, like written speeches rather than legal briefs. Their tone made it clear that Virginia regarded itself as the most important player in this political crisis, and the Virginians sent their resolutions to all the other colonies on the assumption that they set the standard for others to imitate. Given the primacy of Massachusetts in the struggle to date, this was a rather presumptive posture, but it came to the Virginians naturally.[9]

Thus far the referendum on independence had been remarkably harmonious, but the first dissonant sounds were sure to come from the middle colonies, most especially Pennsylvania and New York. Both colonies contained a significant number

of loyalists and an even larger number of reluctant revolutionaries still grasping at the possibility of a last-minute political
reconciliation. The legislatures in both colonies had instructed
their delegates to the Continental Congress, as Pennsylvania
put it, "to dissent from any notion leading to separation from
the Mother Country." And John Dickinson had used these instructions to block all of Adams's efforts in the congress to create a united front for independence throughout the spring of
1776. What was not clear as summer—and the massive British
fleet—approached was whether political opinion in Pennsylvania and New York had changed in response to the escalating
military crisis.

The initial reactions of the Pennsylvania and New York legislatures suggested that it had not. In Pennsylvania, the Quaker
elite remained resolutely committed to a political solution at
all costs. And in New York, many of the wealthiest merchants
remained outspokenly loyal to the crown. Despite the looming
menace of the British invasion, both legislatures refused to alter
instructions to their delegates to the Continental Congress.[10]

What then happened in both colonies exposed the latent
political power of the bottom-up approach. In Pennsylvania,
the radical mechanics of Philadelphia, Thomas Paine's most
ardent constituency, soon supported by petitions from four
surrounding counties, challenged the authority of the current
legislature to speak for the people. In effect, they argued that
the elected representatives had forfeited their right to govern
by ignoring the seismic shift in popular opinion on the independence question over recent months. And, in a dazzling display of political agility, these mechanics, artisans, and ordinary
farmers mobilized enough supporters to create a provisional
government dominated by pro-independence representatives.

(Their key reform was to expand the electorate by limiting the property qualification to vote, thereby ensuring a comfortable majority in the constitutional convention and the new legislature.) One of their first acts was to register their "willingness to concur in a vote of the [Continental] Congress declaring the United Colonies free and independent States."[11]

Something similar, though not quite as dramatically decisive, happened in New York. In New York City as in Philadelphia, organized associations of mechanics, again with the support of petitioners from surrounding counties, mounted a campaign to challenge the legitimacy of the elected government. In New York, however, opponents of independence were sufficiently powerful to block the calling of a constitutional convention on the grounds that the petitioners themselves were an extralegal body "without any authority whatsoever in the public transactions of the present times." Though it was clear by mid-June that the provincial legislature was fighting a losing battle against a surging popular movement outside New York City, it resisted the inevitable until July 9, endorsing independence a full week after the Continental Congress made the dramatic move and even then lamenting "the cruel necessity which had rendered that measure unavoidable." By then "cruel necessity" referred to the veritable forest of British masts bobbing up and down in Long Island Sound.[12]

And so, even in colonies where resistance to independence enjoyed considerable support, pro-independence forces captured the elected governments on the basis of superior organizational skills and greater political energy. If the spears being handed out to militia units on Long Island were an ominous sign for the military prospects of the Continental Army, the speed with which the supporters of independence seized control of the political agenda in Pennsylvania and New York was an ominous sign for the prospects of Great Britain's imperial agenda.

As it turned out, all the new state governments in the former United Colonies eventually came under the control of dedicated patriots fully committed to American independence. This was not an accurate reflection of popular opinion as a whole, which was more divided, with perhaps a significant minority south of the Hudson wishing the crisis would somehow end, the armies disappear, so they could get on with their splendidly ordinary lives. But at the moment, political control rested with the more actively involved local leaders and citizens. And if their words are to be believed, their conversion and subsequent commitment to "The Cause" was a choice literally forced on them by the nonnegotiable policies of George III and that approaching flotilla of redcoats and foreign mercenaries.

. . .

JOHN ADAMS COULD NOT have imagined a better outcome. As the resolutions and petitions rolled into the Continental Congress in late May and June, they amounted to close to a unanimous consensus on independence. But as in the Sherlock Holmes short story, the dog that did not bark pleased him almost as much. Which is to say that all responses from the states stayed on point, meaning they focused on the core question of independence and did not append a complicating catalog of demands about ending slavery, granting women their rights, or removing property qualifications to vote. The prevailing attitude seemed to be that independence was the all-important immediate question and that collateral concerns about the shape of the American republic should be postponed for another day. As the citizens of Topsfield so nicely put it: "As innovations are always dangerous, we heartily wish that the ancient rules in the [Massachusetts] Charter might be strictly adhered to until the whole of the People of this Colony have liberty to express their sentiments in respect to that affair as fully as they have in the case of independence."[13]

The only exception seemed to be the Philadelphia mechanics, who were busy writing a Pennsylvania constitution that called for the expansion of the franchise to include artisans and mechanics like themselves. But instead of clouding or complicating the independence question—the great Adams fear—adding propertyless men to the rolls of the citizenry only enlarged the pool of patriots. Indeed, without them Pennsylvania might well have remained a huge obstacle in the road to independence. Adams was so thrilled to get Pennsylvania into the fold that he temporarily abandoned his long-standing belief in the property qualification to vote: "The Province of Pennsylvania . . . will soon become an important Branch of the Confederation," he wrote a friend in New York. "The large Body of the People will be possessed of more power and Importance, and a proud Junto of less. And yet Justice will I hope be done to all."[14]

For nearly a year, Adams had imagined the arrival of this climactic moment, and in his mind's eye he had pictured the proper sequence of events that would permit its orderly management. First, state constitutions, then a confederation of the states, then an alliance with France; then, and only then, once all these pieces were in place, independence would be declared. But now events were making a mockery of this orderly sequence. Up and down the Atlantic coast, new state constitutions were being debated, delegates to the Continental Congress were shuffling in and out of Philadelphia with new instructions from their state governments, and the British fleet was expected to arrive at New York at any moment. As Adams explained to Patrick Henry, he now realized that his hopes of managing a political explosion had always been a pipe dream. "It is now pretty clear," he wrote on June 3, "that all these Measures will follow one another in rapid succession, and it may not perhaps be of much Importance which is done first."[15]

It was also "pretty clear" that when history was happening at such breakneck speed, any effort at management was an illusion. Adams did not like that realization—it defied all his conservative instincts—but he had no choice but to accept it. And if he could not control events, he could at least record them for posterity—perhaps the ultimate form of control. "In all the Correspondencies that I have maintained," he wrote to Abigail, "I have never kept a single Copy. . . . I have now purchased a Folio Book, in the first Page of which . . . I am writing this Letter, and intend to write [i.e., copy] all my Letters to you from this time forward." He urged Abigail to do the same thing, "for I really think that your Letters are much better worth preserving than mine."[16]

He had a keen sense of being present at the creation. As he explained to an old Boston colleague: "Objects of the most Stupendous Magnitude, Measures in which the Lives and Liberties of Millions, born and unborn are most essentially interested and now before Us. We are in the very midst of a Revolution, the most compleat, unexpected, and remarkable of any in the History of Nations."[17]

In the crowded character of the moment, Adams could be excused for an overexcited assessment. But, in fact, he was not exaggerating. No republic—or confederation of republics—on this scale and magnitude had ever been attempted. Adams truly was living "in the very midst of a Revolution," and in June 1776 he also felt as if he were standing in the center of a windstorm as the currents of history swept past him.

As Adams's correspondence during those hectic weeks reveals, his mind was mostly occupied with his duties as chair of the Board of War and Ordnance. These involved several postmortems on what had gone wrong at the Battle of Quebec, questions about where to acquire sufficient supplies of sulfur and saltpeter for gunpowder, proposals for the creation of an infant American navy, and worries about the neglected defenses around Boston. Strangely, Adams paid almost no attention to the military buildup in New York, perhaps believing that the conference with Washington had settled all outstanding problems so that there was nothing to do now but trust in Washington's leadership and wait for Howe's fleet to arrive. At least part of his mind was on Abigail and their four children, who were living outside Boston amid a raging smallpox epidemic. On the political front, his chief focus was on sketching the outline for a new American foreign policy, with an eye toward attracting France as an invaluable European ally.[18]

He made no mention of his appointment to a five-person committee charged with drafting a document announcing American independence to the world. Such a committee seemed like a sensible idea because of the calendar of the congress. The vote on the Virginia Resolution, officially proposed by Richard Henry Lee on June 7, had been delayed until July 1, in deference to several delegations that were obliged to confer with their state legislatures before any binding vote on independence could be cast. If and when the Virginia Resolution passed, a document should be ready so that the congress could proceed without pause to publish the decision. Adams convened the committee to draft that document on June 11.

The other members were Benjamin Franklin, Thomas Jefferson, Robert Livingston, and Roger Sherman. None of them regarded the assignment as particularly important. Depending on where you stood, the chief business was going on back in the state conventions, in the still-divided Pennsylvania and New York delegations at Philadelphia, and on the shorelines of Long Island and Manhattan.[19]

The obvious choice to draft the document was Benjamin Franklin, who was generally regarded as the most accomplished prose stylist in America. But Franklin refused, first taking refuge in a painful case of gout, then claiming that, on the basis of several bitter experiences, he had vowed never to write anything that would then be edited by a committee. Adams also declined the honor, explaining that his prominence as a leader of the radical faction in the congress would subject the document to greater scrutiny. He was overwhelmed as well by his more pressing duties as head of the Board of War and Ordnance. Jefferson was the next choice, in part because he was a Virginian and the resolution was coming from Virginia, in part because he was more innocuous than Adams. It would turn out to be one of the most consequential accidents in American history.[20]

· · ·

JEFFERSON HAD RETURNED to his post at Philadelphia on May 14 after a five-month absence back at Monticello, his mansion-in-the-making just outside Charlottesville. His wife of four years was having a difficult pregnancy, his mother had died suddenly in March, and Jefferson himself was suffering from migraine headaches, the first occurrence of what proved to be a chronic condition. As soon as he arrived, he wanted to leave, believing that the main business was occurring in Williamsburg, where the Virginia Convention was drafting a new state constitution. "It is a work of the most interesting nature and such as every individual would wish to have his voice in," he explained to a Virginia friend. "In truth, it is the whole object of the present controversy." When Jefferson talked about "my country," he was referring to Virginia, and he harbored a Virginia-writ-large view of America in which the momentous events now cresting in Philadelphia were a mere sideshow. Based on his correspondence of May and June, it appears the imminent battle at New York never even crossed his mind.[21]

Almost exactly a year earlier, he had made what might be called a provincial version of the grand entrance, arriving in Philadelphia aboard an ornate carriage called a phaeton, drawn by four horses and accompanied by three slaves. Within the carefully calibrated hierarchy of the planter class in Virginia, he did not make the top tier, in part because of his age—he was only thirty-two—and in part because he was a notoriously poor public speaker. At slightly over six foot two, with reddish blond hair and an erect posture described as "straight as a gun barrell," he possessed the physical attributes of a Virginia grandee, but he had a weak and "reedy" voice that did not project in large spaces. He was also by disposition self-contained, some combination of aloof and shy, customarily standing silently in groups, with his arms folded tightly around his chest as if to ward off intruders.[22]

He had made his political reputation with his pen, chiefly with a pamphlet titled *A Summary View of the Rights of British America* (1774), in which he was one of the first to argue that Parliament lacked the authority not just to tax the American colonies but to legislate for them at all. (In hindsight, *Summary*

View also contained some sharp criticisms of George III, an early rehearsal for the more expansive indictment in the Declaration of Independence.) Adams had immediately recognized the young Virginian as a kindred spirit within the radical faction of the Continental Congress, silent but staunch in committees, and a "penman" who could be called upon to draft reports. The leadership in the congress selected him to draft an address to George III titled *Declaration of the Causes and Necessity for Taking Up Arms* (1775), an important assignment that reflected Jefferson's reputation as a literary craftsman who could make his greatest contribution behind the scenes.[23]

Jefferson's selection to draft what would become the most famous and revered document in American history was, then, part of a prevailing pattern. He had become the unofficial draftsman of the Continental Congress. But it is important to recognize that the golden haze that eventually enveloped the Declaration had not yet formed. Its subsequent significance was lost on all the participants, including Jefferson himself. All assumed that more important business was going on elsewhere, either in other committees meeting in Philadelphia or, in Jefferson's case, down in Williamsburg. What became the great creative moment was perceived by all concerned as a minor administrative chore.

Most probably, which is to say that historians are not sure, the full committee met at Franklin's lodgings on or shortly after June 11 to discuss the content and shape of the document. After reaching agreement on its general framework, they handed the task of composition to Jefferson. Much later, when the historic significance of the Declaration had become clear, he claimed that he had "turned to neither book nor pamphlet while writing," nor had he "copied from any particular or previous writing." While literally true, the remark was misleading and fed the emerging mythology of a solitary Jefferson, communing with the gods in some quasi-religious séance.[24]

In fact, he had before him, or at least in his mind's eye, his recent draft of a new constitution for Virginia, which contained a long list of grievances against George III. His draft of the Declaration represented an expansion of that list, following a well-established formula enshrined in English history whenever a king needed to be restrained or deposed. Upon reading the published version of the Declaration, Edmund Pendleton, who was chairing the Virginia Convention, apprised Jefferson that the bill of indictment against George III in the draft constitution he had sent to Williamsburg had apparently "exhausted the Subject of Complaint against Geo. 3d. and [I] was at a loss to discover what the Congress could do . . . without copying, but find that you have acquitted yourselves very well on that score." Jefferson had, in truth, been practicing the long grievances section of the Declaration ever since *Summary View,* had refined the draft in his version of Virginia's constitution, and had then made his final revision for the Continental Congress. In that sense, he was the most experienced prosecutor the congress could have appointed to make the case against George III.[25]

Jefferson completed his draft of the Declaration sometime during the third week of June. (Adams later remembered, perhaps exaggerating, that it took him only "a day or two.") He showed that draft to Adams and Franklin, two of the most prominent leaders in the congress, whose judgment he respected. They suggested only one change. Instead of "We hold these truths to be sacred and undeniable," they made the truths "self-evident," an alteration that Jefferson apparently accepted as an improvement.[26]

Then the committee placed the document before the full

congress on June 28. (The famous painting by John Trumbull that hangs in the Capitol Rotunda, titled *The Declaration of Independence,* depicts this moment, not July 4, as most viewers presume.) A debate then ensued (July 1–2) on the Virginia Resolution for independence, in which John Dickinson spoke eloquently for delay, repeating the moderate mantra that diplomacy had not yet run its course, that secession from the British Empire meant war against the most formidable military power on the planet, and that any attempt to conjure up the vision of an independent American republic produced only a series of political nightmares in his mind. Unfortunate for Dickinson's message, indeed fatal for his increasingly anachronistic agenda, was the quite real nightmare of British troops and ships assembling on Staten Island, which did not need to be conjured up. Adams argued, in his best Ciceronian style, that the time for American independence had obviously arrived. (It was the most significant speech in Adams's long political career but was delivered without notes, and no record of it exists.) The vote was nearly unanimous, 12–0, with the New Yorkers abstaining on the grounds that they were still bound by the instructions of their legislature. Then the congress immediately put itself into a committee-of-the-whole format in order to debate Jefferson's draft.[27]

Over the next two days, the committee made eighty-five revisions or deletions in the text, a rather remarkable editorial feat that, most historians have concluded, improved the clarity and cogency of the final document. Jefferson, on the other hand, sat silently and sullenly throughout the debate, regarding each revision as a defacement. At one point Franklin leaned over to console him, reminding Jefferson that this was the reason he never wrote anything that would be edited by a committee. On July 4 the congress approved its revised version, and the Declaration of Independence was sent to the printer for publication. There was no signing ceremony on that day, as Jefferson later claimed. The parchment copy was signed by most members on August 2.[28]

The major editorial changes all occurred in the lengthy grievances section of the document, which the delegates focused on for the understandable reason that it provided the political and legal rationale for independence; this was, after all, the whole point of the Declaration. The delegates found three of the charges against George III either too Virginian or too Jeffersonian for their taste.

First, Jefferson accused George III of waging "cruel war against human nature itself, by rejecting efforts to end the slave trade," then "exciting those very people [i.e., slaves] to rise in arms against us . . . by murdering the people on whom he has also obtruded them." This was Jefferson's attempt to rephrase Virginia's somewhat tortured claim that the slave trade, and implicitly slavery itself, was the fault of George III, and that he was also to blame for Lord Dunmore's offer of emancipation to Virginia's slaves, a purportedly criminal act.

This might have made sense in the Old Dominion, where the plantations were overstocked; so ending the slave trade was popular among the Tidewater elite, though ending slavery itself was unimaginable. But in the Deep South, most especially in South Carolina, ending the slave trade was a deal breaker. And for all the states north of the Potomac, the very inclusion of slavery in the bill of indictment was inadmissible, even more so when coupled with condemnation of Dunmore's emancipation proposal, which contradicted the antislavery implications of the paragraph. Best to delete the entire passage and let slavery remain the unmentionable elephant in the center of the room.[29]

Second, Jefferson attempted to insert one of his own fondest beliefs into the draft, which he had developed more fully in *Summary View*. He called it the doctrine of "expatriation," and it claimed that the original English migrants to America came "at the expense of our own blood and treasure; unassisted by the strength of Great Britain . . . but that submission to their parliament was no part of our constitution." In Jefferson's scenario, the American colonists were all descendants of the Saxon race, itself with origins in the Germanic forests, where all coercive forms of government were rejected as despotic, so all claims of royal or parliamentary authority over American colonists were latter-day violations of the original understanding. This represented a rather preposterous rewriting of American colonial history in the once-upon-a-time mode, and the Continental Congress struck it out as an embarrassing piece of romantic fiction.[30]

Third, and finally, the end of Jefferson's draft featured a highly emotional condemnation of George III for abdicating his role as affectionate parent by "sending over not only soldiers of our common blood but Scotch & foreign mercenaries to invade and destroy us." Parental love had somehow been replaced by despotic cruelty: "These facts have given the last stab to agonizing affection, and manly spirit bids us to renounce forever these unfeeling brethren." Jefferson was trying to give expression to the multiple resolutions from state, town, and county precincts that lamented the sudden transformation of George III from benevolent monarch into belligerent tyrant. That really was the dominant message conveyed by ordinary Americans, and its inclusion suggests that Jefferson had been reading the resolutions pouring into the congress in response to the May 15 request. But the Jeffersonian version of the message struck most members of the congress as excessively sentimental. So it too was deleted.[31]

. . .

THE MOST IMPORTANT OCCURRENCE during the editorial
debate within the congress was an event that did not happen,
another dog that did not bark. Fixated as they were on the long
grievances section, the delegates ignored altogether the first
two paragraphs of the text, which they presumably regarded as
Jefferson's rhetorical overture, the flamboyant windup before
the real pitch. They made no comment whatsoever on the following words:

> We hold these truths to be self-evident; that all men are
> created equal; that they are endowed by their Creator with
> certain inalienable rights; that among these are life, liberty,
> and the pursuit of happiness; that to secure these rights,
> governments are instituted among men, deriving their just
> powers from the consent of the governed.[32]

Since these were destined to become the most important
fifty-five words in American history, the seminal statement of
the "American Creed," and perhaps the most inspiring words
in all of modern history, it is difficult for us to comprehend
the total indifference and inattention of the delegates. But that
is because we possess the advantage of hindsight and therefore realize what the natural rights section of the Declaration
would eventually become. Starting in the 1790s, several prominent Americans began to notice the implications of Jefferson's
language, but the culmination of the creeded interpretation of
the document was articulated by Abraham Lincoln in 1859:

> All honor to Jefferson—to the man who, in the concrete
> pressure of a struggle for national independence by a single

people, had the coolness, forecast, and capacity to introduce into a merely revolutionary document, an abstract truth . . . and so to embalm it there, that to-day and in all coming days, it shall be a rebuke and a stumbling-block to the very harbingers of re-appearing tyranny and oppression.[33]

But what Lincoln, surely with tongue in cheek, called "a merely revolutionary document" was for all the delegates in Philadelphia the whole point of the exercise and the major reason why the document is called the Declaration of Independence. Lincoln's phrase "embalm it there" implies that Jefferson knew what he was doing, but there is no evidence that he did. His primary attention over the ensuing weeks was devoted to ensuring that his unedited draft—that is, before it was "mangled" by his fellow delegates—was preserved for posterity, but that meant focusing exclusively on his language in the grievances section.[34]

Nevertheless, what Jefferson had done, albeit inadvertently, was to smuggle the radical implications of the American Revolution into the founding document, planting the seeds that would grow into the expanding liberal mandate for individual rights that eventually ended the property qualification to vote, ended slavery, made women's suffrage inevitable, and sanctioned the civil rights of all racial minorities. Adams had worried himself sick that all the state, county, and town resolutions of May and June would raise this radical agenda, and in the process complicate the all-important vote on independence. Now Jefferson's lofty and lyrical prose had surreptitiously inserted the latent implications of the American Revolution into the Declaration so deftly that no one noticed. Before he died in 1826, Jefferson had begun to glimpse ever so faintly what he had done, insisting that "Author of the Declaration of Independence" top the list of achievements engraved on his tombstone.

As the core statement of America's most elemental principles, the natural rights section of the Declaration has stood the test of time, just as Lincoln predicted it would. And it has done so for reasons that Lincoln was one of the first to fully comprehend.

For while the idea that governments derive their authority from the consent of the governed is clearly indebted to John Locke's formulation of the doctrine and "the right of revolution" that followed from it in his *Second Treatise on Government* (1688), a more utopian dimension lurks in the second paragraph of the Declaration that is very much an expression of Jefferson's imagination. It envisions a perfect world, at last bereft of kings, priests, and even government itself. In this never-never land, free individuals interact harmoniously, all forms of political coercion are unnecessary because they have been voluntarily internalized, people pursue their own different versions of happiness without colliding, and some semblance of social equality reigns supreme. As Lincoln recognized, it is an ideal world that can never be reached on this earth, only approached. And each generation had an obligation to move America an increment closer to the full promise, as Lincoln most famously did. The American Dream, then, is the Jeffersonian Dream writ large, embedded in language composed during one of the most crowded and congested moments in American history by an idealistic young man who desperately wished to be somewhere else.

. . .

IN ONE OF THOSE chronological coincidences that would not be believed in fiction, the first wave of the British fleet carrying

General William Howe and his 9,000 troops was sighted off the Long Island coast on June 28, the day the drafting committee presented the Declaration to the Continental Congress. As the fleet approached, sentries in the Continental Army were stunned by its size: 113 ships led by Howe's flagship, *Greyhound*. "I thought all London was afloat," exclaimed one of the sentries. Little did he know that Admiral Howe was coming on with an even larger fleet.[35]

After an initial probe of the Long Island coast, General Howe decided that Staten Island was a more secure location. Troops began to disembark there on July 2, the day the congress voted on independence, and completed the landing on July 4, the day the Declaration was approved and sent out to the world. As the Howes were soon to discover, by arriving just as the climactic vote on independence was cast, their preferred role as peace commissioners became decidedly more problematic, because now they would not be asking American colonists to avoid taking that fateful step, but rather asking Americans who no longer regarded themselves as colonists to reconsider their decision.

Although Washington had been worried about New York's tactical vulnerability for weeks, the actual presence of the enormous British force was now striking home much in the manner of his worst nightmare. He put his entire army on alert, assuming that Howe intended to attack immediately, especially after loyalist spies had apprised him of the location and unfinished condition of the American defenses. He did not yet realize that Howe had prudently decided to wait for his brother's arrival with a much larger force.

The political drama reaching a climax in Philadelphia now had its military equivalent in New York, with the sharp edge of life-and-death danger building up for all to see. Obviously shaken, and not yet aware of what was transpiring in Philadelphia, Washington summoned up his own rhetorical energies in his General Orders on July 2, in his own way matching Jefferson's visionary message and tone:

> The time is now at hand which must probably determine, Whether Americans are to be, Freeman, or Slaves; whether they are to have any property they can call their own; whether their Houses and Farms are to be pillaged and destroyed, and they consigned to a State of Wretchedness from which no human efforts will probably deliver them. The fate of the unborn Millions will now depend, under God, on the conduct of this army. . . . Let us therefore animate and encourage each other, and show the whole world, that a Freeman contending for Liberty on his own ground is superior to any slavish mercenary on earth.[36]

This was Washington's own declaration, rendered pressingly relevant by the recognition that Jefferson's Declaration would be quickly forgotten if the war was lost that same summer. The ideals that Jefferson had so eloquently articulated were designed to be universal and eternal. But whether they would endure forever or die an early death over the next few weeks was a question soon to be decided by soldiers on the battlefield and not by an inspired young statesman in his study.

4

Etc., Etc., Etc.

I consider this War against us therefore, as both unjust, and unwise, and I am persuaded that cool dispassionate Posterity will condemn to Infamy those who advised it; and that not even Success will save from some degree of Dishonour, those who voluntarily engaged to conduct it.

—BENJAMIN FRANKLIN TO LORD RICHARD HOWE, July 20, 1776

The men disembarking onto Staten Island had just endured a harrowing monthlong ordeal at sea that eventually proved more dangerous than any of the battles they would fight on land. The close quarters, poor diet, and bad sanitary conditions had created outbreaks of malaria and accompanying high casualty rates. Slightly more than 1,000 soldiers and sailors had been buried at sea, together with almost as many horses and livestock. In most military histories, the term *killing zone* refers to that most lethal location on the battlefield where advancing troops are exposed to waves of metal projectiles propelled at high velocity from the state-of-the-art weapons of mass destruction. But in the late eighteenth century, and for more than a hundred years thereafter, the most lethal "killing zones" were the hospitals and confined conditions aboard ships, where the weapons of mass destruction were germs, microbes, and viral strains against which medical science had yet to develop any defensive network of prevention or cure. Leaving those disease-ridden ships for the bucolic hills and clean air of Staten Island meant that for the British Army the most dangerous part of the American campaign was over.[1]

Ambrose Serle, the secretary to Admiral Howe, has left the fullest account of his impressions of Staten Island. "The People of this Island, like their Soil, are thin and meager; the Voices faint, and their whole Frame of a loose and languid texture," Serle observed, adding that "the Soil is mostly poor, and receives a very inferior Cultivation than our Lands in G. Britain." Serle obviously observed the people and overall American environment, which he had never seen before, through the lens of presumed superiority and studied condescension appropriate for an overbearing British aristocrat. It was all part of the mental package he carried from the London courts and Whitehall corridors, where American resistance to British authority was regarded as a preposterous violation of the divinely sanctioned political order and George Washington was viewed, in Serle's words, "as a little paltry Colonel of Militia at the Head of a Banditti of Rebels."[2]

If Serle's political prejudices were just as predictable as they were insufferable—and, in truth, they provided a nice window into one reason American independence had become inevitable—ordinary British soldiers harbored several strange preconceptions of their own. Some were surprised that the colonists wore clothes, thinking they would dress like Indians. Others had expected to encounter roving bands of wild animals in the manner of African jungles. And when a loyalist came aboard one ship to help pilot it into port, the British crew and troops were dumbfounded. "All the People had been of the Opinion," they exclaimed, "that the inhabitants of America were black."[3]

But the dominant impressions were more sensible and strategic. The Staten Island landscape was dotted with highly productive farms and impressive herds of cattle and sheep that—Serle's comments to the contrary notwithstanding—ensured an immediate improvement in the diet of the soldiers of the British Army. Indeed, given their recent experience crossing the Atlantic, the British troops could be excused for believing that they had arrived at paradise.

To top it off, the local inhabitants greeted them as long-awaited rescuers rather than as hostile invaders. Over the preceding months, all attempts to assess the political allegiance of farmers on Long Island and Staten Island had produced only muffled guesses, which accurately conveyed the multi-layered political disposition of the populace. Outright loyalists and patriots were vastly outnumbered by simple farmers who only wished that the two armies would go somewhere else to kill each other. But with the arrival of General Howe's massive force, popular opinion shifted overnight. American sentries looking through their telescopes from the southern coast of Long Island reported that the residents of Staten Island had not really surrendered so much as converted, enthusiastically joining the other side. Very soon the various "joinings" included sexual unions occurring throughout the rolling hills and apple orchards of the island. "The fair nymphs of this isle are in a wonderful tribulation," reported one British officer. "A girl cannot step into the bushes to pluck a rose without running the imminent risk of being ravished." Court-martial cases involving accusations of rape became daily occurrences at British headquarters.[4]

To a surprising degree, the British soldiers encamped on

Staten Island resembled their American counterparts on Long Island and Manhattan. Contrary to a negative stereotype that developed in the next century during the emergence of the British Empire at the height of its power, the British Army was not a collection of outcasts, criminals, and psychopaths swept into service from the jails and bars of London or dragooned from English towns and villages. They were, instead, working-class Britons—former day laborers, farmers, carpenters, and shoemakers—who had the misfortune to have become victims of the Industrial Revolution, their jobs displaced by machines, thereby making the army the employer of last resort. They were almost all volunteers.

The big difference between the enlisted men of the British and American armies was age and experience. The typical British soldier was twenty-eight years old, his American counterpart almost eight years younger. And most important, the redcoat had seven years of experience as a soldier, while the American had less than six months, and those in several units of the Continental Army had none whatsoever.[5]

It came down to proven experience in battle, which on the eighteenth-century battlefield placed a premium on remaining calm amid scenes of unspeakable carnage and horror. "To march over dead men, to hear without concern the groans of the wounded," Nathanael Greene meditated, "I say few men can stand such scenes unless steeled by habit or fortified by military pride." Many of the British soldiers, and even more of the Hessians, had shown they could pass that test. The Americans were as yet untried.[6]

In an effort to buoy the spirit of his troops, Washington had on several occasions questioned the motivation of British regulars. They were mere mercenaries fighting for money.

The Americans were patriots fighting for the noble goal of independence. This quasi-religious message had a point, but it misconstrued the motivation of ordinary soldiers on the British side, who shared a deep-felt affection for their respective regiments and for the men standing to the right and left of them in battle. British soldiers saw and felt themselves as a brotherhood prepared to share some of the most excruciating experiences of life together. The regiment was their family, and they were prepared to defend its honor whatever the cost.

. . .

ON JULY 9, Washington received a packet of documents from Hancock, along with the following cover letter:

> The Congress have judged it necessary to dissolve the connection between Great Britain and the American Colonies, and to declare them free & independent states; as you will perceive by the enclosed Declaration, which I am directed to transmit to you, and to request that you will have it proclaimed at the Head of the Army in the Way you shall think it most proper.[7]

News that independence had been declared had reached Washington two days earlier, but this was the official communication from the civilian head of the government to the military commander, along with the document itself. Washington made no comment on the language of the Declaration, preferring to regard the words as the long-awaited political commitment that at last aligned the Continental Congress with the Continental Army. He ordered it read aloud to all the troops after dinner that evening on the New York City Commons and on several brigade parade grounds.

The reading on the commons was greeted with "three Huzzas from the Troops," who then joined a large crowd of civilians that marched down Broadway to Bowling Green to tear down a massive statue of George III. It was made of lead gilded in gold and depicted the king on horseback clad as a Roman emperor. Only a strenuous effort with crowbars and ropes could budge the two-ton monument. After beheading their former sovereign, the lead was hauled away to make 42,000 musket balls, one witness relishing the prospect that "redcoats will have melted majesty fired at them." In his General Orders the following day, Washington reprimanded his troops for joining the crowd in the wanton act of destruction against the last vestige of royal authority. No one took this reprimand seriously, including Washington himself, who ordered no investigation or punishment of the offenders.[8]

. . .

DURING THE WANING WEEKS of July, Washington continued his practice of building up his networks of defense, both on Long Island and inside his own soul. As ominous as the British encampment on Staten Island appeared, it soon began to provide reliable intelligence, from British deserters and from American loyalists on the island having second thoughts. Greene obtained information about the size and arrival time of Admiral Richard Howe's approaching fleet, plus General William Howe's tactical plans to launch his main invasion on Long Island.[9]

These precious bits of information allowed Washington to fill in the blanks of his defensive scheme with more confidence than guesswork. Moreover, by mid-July he had obtained accurate intelligence about Germain's strategic plan for the conduct of the entire war. "As it now seems beyond question," Washington informed Hancock, "that the Enemy mean to direct their Operations against this Colony, and will attempt to unite their two Armies, that under General Burgoyne [coming down from Canada] and the one arrived here." The looming invasion of New York, then, was the southern half of a coordinated British strategy to capture the Hudson corridor and isolate New England.[10]

This helps explain the otherwise inexplicable attention Washington devoted to the hapless and apparently hopeless American military efforts in upstate New York commanded by General Philip Schuyler, which dominated his correspondence for days at a time at the expense of attention to the more conspicuous and visible British threat only six miles away. Knowing Germain's overall strategy forced Washington to broaden his vision in order to counter the British buildup north of Lake Champlain. In retrospect, he would have been better off concentrating his attention on his more immediate adversary.[11]

On July 12 he proceeded to do precisely that. Knowing as he did that Admiral Howe's fleet was due later that very day, Washington convened a council of war to consider a strike against the British garrison in Staten Island before it was reinforced. Rather than just sit and watch as the flower of the British army and navy assembled and prepared to deliver a crushing blow, Washington proposed that the Continental Army take the offensive and deliver its own blow before Admiral Howe's fleet was securely ensconced.

It was a bold idea that accurately reflected Washington's aggressive military instincts. A plan was drafted in Lord Stirling's hand calling for a coordinated assault on Staten Island by 3,300 American troops at six separate landing spots. It presumed split-second timing and a wholly unrealistic level of coordination that would have tested the most experienced professional army in the world. Given the inexperience and conspicuous disarray throughout the Continental Army, the plan resembled a textbook example of how to orchestrate a disaster. It was also the first of Washington's inherently overcomplicated offensive schemes that would bedevil the Continental Army throughout the war. The question put to the council of war was clear and succinct: Should the army mount an attack on Staten Island? The answer came back with equivalent clarity: "Agreed unanimously that it should not." Complicated tactical attacks were not yet part of the Continental Army's repertoire. Washington backed off.[12]

Even before that decision could be digested, Admiral Howe's flagship, the *Eagle,* was sighted on the horizon, signaling the arrival of the main British fleet and force. A few hours later two British men-of-war, the *Phoenix* and the *Rose,* accompanied by three tenders, took advantage of the favorable winds and tides to sail past Red Hook and Governors Island up the Hudson, guns blazing all the way up the west side of Manhattan. Cannonballs came crashing through houses, scattering the terrified residents in the streets, while the soldiers in the Continental Army watched in disbelief from the shoreline as the Royal Navy offered an exhibition of its matchless firepower. American batteries got off nearly two hundred shots as the ships glided past, but to little avail—they swept past the major gun emplacements at Fort Washington and cruised thirty miles upstream before dropping anchor at the Tappan Zee that evening.[13]

A recently arrived recruit from Connecticut, only fifteen years old, by the name of Joseph Plumb Martin, noted that he had just seen his first action, which struck him as complete chaos. He had never witnessed cannonfire before but was prepared to testify that "the sound was musical, or at least grand." He was mesmerized.[14]

In his General Orders the next day, Washington focused on the dazed response of troops, like Private Martin, who did not behave according to orders by repairing to their posts but instead just stood there in frozen amazement. "Such unsoldierly conduct must grieve every good officer," Washington lectured, noting that it did not bode well for "The Cause" once serious fighting started.[15]

But the most foreboding fact about the action that day was the ease with which the British ships had sailed past all the American batteries. In this first test of those elaborately constructed forts and gun emplacements designed to limit British naval mobility around Manhattan, the American defenses had failed miserably. This meant that British ships could move with virtual impunity throughout the New York archipelago, delivering troops and firepower wherever they wished, making a mockery of Washington's static defenses. Most ominously, it meant that if Manhattan was a bottle, the British could cork it at their pleasure, landing troops on the north end of the island and trapping Washington's entire army without any avenue of escape. It meant that General Lee's original assessment was correct: British naval supremacy made New York indefensible.

Hindsight suggests that these revelations should have prompted a fundamental review of American strategy, leading to the abandonment of New York and withdrawal of the Continental Army onto the American mainland in either New Jersey or Connecticut. But hindsight was not available to Washington, who was trapped in the moment much as his army was trapped on two islands. It was clear that the Continental Congress expected him to defend New York at all costs. It was equally clear that his civilian superiors in Philadelphia did not understand what "at all costs" might mean.

Throughout July he devoted his fullest energies to assessing several schemes designed to limit British naval mobility on the Hudson and East rivers. He responded enthusiastically to a proposal from the Pennsylvania Committee of Safety for the creation of six "fire ships" that would ram and sink British frigates in a naval version of "forlorn hope," or suicidal tactics. He entertained the prospect of blocking ships in the channels of the Hudson with huge piles of debris called chevaux-de-frise, creating underwater blockades that would force British vessels to slow down and maneuver within the range of American guns at strongpoints like Fort Washington. He even listened to a proposal, forwarded to him through Benjamin Franklin, for the deployment of a new kind of ship called a submarine, which would sink beneath the surface, then pop up to wreak havoc among unsuspecting British ships. He was obviously searching for a way to offset the tactical advantages enjoyed by the British fleet, grasping at straws to reduce the odds against him.[16]

The sheer volume of requests landing on his desk made it impossible for Washington to concentrate his attention on the larger picture. There were, it turned out, about fifteen thousand cattle, sheep, and horses on Long Island, all belonging to local farmers. Should his army confiscate them to prevent them from falling into British hands? What impact would such confiscation have on the political allegiance of the farmers? After much back-and-forthing, all the livestock on Long Island were rounded up and slaughtered, which amounted to Washington's tacit recognition that Long Island was likely to fall into British hands.[17]

Then there was the pressing and awkward question of

what to do about the local loyalists. It was pressing because, according to Greene's estimate, several hundred residents of Long Island were currently hiding in the woods and swamps, waiting to join the British invasion force once it landed. It was awkward because within New York City, a substantial segment of the population, including some of the most prominent citizens, refused to acknowledge the new reality created by the Declaration of Independence and insisted on straddling the divide as British Americans who refused to choose. Eventually it was decided that all straddlers should be treated as loyalists and jailed, and the most suspicious characters should be transported to Connecticut in order to prevent their liberation if the British should occupy the city. Greene ordered a clean sweep of all the households on Long Island, done with decorum in order to avoid the appearance of harshness or insensitivity toward sincere neutrals. The arresting officers should be "decently dressed" and should avoid any expression of "indecency or abuse to any person." The sheep had to be separated from the goats for obvious military reasons, but Greene wanted to accomplish his mission without becoming the American bully who alienated the very people he hoped to rescue.[18]

Washington's chief accomplice in managing the cascading array of daily demands was Joseph Reed, a thirty-five-year-old veteran of the Boston Siege whom Washington had plucked from the ranks to serve as an aide because of his obvious intelligence and educational background. (Reed had studied law at London's Middle Temple.) When Reed decided in April to return to his family and law practice in Philadelphia, Washington was disappointed, since he had come to regard the young man as an indispensable member of his official "family," whose judgment and writing ability had become invaluable. In June he lured him back into service with an offer of higher rank, as adjutant general, the chief administrative office in the Continental Army. Almost immediately Reed recognized that he was in over his head. "The office I am in," he wrote his wife, "is so entirely out of my line, that I do not feel myself so easy in it."[19]

In addition to his inexperience—like Greene and Knox, Reed was another one of Washington's gifted amateurs—he was responsible for administering an army that lacked time-tested procedures and routinized policies, so that every decision became an improvisational act. The intense concern within the officer corps about rank, for example, reflected the evolving criteria for promotion, which produced persistent bickering, mountains of paperwork, and scores of bruised egos. Militia units from Connecticut that insisted on bringing their horses had to be sent home because the Continental Army had no way of accommodating a cavalry regiment. Reed tried to transform the lack of cloth for uniforms into an advantage, ordering the soldiers to make their own "Hunting Shirts," which might terrify the British, "who think every such person a complete marksman." Knox's artillery regiment had more cannons than men who could load and fire them safely. The standard-size musket balls and flints used in the Continental Army did not fit the muskets carried by several militia regiments. Surgeons at the regimental hospitals demanded the authority to admit or dismiss patients without approval from superior officers, but to no avail.[20]

Reed's main job was to prevent all these nettlesome problems from landing on Washington's desk. He surely did the best he could, but given the inexperienced condition of the army, even the most experienced British officer would have been hard-pressed to manage the flow. And beyond the unscripted administrative burdens, the Continental Army itself was actually designed as a permanently transitory improvisation that would expand and contract on a battle-by-battle basis, when the core force of regulars would be supplemented by militia from proximate states.

This meant that over half the total strength of the army was comprised of newly arrived volunteers who somehow had to be folded into the military plans and organizational charts at the last minute. This logistical nightmare defied any coherent solution, only adding a final layer of confusion and loose ends to the tangled mass of men and equipment called the Continental Army. No single mind could comprehend it all, much less control it. Swamped every day with vexing requests from countless quarters, Washington took refuge from the incessant barrage in the impenetrable bunker of his own mind, where all the options were uncompromisingly clear and blissfully elemental. "If they will stand by me, the place cannot be taken without some loss," he wrote his brother, adding the caveat, "notwithstanding we are not yet in a posture of defense I should wish."[21]

. . .

CONSIDER THE FOLLOWING SEQUENCE of events: on July 12, Lord Howe's fleet with 20,000 British troops arrived in Long Island Sound; on that same day, His Majesty's *Phoenix* and *Rose* blazed their way up the Hudson, demonstrating the tactical supremacy of the British navy and the abiding vulnerability of the American defensive scheme; the following day, Lord Howe sent a letter to Washington via a courier, announcing "the Commission with which I have the honor to be charged," referring to his appointment as one of the two peace commissioners—his brother was the other—purportedly carrying proposals from George III and the British ministry for diplomatic negotiations that would render all those ships and soldiers superfluous. "I trust that a dispassionate consideration of the King's benevolent intentions may be the means of preventing the further Effusion of Blood," Lord Richard fondly hoped, "and become productive of Peace and lasting Union between Great Britain and America." One would be challenged to find a more dramatic example of the iron fist and the velvet glove—or perhaps the sword and the olive branch—in all of ancient and modern statecraft.[22]

But the letter could not be delivered. Howe's courier and Joseph Reed met in rowboats between Staten Island and Governors Island. After pleasantries were shouted over the wind and waves, Reed refused to accept the letter because it was addressed to "George Washington Esq. &c, &c, &c." No such person existed in the Continental Army, Reed declared, adding that "all the World knew who Genl. Washington was since the transactions of last summer," presumably referring to Washington's appointment as commander in chief of the Continental Army. Reed's legal training served him well during this diplomatic exchange, emboldening him to reject any solicitation that failed to acknowledge the legal status of his client.[23]

So the courier returned the letter undelivered, prompting a tantrum from Ambrose Serle, Lord Howe's secretary. "So high is the Vanity and Insolence of these Men," Serle recorded in his journal, "they Dare to rebut Lord Howe, whose Bravery & Honor are So well known . . . [and] they pretend (or rather have pretended) to seek Peace, and yet renounce it." Washington wrote to Hancock the next day to justify Reed's conduct during the interview, explaining that the decision to reject Howe's letter involved more than mere etiquette. "I would not upon any occasion sacrifice Essentials to Punctilio," Washington observed, "but in this Instance . . . I deemed it a duty to my

Countrymen and my appointment to insist upon that respect which in any other than a public view I would willingly have waived."[24]

In truth, Lord Howe's inability to address Washington by rank, though only symbolic, captured the essence of the diplomatic impasse, for Germain's instructions explicitly prohibited Howe from treating the Americans as equals or even from negotiating at all until *after* the rebels threw down their arms and surrendered. Both Howe brothers would have preferred a more roving mandate, but both had been forced to come to terms with Germain's narrow restrictions, and they had reluctantly concluded that any peace initiative could occur only after inflicting a decisive defeat on Washington's army.

Apparently, Lord Howe had decided to make one bold effort before the battle. Perhaps he thought that the very sight of the massive invasion force might weaken Washington's resolve. And it is possible, though pure speculation, that Howe dispatched the two warships up the Hudson in order to demonstrate to Washington the hopelessness of his military situation. Whatever Howe's motives, they had no effect on Washington's resolute posture of defiance, nor on his long-standing conviction that the whole business of peace commissioners was a political ploy designed to give false hope to die-hard reconciliationists: "Lord Howe is arrived," Washington informed General Horatio Gates, currently trying to impose some semblance of discipline on the northern detachment of the Continental Army. "He & the Genl his Brother are appointed Commissioners to dispense Pardons to Repenting Sinners."[25]

Lord Howe was obviously exasperated, on the one hand by the short leash that Germain had allowed him, and on the other by the apparent obliviousness of Washington, who was rejecting the opportunity to avert what was most assuredly going to be a military catastrophe. He decided to make one final attempt a week later, this time sending his adjutant general, James Patterson, with the same letter, plus a generous proposal about prisoner exchange. Reed determined that the prisoner issue afforded a pretext for a face-to-face interview with Washington, so Patterson was led, blindfolded, to Washington's headquarters on Manhattan. Patterson had been briefed to address Washington as "His Excellency," to treat him with the utmost respect, and to assure him that the Howes had been granted great powers to effect an accommodation. This was demonstrably untrue, as Washington was quick to point out, observing that George III's vaunted generosity lay on the other side of American capitulation, so all the Howes had to offer were pardons, "and that those who had committed no Fault, wanted no Pardon." Patterson conveyed Lord Howe's deep disappointment that matters could not move past this initial sticking point, reiterated the regret of both Howes about not recognizing the rank of a man whose "Person & Character they held in the highest Esteem," then bowed himself out the door, "Sociable and Chatty all the way."[26]

The chasm between the British and American positions was now exposed more fully than ever before. From the British side of the divide, all assumptions remained resolutely imperial. Despite over ten years of political conflict during which the colonies challenged Parliament's sovereignty and called for some kind of semiautonomous American presence within the British Empire, then fifteen months of bloodletting that raised the stakes for both sides, George III and his ministers continued to insist that the colonists were subjects, not citizens, and that Parliament's sovereignty was nonnegotiable. No compromise was possible because nothing less than the survival of the British Empire in North America was at stake. And no compromise was necessary because the British army and navy, so conspicuously poised on Staten Island, were invincible.

Only within this imperial context was George III prepared to be charitable, not because he was required to do so but because, so the Howes claimed, he retained a benevolent sense of affection for his American subjects and wished to envelop them once again within the protective folds of his kingship. That meant that he was prepared to issue a blanket pardon to the vast majority of American colonists once they relinquished their misguided claim to independence, disbanded their army, and disavowed those radical ringleaders in the Continental Congress and Continental Army who had generated so much of the recent mischief. These were the true culprits, who must, of course, be rounded up, be tried for treason, and suffer the consequences. After the old order was restored, George III was prepared to listen to fresh proposals for some sensible framework of political reform designed to keep his subjects happy.

The view from the American side of the divide was most eloquently expressed by Benjamin Franklin, who knew Richard Howe from their days together in London, when they were both vainly seeking a political compromise that avoided an open break. Writing from Philadelphia on July 20, Franklin commiserated with Lord Richard's predicament, lamenting that he was precluded from offering any peace terms other than "Offers of Pardon upon submission; which I was sorry to find, as it must give your Lordship Pain to be sent so far on so hopeless a Business."

No other delegate—indeed, no other American—could have written such words, which deftly reversed the British and American roles, commiserating with Lord Richard for the hopelessness of his position. The style came naturally to Franklin, who had been practicing it for nearly fifty years, first as the folksy Poor Richard with his arsenal of witty maxims (e.g., "Let all men know thee, but no man know thee thoroughly"), most recently in a devastating satire of British statecraft, *Rules by Which a Great Empire May Be Reduced to a Small One* (1773).

Franklin was, in fact, a latecomer to the cause of American independence. For most of the last two decades he had lived in London, lobbying for a royal charter for Pennsylvania, receiving the accolades of the Royal Society for his pioneering work on electricity, and rubbing elbows with the leading figures of British society, Lord Richard included. He presumed that the British Empire was really an Anglo-American empire of partners, bound together by mutual consent and common interest. When the recently crowned George III and a succession of British ministries began to tighten restrictions on colonial trade, impose new taxes, and station a standing army in America, Franklin regarded these changes as a temporary aberration. Only a pack of fools would seek to destroy an imperial relationship that worked so smoothly and boded so well for both sides as members of an emerging global power.

By 1773 he was beginning to conclude that the British government no longer knew its own interest. The clinching moment came in January 1774, when he was required to sit silently in the House of Lords while he was pilloried and personally insulted for advocating his vision of a British Empire based on the principle of mutual consent. This searing experience prompted a conversion to the goal of American independence. He returned to America in 1775, was immediately elected to the Continental Congress, and never looked back. If John Adams was the hands-on architect of the movement for independence in the congress, Franklin was the acknowledged elder statesman, a generation or two older than most other delegates, who brought the resolve of a recent convert, the weight of his reputation, and even the status of a celebrity to the deliberations. If Washington was the new American hero, Franklin was the most familiar and famous American of the century.[27]

His message to Lord Richard Howe, then, carried a special resonance that could not be dismissed, even though it undermined everything that Lord Richard hoped to accomplish. The notion that the British government was prepared to pardon the recalcitrant colonists was preposterously presumptive, Franklin observed, since that very government "had behaved with the most wanton Barbarity and Cruelty, burnt our defenseless Towns in the midst of winter, excited the Savages to massacre our farmers . . . and is even now bringing foreign Mercenaries to deluge our Settlements with Blood." The moral leverage to grant pardons belonged to the American side, "since it is not possible for you (I mean the British Nation) to forgive the People you have so heavily injured."

If Lord Richard had carried proposals for peace between two sovereign powers currently at war, Franklin continued, then perhaps negotiations would be possible. "But I am persuaded you have no such Powers," he observed, because Britain could not recognize the separate and independent existence of her former colonies as equal states without abandoning her presumed supremacy. And if that supremacy then took a military form, as it was now doing, it only exposed the hypocrisy of all British claims of generosity. It did not help the good lord's cause that he was simultaneously a peace commissioner and co-leader of an invasion.

Whatever the outcome of the current contest at New York, Franklin predicted that Britain's war against America would prove unwinnable and "so destructive both of Lives and Treasure, that must prove as pernicious to her in the End as the Croisades [Crusades] formerly were to most of the

Nations of Europe." Like all his former predictions, this one, Franklin realized, would not be believed "till the Event shall verify it." Rather than invincible, British arms would prove inadequate.

Franklin concluded with a piece of unsolicited advice to Howe. It pained him to find his former friend prosecuting a war destined to go down in history as unnecessary, unwise, and unjust. "Posterity will condemn to Infamy those who advised it," he warned, "and that not even Success will save from some degree of Dishonour, those who voluntarily engaged to conduct it." Franklin was prepared to grant that Howe's "great Motive in coming hither was the Hope of being instrumental in a Reconciliation." Now that it was clear that reconciliation was impossible on the terms Lord Richard was permitted to propose, he should "relinquish so odious a Command and return to a more honourable private station."[28]

Of course, Lord Richard could hardly hear Franklin's advice, much less take it. A few weeks later he wrote Germain: "The interview [with Washington] was more polite than interesting; however it induced me to change my subscription for the attainment of an end desirable." This was his elliptical way of acknowledging that no peace was possible until the Americans had been taught a painful and bloody lesson, which would now become his chief task.[29]

At Franklin's urging, the Continental Congress forwarded Lord Richard's peace proposals to several major newspapers, in order to expose his limited powers and dash any false hopes that still lingered in the ever-dwindling number of moderate minds. If there ever had been a middle position, a bridge over the chasm, it was now completely gone.[30]

. . .

IN EARLY AUGUST, the gathering storm continued to gather. On August 1, Greene reported the arrival of thirty ships at Sandy Hook, which he took to be the German mercenaries but turned out to be generals Clinton and Cornwallis coming up from South Carolina. Another small fleet arrived a week later, containing the first wave of Hessians and several regiments of Scottish Highlanders. The main body of Hessians, 8,000 strong, landed on August 12. All in all, the Howe brothers now commanded a strike force of 42,000 soldiers, marines, and sailors, by far the largest military operation ever mounted in North America.[31]

Back in Philadelphia, Adams concluded that Lord Howe's peace initiative had always been a delaying tactic: "He has let the cat out of the Bag . . . , throwing out his Barrells to amuse Leviathan until his Reinforcements shall arrive."[32] This was not really correct. Lord Richard's last-minute diplomatic effort was utterly sincere, though equally hopeless. The more prosaic truth was that William Howe, fully aware that Germain had spent a small fortune to acquire the Hessian mercenaries, saw no reason to launch his attack before they arrived. And given the tactical and manpower advantages that he enjoyed, he felt no pressure to move according to any schedule but his own.

For his part, Washington might be forgiven for regarding each new arrival of British and Hessian troops as nails in the proverbial coffin. He wrote in a nostalgic tone to a fellow veteran of earlier campaigns in the French and Indian War, recalling their providential escapes at "the Meadows [Fort Necessity] and on the Banks of the Monongahela." Since both of these battles had been crushing defeats, they were strange memories to be conjuring up on the eve of the looming battle. Watching the British buildup enhanced his fear that the forces at his disposal were going to be seriously overmatched. He confessed that "I cannot help but feeling very anxious Apprehensions."[33]

Part of his problem was that he did not know for sure how many troops he had at his disposal. Under the implicit "balloon theory," the size of the Continental Army would be slightly more than doubled if and when militia units from Connecticut, New York, and New Jersey arrived, bringing his total force to about 25,000. But it was harvesttime, so many of the farmer-soldiers were late to the task or did not show up at all. Washington dashed off last-minute exhortations to state governors and militia officers to have the troops come on, leaving the crops to rot in the field if necessary, emphasizing the historical urgency of the current crisis. "The Deficiency of Regiments . . . is far short of its intended Compliments," he warned. "Since the Settlement of these Colonies there has never been such just occasion of Alarm or such an Appearance of an Enemy both by Sea and Land."[34]

Moreover, he did not know how many of his troops already present were fit for duty. Contaminated water supplies had produced widespread dysentery on Manhattan, and Greene reported an outbreak of smallpox on Long Island in late July. Within the week, Washington estimated that 20 percent of his army was too sick to fight.

Adams broke into a frenzy when he heard about the smallpox epidemic: "The small Pox has done us more harm than British Armies, Canadians, Indians, Negroes, Hannoverians, Hessians, and all the rest." The disease was on his mind for personal reasons as well, since Abigail and their four young children were currently undergoing inoculation up in Boston at that very same time. He was juggling his responsibilities as statesman and his obligations as husband and father, in the same letter expressing guilt about being distant while his family was in danger, then adding that "our Army is also rather sickly at N. York."[35]

The General Orders emanating from headquarters continued to sound an upbeat note, despite the overwhelming British superiority in numbers. "The enemy will endeavor to intimidate by show and appearance, but remember how they have been repulsed on various occasions, by a few brave men," read the order for August 13. "Their Cause is bad; their men are conscious of it, and if opposed with firmness, and coolness . . . Victory is most assuredly ours."[36]

Washington did not really believe these words, though he did believe that he was personally and professionally obliged to write them. He was more candid with Hancock, cataloging the manpower and sickness problems, acknowledging that it was unlikely that he could prevent the Howes from capturing New York. But he found final refuge in the Bunker Hill scenario, in effect another ruinous British victory: "These considerations lead me to think, that though the Appeal may not terminate so happily in our favor as I could wish, that they will not succeed in their views without considerable loss. Any advantage they may get, I trust will cost them dear." Left unsaid was how many men he could afford to lose in order to produce a Pyrrhic British victory.[37]

Not yet sure how his family had made it through the inoculation process, Adams assured his recovering Abigail that his every thought was with her. But at least one eye was looking north: "We are in daily expectation of some decisive strike at New York."[38]

5

After Virtue

Thus we are sowing the Seeds of Ignorance, Corruption, and Injustice, in the fairest Field of Liberty ever appeared upon Earth, even in the first attempts to cultivate it.

—JOHN ADAMS TO JOSEPH HAWLEY, August 25, 1776

Back in the spring, John Adams had on several occasions outlined the political steps the Continental Congress should take in order to manage the movement toward American independence responsibly. His primary concern had been to create a stable political platform of confederated states before launching the movement for American independence.

The central flaw in this wholly logical scheme—apart from the assumption that a political earthquake could be managed—was the belief that you could set the stage for an independent government before you knew for sure that there would be an independent America to govern. After the decisive vote of July 2 provided that assurance, the delegates then decided to proceed without pause to address the ambitious political agenda that Adams had outlined earlier, albeit in a different order than he had envisioned.

If only in retrospect, it was a preposterously presumptive decision, surely a measure of the free-flowing confidence that accompanied the resounding triumph on the independence question. For the Continental Congress was proposing to draft a new constitution for the former United Colonies, now the United States, and at the same time to define the foreign policy goals of whatever government was created, all this to be accomplished by two committees in a matter of weeks in late July and early August.

The revolutionary fires were obviously burning brightly, warming up "the spirit of '76" to a fever pitch that defied any prudent assessment of the possible. In fact, the political questions the Continental Congress proposed to resolve so quickly would continue to haunt and befuddle the infant American republic for the next decade and beyond and would not reach resolution until the Constitutional Convention, and even then only tentatively.[1]

Moreover, these daunting political conversations would occur in the shadow of the looming British invasion at New York, which had been designed, and then artfully organized, to deliver a crushing blow to the American rebellion before it got off the ground, thereby rendering all the deliberations in Philadelphia irrelevant. Given the escalating size of the two armies gathering on the waters and islands of New York, and given the "all-in" mentality of both sides, the apparent nonchalance of the Continental Congress is striking. While the British ministry regarded the military outcome at New York as decisive, the delegates in Philadelphia viewed the political agenda of an independent America as a priority not to be halted or hampered by worries about what would transpire on the battlefields of Long Island and Manhattan.

Part of the overconfidence was rooted in some combination of ignorance and misguided faith in Washington's ability to best Howe in New York, as he had done in Boston. Except perhaps for Adams, whose role as chair of the Board of War and Ordnance made him privy to more accurate intelligence, most delegates believed that "swarming militia" had enhanced Washington's army to nearly double the size of Howe's. "Washington's numbers are greatly increased, but we do not know them exactly," Jefferson wrote a Virginia relative. "I imagine he must have from 30 to 35,000 by this time." In fact he had about half that number, of which 20 percent were sick and "unfit for duty." Jefferson noted in passing that British ships had demonstrated their ability to navigate past American batteries on the Hudson, but he did not realize the tactical implications of British naval supremacy. "I imagine that General Washington, finding he cannot prevent their going up the river," he observed with confidence, "will prepare to amuse them wherever they shall go," not recognizing that without a navy, Washington was tactically incapable of amusing anyone. Even after the full British force, absent the Hessians, had arrived on Staten Island, totaling 25,000 troops, Jefferson was reporting to Virginia correspondents that "the enemy there is not more than 8 or 10,000 strong."[2]

By and large, then, the view from Philadelphia was that Washington had the situation well in hand in New York, which he clearly did not, and that the Continental Army had been sufficiently reinforced by militia to possess comfortable numerical superiority over Howe's army, when in fact the exact opposite was true. One wild rumor had Washington commanding a force of more than 60,000.[3]

Another optimistic train of thought circulating within the Continental Congress had more far-reaching implications than any rough estimate of Washington's and Howe's armies. After returning from a tour of the eastern states, the Massachusetts delegate Elbridge Gerry reported to Adams that, by his reckoning, there were 111,000 militia armed and ready to fight from New Jersey northward, "a force sufficient to repulse the Enemy if he were 40,000 strong at New York and Canada." Even if Washington suffered a catastrophic defeat, even if his entire army was destroyed or captured in New York, a virtually bottomless supply of men was available to take their place. In response to British pretensions of invincibility based on the supremacy of their army and navy, an American sense of invincibility was now emerging, based on the manpower potential of the American population.[4]

From the British perspective, a decisive victory in New York, then the union of Howe's and Burgoyne's armies along the Hudson, would end the war. From the American perspective, no single defeat would prove decisive until the entire American population had been subjugated, an outcome no imaginable British army could possibly achieve. As Franklin put it: "If the Enemy is beaten, it will probably be decisive for them; for they can hardly produce another Armament for another Campaign. But our growing Country can bear considerable Loses, and recover them, so that a Defeat on our part will not by any means occasion our giving up the Cause."[5]

Franklin's formulation reflected his values as a long-standing student of American demography, whose *Observations on the Increase of Mankind* (1751) had predicted—accurately, it turned out—that the American population was doubling every twenty to twenty-five years, over twice as fast as the population of Great Britain. In a century or so, Franklin observed with that ever-present twinkle in his eye, the capital of the British Empire would probably have moved to somewhere in Pennsylvania. But the more immediate implication of his demographic perspective—one could see overtones of this idea in Paine's *Common Sense* as well—was that the American and

British armies were merely the military projections of two different societies and populations. Whatever advantage the British enjoyed as a consequence of their superior army and navy was offset, and would eventually be overcome, by the size and supremacy of America's exploding population. Whether they knew it or not, the Howe brothers were on a fool's errand.

But even within the optimistic framework of this emerging American perspective, the outcome at New York remained crucial. A humiliating British defeat would be vastly preferable, because it would mean a short war. A calamitous American defeat obviously would be painful, because it would mean a long war. A hard-earned British victory along Bunker Hill lines—the most likely conclusion, in Washington's opinion—would mean something in between. Whatever the result, the delegates in Philadelphia believed the American Revolution should continue to move forward politically regardless of the military outcome in New York. For them that meant deciding what a government of the United States should look like, even while the armies squared off.

· · ·

IN LATE JULY and early August, the Continental Congress put itself into committee-of-the-whole posture in order to debate the recommendations of a large, thirteen-man committee, chaired by John Dickinson, charged with providing the framework for an American government that would replace the Continental Congress. For over a year, the congress had been functioning as a provisional government, with broad emergency powers that were implicitly justified by the dire circumstances of the ongoing if undeclared war and the looming prospects of secession from the British Empire. A more permanent central government was obviously necessary once independence was declared, so on June 12 the congress had appointed delegates from each of the colonies to a committee that would provide the political architecture for that new government, if and when independence was declared. The committee met off and on for a month, then submitted what was called the Dickinson Draft on July 12. No record of the committee's deliberations exists, because none was kept.[6]

But some glimpse of the issues at stake is preserved in the correspondence between delegates at the time. Josiah Bartlett of New Hampshire apprised a colleague that the conversations within the committee were edgy: "As it is a very important business, and some difficulties have arisen, I fear it will take some time before it will be finally settled." Edward Rutledge of South Carolina hinted at the core difficulty, objecting to "the idea of destroying all Provincial Distinctions and making every thing . . . bend to what they call the good of the whole." There was obviously a deep disagreement among delegates over how powerful the new central government should be.[7]

The charge of the committee was to draw up "Articles of Confederation," suggesting a voluntary alliance of sovereign states. The Continental Congress had been created in 1774 as just such a confederation, and the constitutional arguments made against Parliament's authority had identified the colonial assemblies as the sanctioned voice of popular opinion, thereby locating sovereignty in the respective colonial (soon state) governments.

But over the past fifteen months, the Continental Congress had been functioning as a sovereign national government, adopting emergency powers to raise an army, orchestrate a collective response to British military and political policies, and put a common face on the thirteen separate colonies. This quasi-national status, to be sure, had been achieved pragmati-cally, on the run, in response to the mounting British challenges currently embodied in all those ships and soldiers commanded by the Howe brothers.

Clearly, a faction within the committee wanted the new American confederation to build on the embryonic union cre-ated in the imperial crisis and establish a central government sufficiently empowered to provide the political foundation for an emerging nation rather than a mere clearinghouse for thirteen separate sovereignties that would presumably each go their own way after the war was won.

The Dickinson Draft is difficult to interpret, even to com-prehend, because it represents a series of accommodations between delegates with fundamentally different visions of postrevolutionary America. The very term *confederation,* as mentioned, implied a loose alliance of sovereign states. But then Article 2 referred to former colonies that "unite themselves into one Body politic." Article 3 seemed to suggest that each state was sovereign over its own internal affairs, reserving "to itself the sole and exclusive regulation and Government of its inter-nal Police," but then added the qualifying clause "in all Matters that shall not interfere with the Articles of Confederation."[8]

The Dickinson Draft placed one unqualified restriction on the congress, namely that it could never impose any taxes or duties on the states. The new congress, in short, could not become an American version of Parliament, a principle that clearly reflected the core grievance of the colonies over the past decade. But Article 19 provided a long list of powers the con-gress could exercise, most of them related to foreign policy, and taken together they suggested a central government that was a good deal more than the passive plaything of the states.[9]

No official record of the debate over the Dickinson Draft was kept, but both Adams and Jefferson took notes that were preserved in their private papers. These provide a snapshot of the rivalries swirling among the different states and regions. Such deep disagreements had been suppressed until now in order to sustain a united front against the British ministry and on behalf of a common commitment to that elevated ideal simply called "The Cause." But if the core meaning of "The Cause" was American independence, once all the former colonies embraced that goal, the different interests of the new states rose to the surface in a dramatic display of conflicting assumptions about the meaning of "the United States" after independence was won. The chorus quite quickly became a cacophony.

There were, in effect, three fundamental disagreements: first, a sectional split between northern and southern states over slavery; second, a division between large and small states over representation; and third, an argument between proponents for a confederation of sovereign states and advocates for a more consolidated national union. All the political and constitutional questions that would bedevil the emerging American republic until the Civil War were thrown onto the agenda for the first time. For five days in late July and early August 1776, the Continental Congress engaged in spirited debates that proved to be a preview of coming attractions in American history.

Although slavery was too explosive an issue to be addressed directly, it was also too embedded in the economy of the southern states to avoid altogether. The forbidden subject came up in the debate over Article 12 in the Dickinson Draft, which proposed that "the expenses for the war and the general welfare shall be defrayed out of a Common Treasury, which shall be supplied by the several colonies in proportion to the Number of

Inhabitants of every Age, Sex and Quality, except Indians." An argument then ensued over how to count "Inhabitants," which quickly became an argument over slaves: Were they persons or property?[10]

The southern delegates insisted that slaves were like horses and sheep and therefore should not be counted as "Inhabitants." Franklin countered that, the last time he looked, slaves did not behave like sheep: "Sheep will never make any insurrections." This bit of humor was not appreciated by the South Carolina delegation, which then proceeded to issue the ultimate threat: if slaves were defined as persons rather than as property, "there is an End of the Confederation." Sensing a southern secession movement, Samuel Chase of Maryland urged all delegates to calm down, then proposed that the term "white" be inserted before "inhabitants" in order to appease his southern brethren. But Chase's proposed amendment only provoked outrage from northern delegates, including Adams, who accused South Carolina of trying to avoid its fair share of the tax burden to finance the war. In a thoroughly sectional vote, Chase's amendment was defeated.[11]

Since any resolution of the matter would risk a sectional split at the very moment when a united front against Great Britain was utterly essential, the delegates simply tabled it. It was resolved, if that is the correct term, in 1783, when the Confederation Congress voted to count slaves as three-fifths of a person for purposes of taxation and representation, an awkward compromise that was subsequently adopted at the Constitutional Convention.

The question of representation in the new government generated an equally spirited and divisive debate as the argument over slavery, though the split was not sectional but rather between large and small states. In the Continental Congress, each colony had one vote, no matter how large its population. And Article 18 of the Dickinson Draft recommended a continuation of the one-vote-per-state principle.[12]

But when the Dickinson Draft came before the full congress, delegates from Virginia, Pennsylvania, and Massachusetts launched a frontal assault on state-based representation, arguing that population should determine the electoral power of the respective delegations. Franklin was most outspoken on the issue, warning that any new government based on equal representation by state "will never last long," because the disproportionate political power of the smaller states defied the economic realities. It was, Franklin argued, a simple matter of justice: "Let the smaller Colonies give equal Money and Men, and then have an equal Vote."[13]

Advocates for proportional representation also wanted the new confederation to build on the intercolonial alliance against British imperialism forged during the past year. Benjamin Rush of Pennsylvania put it most provocatively: "We are now a new Nation . . . We are dependent on each other—not totally independent states." As Rush described it, Americans were now united in common cause as a single people. Only a representative government based on population could reflect this new reality. Thinking as Virginians or Rhode Islanders was passé. The new name for the government, "the United States," needed to become a singular rather than plural noun.[14]

Delegates from the smaller states found Rush's national vision a political nightmare that exchanged the despotic power of Parliament for a domestic version of the same leviathan. Roger Sherman of Connecticut warned that his constituents would never surrender their liberties to some distant government that did not share their values. Coming together to oppose the British invasion was one thing, but Sherman described "the United States" as a plural noun, and any national ethos was a pipe dream that defied state-based loyalties, which were as far as most Americans were prepared to go. Though there was such a thing as "The Cause," there was no such thing as "We, the people of the United States."[15]

Because voting in the Continental Congress remained state-based, Sherman and the other small-state delegates knew that they could carry the day despite opposition by such powerful opponents as Franklin and Adams. And they did.

The latent disagreements about the powers of the new central government rose to the surface most menacingly in the debate about jurisdiction over the ill-defined western borders of the states. Several states cited colonial charters that placed their western borders at the Mississippi, or even more preposterously in Virginia's case, at the Pacific. A consensus in the congress held that these extravagant claims were based on charters that had been drafted before anyone realized the size of the North American continent. But there was no consensus on the question of whether the states or the new central government possessed the authority to decide the matter. And the landed states like Virginia and the landless states like Maryland were seriously split over how the matter should be resolved.[16]

Jefferson was under pressure from his colleagues back in Virginia to resist any encroachment on the Old Dominion's right to interpret her own charter claims. His main strategy was to defend Virginia's jurisdiction but assure delegates behind the scenes that "no Virginian intended to go to the South Seas," which was apparently a reference to the Pacific. Edward Pendleton, overseeing the Virginia Convention in Williamsburg, urged Jefferson to drag out the debate, then noted ominously that "perhaps while you are reading this, nay indeed while I am writing it, it may be decided by the sword at New York whether we shall have any land left to dispose of."[17]

In hindsight, the failure to achieve any consensus on the shape and powers of the new American government was eminently predictable. Knowing as we do that enormous political and constitutional controversies over the overlapping questions of sovereignty and slavery would define the history of the emerging American republic for the next eighty-five years, we recognize that the conviction that these problems could be solved rather easily in a few weeks of earnest effort during the summer of 1776 was unrealistic in the extreme. Lacking such hindsight, however, most delegates in the Continental Congress expressed deep disappointment in their failure, coming as it did on the heels of the triumphant vote on American independence.

Adams was especially distraught to discover that unanimity about independence should be followed by total disagreement about what an independent American government might look like. "Thus we are sowing the Seeds of Ignorance, Corruption, and Injustice," he lamented, "in the fairest Field of Liberty ever appeared upon Earth, even in the first attempts to cultivate it." Two conclusions seemed to be clear: first, Americans were united, or at least mostly united, in opposition to the policies of the British ministry; second, they were divided along regional and state lines once their common enemy was taken out of the equation. They knew what they were against, but did not know what they were for.[18]

Adams had been extremely adroit at managing the delegates in the Continental Congress between advocates of reconciliation and proponents of independence in 1775 and 1776. Now, however, the divisions within the congress had become more complicated and cut in several directions. Moreover, the political adrenaline that had energized their collective response to British policy had run its course. Winning the war, of course, remained a common goal. Beyond that, however, the colonists had no agreed-upon political agenda, several competing versions of how an independent American republic should be configured, and some skepticism about whether any union of the states should continue after the war was won. In his capacity as de facto secretary of war, Adams's chief job was to prevent these emerging sectional and state divisions from undermining the military alliance. On the very eve of the battle in New York, he got a glimpse of just how difficult that job had become. Beyond independence, Americans had no consensus on what being an American meant.

The exposure of the deep differences that had lain latent beneath the surface since the outbreak of hostilities at Lexington and Concord fifteen months earlier moved the American Revolution into a new phase. The idealistic, quasi-religious political mentality suggested by elevated expressions like "The Cause," and moralistic references to the superiority of American virtue as contrasted with British corruption, had provided a rhetorical platform on which the different and disparate state and regional interests could congregate as a self-proclaimed collective. Like Joseph Warren at Bunker Hill, patriots were prepared to sacrifice everything—in Jefferson's lyrical rendering, "their lives, their fortunes, and their sacred honor"—on behalf of a higher goal.

The exalted and almost operatic character of this mentality was heartfelt but unsustainable. It was like the honeymoon phase of a marriage, blissfully romantic but of short duration. The divisive debates in midsummer 1776 marked the end of virtue and the beginning of interest as the dominant influence in shaping debates in the Continental Congress. To be sure, the Howe brothers had to be defeated and American independence won. But after that, nothing was clear. And everything would have to be negotiated.

. . .

AMID THESE DISPIRITING political developments came one expected and unqualified success. A committee charged with defining the contours of an American foreign policy, most urgently to explore a Franco-American alliance that would give the wartime government an invaluable European partner, delivered its report on July 18. The committee had delegated the task to Adams, who single-handedly wrote the report, which was titled "A Plan of Treaties." Unlike the Dickinson Draft, which was an incoherent expression of differing opinions, the Plan of Treaties spoke clearly and with a singular voice. Almost inadvertently, it defined the framework for American foreign policy that remained in place for over a century.[19]

The first thirteen articles of the plan described the terms of a wholly commercial treaty "between the most Serene and mighty Prince, Lewis the Sixteenth, the most Christian King, His Heirs and Successors, and the United States of America." Adams adopted the courtly language of European diplomacy in its most affected style, presumably to demonstrate that the upstart American government knew how to play the European diplomatic game. In effect, France was being invited to recognize the freshly created United States, and both countries would eliminate all import duties and tariffs in order to foster a more robust commercial connection.[20]

The Plan of Treaties explicitly rejected any diplomatic or military alliance with France. At least in retrospect, this seems strange, knowing as we do that French military assistance was utterly essential in winning the war for independence. But in July 1776 Adams and the other delegates in Philadelphia did not believe that French troops and treasure would be necessary to defeat Great Britain. Confidence in the prowess of the Continental Army and in a virtually bottomless supply of manpower had yet to be exposed as wishful thinking.[21]

Articles 8 and 9 of the plan underlined the chief reason why any military alliance with France posed potential problems, for they prohibited any French claims to territory on the North American continent. A military alliance that put French troops on American soil ran the risk that, once here, they would never leave. Adams was fully aware of France's desire to recover some portion of its lost American empire, and he wanted to foreclose that possibility.[22]

Two years later, when the military situation on the ground looked more problematic, Adams was dispatched to Paris to negotiate the very diplomatic and military alliance that the Plan of Treaties sought to avoid. (Franklin, in fact, had already negotiated the Franco-American alliance before Adams arrived.) Concern about French imperial ambitions on the North American continent, especially Canada, would not dissolve until the last French ship and soldier sailed home.

The truly visionary contribution of the Plan of Treaties, to which the Franco-American alliance of 1778 was the unavoidable exception, was that the lodestar of American foreign policy for the foreseeable future would be neutrality. All treaties, most especially with any of the European powers, would be exclusively commercial in character, with no binding diplomatic or military commitments. The Plan of Treaties was the first formulation of a neutral and isolationist posture subsequently enshrined in Washington's Farewell Address (1796).

This centerpiece of American foreign policy remained in place until World War I and was not officially abandoned until after World War II.

The debate over the Plan of Treaties went as smoothly as the debate over the Dickinson Draft went badly. The Continental Congress adopted it on September 17 with only a few minor revisions. Its passage created a rather anomalous situation, namely that this new entity called the United States had a reasonably clear vision of how it wished to interact within the world of nations, but lacked anything like a consensus on whether it was a nation itself.[23]

. . .

ANY HISTORICAL RECONSTRUCTION of the crowded political agenda of the Continental Congress in midsummer 1776 inevitably imposes an ex post facto sense of coherence that the delegates at the time, doing their best to manage events that were coming at them from multiple angles and at very high velocity, did not share. They were trying to orchestrate a revolution, which almost by definition generated a sense of collective trauma that defied any semblance of coherence and control. If we wish to recover the psychological context of the major players in Philadelphia, we need to abandon our hindsight omniscience and capture their mentality as they negotiated the unknown.

In Jefferson's case, the editorial changes made in his draft of the Declaration preoccupied him more than the debates over the Dickinson Draft and the direction of American foreign policy. He devoted considerable energy to making copies of his unedited version of the document, restoring the sections deleted by the congress, placing their revisions in the margins so as to differentiate his language from the published version circulating throughout the country. He then sent these copies to friends in Virginia, complaining that the congress had diluted the purity of his message, suggesting that all the revisions were defacements designed to appease the faint of heart, who still harbored hopes of reconciliation with Great Britain. This was not really true—the revisions were intended to clarify rather than compromise—but Jefferson's wounded pride required a more compelling rationale than thin skin.[24]

His obsession with preserving his original language eventually waned, but it never completely disappeared. Near the end of his life, he went back to this moment in his autobiography and reiterated his sense of being badly treated by the congress. At the time, he came off as a rather self-absorbed young man, though his early recognition that the language of the Declaration mattered a great deal proved to be prescient.[25]

If his head was focused on defending his own words, his heart was at Monticello, where he himself desperately wanted to be. "I am sorry that the situation of my domestic affairs renders it indispensably necessary that I should solicit the substitution of some other person here," he explained to Edmund Pendleton back in Williamsburg, adding that "the delicacy of the house will not require me to enter minutely into the private causes which render this necessary." These "private causes" surely referred to his wife's health. Martha Jefferson was pregnant and, in fact, on the verge of suffering a miscarriage. "For God's sake, for your country's sake, and for my sake," he wrote to Richard Henry Lee, "I am under a sacred obligation to go home." Ironically, if his plea to be replaced in the Virginia delegation had been promptly answered, he would not have been present to sign the Declaration on August 2, thereby tarnishing his lasting reputation as its author.[26]

If his correspondence is any indication, Jefferson was more interested in the debates over the Virginia constitution occurring at Williamsburg than in the political debates at Philadelphia. He had sent his own draft constitution to Pendleton, who was chairing the Virginia Convention, and was especially concerned that the right of suffrage be extended to "all who had a permanent intention of living in the country." When rumors began to circulate in Williamsburg that he harbored radical ideas about the inherent wisdom of "the people," Jefferson was quick to point out that he opposed the direct election of senators in his draft constitution. "I have ever observed," he wrote Pendleton, "that a choice by the people themselves is not generally distinguished for its wisdom. The first secretion from them is usually crude and heterogeneous."[27]

Another libelous rumor suggesting that he had no stomach for tough-minded politics against Indian tribes allied with the British produced a spirited response that he would subsequently act on a quarter century later as president: "Nothing will reduce those wretches so soon as pushing the war into the heart of their country. But I would not stop there. I would never cease pursuing them while one of them remained on this side of the Mississippi." He obviously cared most about his reputation back home within the Tidewater elite and did not wish to be regarded as a romantic idealist.[28]

Finally, like all the delegates in the congress, Jefferson received regular updates on the military situation in New York. The new information made him more aware of the discrepancy in troop strength between the British and American armies, but he remained confident that the last-minute arrival of militia would even the odds. "Washington discovers a confidence, which he usually does only on high ground," he reported to Pendleton. "He says his men are in high spirits. Those ordered to Long Island went with the eagerness of men going to a dance." Military matters did not command the fullest attention of his formidable intellectual energies, and he accepted at face value the patriotic propaganda issuing from Washington's headquarters.[29]

. . .

ADAMS HAD A wholly different temperament and a range of responsibilities within the congress that did not allow him the luxury of indulging his personal feelings. If Jefferson preferred to levitate above the waves of political and military challenges roiling through the Continental Congress after independence was declared, Adams was predisposed to dive into them all at once. In the debates on the Dickinson Draft, he favored a more unified American confederation. His leadership in drafting the Plan of Treaties, as we have seen, charted the future course for American foreign policy. On every political issue, he was both prepared and pugnacious, a one-man volcano ready to overwhelm his opponents in a lava flow of words. His stature in the congress was equal to Franklin's, who also had his enemies, and his responsibilities were second to none. Working eighteen hours a day, he came across to his colleagues as the indefatigable and inexhaustible revolutionary spirit, running a marathon at the pace of a sprinter.

Most demanding were his duties as chair of the Board of War and Ordnance, for they made him the pivotal connection between the Continental Congress and the Continental Army. He was burdened with a cascade of specific requests. Washington needed thirty thousand flints for muskets, then an additional five tons of gunpowder; promotion decisions for senior officers created bruised egos that he had to soothe; militia units from Massachusetts originally ordered to the northern front on Lake Champlain had to be diverted to bolster Washington's army in New York.[30]

Beyond managing these pressing if nettlesome details, Adams was literally forced by his position as the civilian most responsible for military affairs to engage with the larger strategic issues. Both Joseph Reed and Nathanael Greene wrote him to warn that confidence that the militia would bolster the fighting strength of the Continental Army was misplaced, arguing that the militia were untested amateurs whose numbers did not translate on equal terms with British or Hessian professionals on the battlefield. Reed and Greene urged larger bounties to recruit more soldiers with longer enlistments into the Continental Army.[31]

Adams agreed with their assessment but apprised them that political opinion in the congress was resolutely opposed to the creation of a large standing army. "I am convince that Time alone, will persuade Us to this measure," he explained. "And in the mean Time We shall be forced to depend upon temporary calls upon Militia." More than anyone else in the congress, Adams recognized that the current model of a relatively small Continental Army, supplemented at each engagement with a surge of militia from surrounding states, was risky. Just how risky was about to be discovered on Long Island and Manhattan.[32]

But he could not afford to focus exclusively on the looming battle in New York. For example, a congressional hearing on the failed campaigns against Quebec became a search for scapegoats. Adams concluded that the debacle at Quebec was the result of several uncontrollable factors, chiefly bad weather and a virulent smallpox epidemic. More significantly, he came to regard the entire Canadian campaign as delusional, a misguided use of America's limited military resources based on the presumption that Canada was somehow destined to become part of the United States.[33]

He ordered General Horatio Gates, recently appointed commander of what was being called the Northern Army, to abandon the Canadian campaign and consolidate his position farther south on Lake Champlain. "We are very anxious, for you and your Army," he wrote Gates, "as well as for the General [Washington] and his at New York." Then he added a highly revealing insight: "We expect some bold Strokes from the Enemy, but I don't believe that Howe and Burgoyne will unite their forces this year."[34]

Adams clearly grasped the central goal of British strategy, which was to isolate New England by capturing the Hudson corridor in a two-pronged campaign, with Howe's larger force coming up from New York and General John Burgoyne's 7,000 troops coming down through Lake Champlain. While Washington contested Howe's capture of New York, Adams wanted Gates to forget Canada and focus on stopping Burgoyne's march down the Hudson Valley. More than any other delegate in Philadelphia, he had a panoramic perspective of the entire American theater.

No one was juggling more political and military responsibilities than Adams. No one else recognized the all-or-nothing character of this decisive moment or raised his pulse to match the impossible demands of that moment. He was the revolutionary spirit incarnate, and despite a lengthy career of considerable achievement, this was his finest hour.

But, like Jefferson, Adams found his overcrowded mind diverted by personal distractions about his family. As we have seen, in mid-July he had learned that his wife, Abigail, and their four young children were undergoing inoculation for smallpox in Boston. Abigail's descriptions of their eleven-year-old daughter, Nabby, nearly brought him to tears. "She has about a thousand pustules as large a great Green Pea," and could neither stand nor sit without pain. Then word arrived that Charles, the younger son, had caught the smallpox "in the natural way," meaning by contagion rather than inoculation, and was "in delirium for 48 hours," on the edge of death.[35]

Adams felt that he was failing in his role as a husband and father in order to fulfill his role as an American statesman and patriot. "It is not possible for me to describe . . . my Feelings on this occasion," he wrote Abigail. "I shall feel like a Savage to be here, while my whole Family is sick at Boston." But despite the temptations to head for home, he was like a soldier who could not leave his post. "My Sweet Babe Charles, is never out of my Thoughts—Gracious Heaven preserve him," he wrote to Abigail, but then concluded that "the two Armies are very near each other, at Long Island."[36]

.   .   .

IF JEFFERSON WAS disposed to levitate above the political struggles within congress, and if Adams preferred to embed himself in them all at once, Franklin brought his own distinctive mix of floating engagement to the task. In any meeting he was always the most famous man in the room—an internationally acclaimed scientist, a renowned essayist and wit, the senior statesman par excellence. "I am glad to find that notwithstanding your Countrymen have had so many good slices of you those forty years past," James Bowdoin wrote Franklin with a wink, "there's enough of you to afford them good Picking Still. . . . They still expect to feast upon you, and to feast as usual most deliciously."[37]

Though he was a latecomer to the cause of independence who had worked tirelessly in London to effect a reconciliation, his conversion was as complete as it was sudden. He was convinced that the decision by George III and the British ministry to, in effect, declare war on the American colonies would go down as the biggest blunder in the history of British statecraft, and he had apprised Richard Howe of that conviction. It was a measure of Franklin's prestige that Lord Richard, instead of feeling insulted, attempted to sustain the friendship. He hoped that "the dishonour to which you deem me exposed by my military situation in this country has effected no change in your sentiments of personal regard towards me; so shall no difference in political points alter my desire of proving how much I am your sincere and obedient humble servant." Franklin wrote back to reiterate his view that Howe's hopes for a reconciliation with America and with him were illusions. But he chose not to send the letter. He conveyed the impression of a prophet who knew which way history was headed. And if you were on the wrong side, as Howe clearly was, no sentimental attachment could bridge the gap between the two political camps.[38]

Franklin applied the same rigorous standard to his own son, William, an illegitimate child whom he had raised as a full-fledged member of his family. William Franklin had been appointed the royal governor of New Jersey, then sided with Great Britain when the Anglo-American argument widened into a war. He was arrested as a dangerous Tory in the spring of 1776 and was eventually sent to Connecticut for safekeeping. William's wife, Elizabeth, wrote to Franklin, begging him to intercede and have William paroled to New Jersey so they could be together. "Consider my Dear and Honored Sir," she wrote, "that I am now pleading the Cause of your Son, and my beloved Husband." Frank-lin did not respond. His son had chosen sides and would have to live with the consequences. At this fateful moment, political commitments were thicker than blood.[39]

On the more controversial issues about the future American government raised by the Dickinson Draft, Franklin was a staunch advocate for proportional representation and therefore a neonationalist who thought that an independent America should become more than a confederation of sovereign states. But he was not willing to insist on the proportionality principle in the face of united opposition from the smaller states. Just as he thought that history was on the American side in the war for independence, he thought that time would prove a state-based confederation inadequate to the task of governance. If that political fruit had to ripen before it could be picked, so be it. If you knew how the journey was going to end, you could afford to be patient along the path.[40]

The same combination of prescience and patience shaped his response to the drafting of the Pennsylvania constitution. Like Jefferson, he took a personal interest in the framing of his own state's constitution. But unlike Jefferson, Franklin enjoyed the advantage of proximity—the Pennsylvania Convention was meeting in Philadelphia, indeed in the same building as the Continental Congress.

In meetings with Pennsylvania delegates on August 13 and 15, he lent his considerable weight to two of the most distinctive and conspicuously democratic provisions of the Pennsylvania constitution, namely the insistence on a bill of rights and the creation of a one-house legislature to be elected by a citizenry that included artisans as well as property owners, thereby giving Pennsylvania the most egalitarian government in the United States. But he let others take the lead in the debates and receive the credit when the final draft was ratified. His suggested revisions were almost entirely stylistic. Given his prestige, his most important contribution was being present to lend legitimacy to the enterprise. In both the Pennsylvania Convention and the Continental Congress, Franklin was an invaluable trophy, more revered and renowned at this stage than Washington; he was the Delphic Oracle of the American Revolution.[41]

It was a role that Franklin took to instinctively, since he was a genius at sensing what the political imperatives of the moment required. In this instance, they required a sagacious pose, embodying the conviction that the cause of American independence had providential winds at its back. They also required him to become involved in the political debates at a higher altitude that preserved and protected his special status by not being drawn into damaging arguments. This made him an intriguing combination of Adams's omnipresence and Jefferson's distancing. He was a singular figure.

But even Franklin, who believed the British course was doomed, recognized that the military outcome in New York would determine whether the eventual American victory would occur quickly—obviously the preferred conclusion—or slowly, in a more drawn-out war that Great Britain would eventually abandon. He lacked the full flow of information that Adams enjoyed about troop strength and the doubts about the fighting prowess of the militia, but one informant serving in the batteries along the Hudson assured him that the British invasion would be repulsed: "Every circumstance here is cheerful and if our Enemies dare attack, they will undoubtedly procure themselves a severe drubbing." Franklin did not believe that a defeat in New York would kill the American cause, but neither did he believe that patriotic estimates of the odds were reliable. He was confident that America would win the war but uncertain that the Continental Army would win the battle for New York. "While I am writing," he told Horatio Gates on August 28, "comes an account that the armies were engaged on Long Island, the event unknown, which throws us into anxious suspense. God grant success." As it turned out, God was not listening.[42]

6

The Fog of War

In general, our Generals were out generalled.
—JOHN ADAMS TO ABIGAIL ADAMS, October 8, 1776

Ever since Lord Richard Howe's fleet had landed on Staten Island in early July, Washington had been expecting an attack. But over the ensuing weeks, as additional waves of troops and ships arrived, it became apparent that Lord Germain and the British ministry intended to assemble a strike force much larger than Washington expected. And the Howe brothers saw no reason to launch an invasion until all of Germain's reinforcements, most especially the highly professional (and very expensive) Hessians, showed up in mid-August.[1]

The delay meant that the military campaign would begin late in the season, leaving the Howes only about three or four months to capture New York and vanquish the Continental Army before going into winter quarters. It also meant that the size of the American force opposing the invasion would grow considerably, because militia units from Connecticut, Pennsylvania, Delaware, and Maryland would flow into New York in early August, latecomers who had harvested their crops before shouldering their muskets.

Though mystified by the delaying tactics of the Howes, Washington welcomed the opportunity to even the odds:

"They [the British troops] have been stronger than the Army under my Command, which will now, I expect, gain greater strength than theirs, as the Militia are beginning to come fast, and have already augmented our numbers . . . to about 23,000 men." A week later, on the eve of the battle, they totaled about 28,000.[2]

The militia surge bolstered the confidence of several American officers, including even Greene, despite his skepticism about the fighting prowess of militia. Writing from the front lines on Long Island, Greene assured Washington that all was under control: "I have the Pleasure to inform you that the Troops appear to be in exceedingly good Spirits, and have no doubt that if they should make their attack here we shall be able to render a very good account of them." Lord Stirling, who was supervising the defensive preparations on Long Island, concurred with Greene. The forts, redoubts, and trenches were so formidable that Stirling actually hoped, as he put it, "that General Howe would come here in preference to any other spot in America." Eight months earlier Charles Lee had rendered the judgment that New York was indefensible. Now Stirling thought it impregnable.[3]

Stirling's excessive enthusiasm often made it difficult to distinguish between bravado and confidence. But subsequent testimony from British and Hessian officers confirmed that the layered defensive scheme on Long Island was sufficient to repel a frontal assault by 50,000 troops. And even Germain had not seen fit to gather a British force that large.

Given the capacity for carnage building up on both sides, the final exchange of letters between William Howe and Washington seemed to suggest that Howe deeply regretted the whole bloody business. "I cannot close this letter," he confided to Washington, "without expressing the deepest Concern that the unhappy state of the colonies, so different from what I had the Honor of experiencing in the Course of the last war, deprives me of the Pleasure I should otherwise have had in a more personal Communication."[4]

Washington recognized this as a nostalgic postscript to the failed effort at reconciliation a month earlier. But he felt obliged to respond in the same aristocratic style, maintaining the etiquette of honor between two gentlemen who wished to disassociate themselves from the looming slaughter they were about to oversee. "Give me leave to assure you, sir," Washington replied, "that I feel myself greatly obliged by the polite conclusion of your letter . . . and have a high sense of the honor and satisfaction I should have received from your personal acquaintance. The different state of the colonies from what it was in the last War & which has deprived me of that Happiness, cannot be regretted by any one more than Sir Your Most Obedt Servt." The courtesies having been properly exchanged, the bloody work could now begin.[5]

.   .   .

ANTICIPATING JUST WHERE that work would occur was Washington's primary dilemma. On August 14, two British deserters reported that the main British attack was aimed at Long Island. Another intelligence report a few days later predicted coordinated attacks on Long Island and the northern tip of Manhattan. Although one of the cardinal principles of military tactics was never to divide your army in the face of a superior force, Washington was forced to violate it because he was defending two islands against an opponent with total naval supremacy. He chose to regard any British attack against Long Island as a likely diversion; placed 6,000 troops, only a third of his men "fit for duty," there; and kept the remainder on Manhattan, which after all was the ultimate British objective.[6]

Meanwhile, over on Staten Island, a lively debate was occurring between Howe and Henry Clinton, his second-in-command, over their strategic options. In truth, Howe had little respect for Clinton either as a general or as a man, so there was never a serious chance that Clinton's preference would prevail. They had served together at Bunker Hill and in the Boston Siege, where Clinton had displayed his lifelong tendency to make enemies of all his superiors, who never seemed to appreciate his advice as much as he thought it deserved. Clinton, it seems, possessed a truly unique talent for making himself obnoxious; he was the kind of insufferable character who always knew he was right. In this instance, however, all the advantages of hindsight make it abundantly clear that, in fact, he was.[7]

Clinton favored a British invasion at King's Bridge, at the northern end of Manhattan, where the Harlem River separates the island from the mainland. If successful, this option would block the escape of the Continental Army on both Manhattan and Long Island, presuming British naval control of the Hudson and East rivers. Once trapped, the Continental Army could be gradually eroded and eventually annihilated in a single campaign. Clinton's strategy was based on the assumption that the proper target was not the city and port of New York but the Continental Army itself. If it ceased to exist, the American rebellion would follow suit.[8]

Howe disagreed. He believed that the Continental Army had to be decisively defeated but not destroyed. His orders from Germain were to capture New York, which would then become the base of operations for the British army and navy for the decisive campaign to close the Hudson corridor and isolate New England. If the city and port of New York were the target, then Long Island was the obvious avenue to reach it, since command of Brooklyn Heights would render southern Manhattan indefensible. If the Continental Army was sufficiently humiliated in the process to break the will of the rebellion, so much the better. But the strategic goal was the occupation of New York, not the annihilation of the Continental Army. Howe had the final say, of course, so the invasion on Long Island was scheduled for August 22, by which time the recently arrived Hessians should be ready to go.[9]

In hindsight, Howe's decision to reject Clinton's preferred strategy may have meant that Great Britain lost a golden opportunity to end the American rebellion at its very inception. We can never be sure about this might-have-been, because we cannot know whether the total destruction or capture of the Continental Army would have broken the will of the rebellion. Perhaps, as both Adams and Franklin sincerely believed, the Continental Congress would have defiantly raised another army and appointed another version of Washington to lead it. What is clear is that both armies would have been better served if their respective commanders had exchanged places. For Howe, in targeting the territory rather than the Continental Army, pursued the cautious strategy when he should have been bold. And Washington, in his very decision to defend New York, pursued the bold strategy when he should have been cautious.

· · ·

AN IMPROBABLE PIECE of bad luck then struck at the worst possible time, when Greene informed Washington that he was "confined to my Bed with a raging fever" on August 15. Washington's ablest and most trusted officer, just appointed a major general, Greene had also designed and built the defensive network on Long Island and made himself thoroughly familiar with the terrain. Now he had to be evacuated to Manhattan. To replace Greene, Washington chose John Sullivan, not because he knew and trusted him but because he was the only senior officer without a command, having just come down from Albany after threatening to resign rather than serve under Horatio Gates. Sullivan was a former New Hampshire lawyer of boundless confidence, limited military experience, and total ignorance of the troops he was to command and the ground he was to defend.[10]

The British Army had been practicing amphibious operations on Staten Island for two weeks. On August 22, more than 300 transport vessels carried 15,000 troops into Gravesend Bay in southwestern Long Island without a hitch and without any appreciable resistance. Lord Howe's secretary, Ambrose Serle, described the scene as breathtaking: "In a Word, the Disembarkation of about 15,000 Troops upon a fine Beach, their forming upon the adjacent Plain . . . exhibited one of the finest & most picturesque Scenes that the Imagination can fancy or the Eye behold." Three days later another 5,000 Hessians were ferried across. Although Washington moved another 2,000 men over the East River to reinforce the Long Island garrison, the Americans were outnumbered more than two to one. Washington was still hedging his bets that the invasion of Long Island was a feint and the main British attack would come on Manhattan.[11]

In his General Orders the next day, Washington announced that the long-awaited testing time for the Continental Army had finally arrived: "The Enemy has now landed on Long

Island, and the hour is fast approaching, on which the Honor and Success of this army, and the safety of our bleeding Country depend. Remember officers and Soldiers, that you are Freemen, fighting for the blessings of Liberty—that slavery will be your portion, and that of your posterity, if you do not acquit yourselves like men." In case these inspiring words proved insufficient, all the troops should also know that "if any man attempt to skulk, lay down, or retreat without orders, he will instantly be shot down as an example."[12]

. . .

GREENE HAD DEVISED a three-tiered defensive scheme for Long Island designed to inflict an unsustainable level of casualties on the British as they moved through each killing zone. Sharpshooters would be positioned in the thickly wooded area north of Gravesend Bay, concentrated along the three passes that afforded space for British horses and artillery to advance. The American troops would then fall back to a necklace of trenches and redoubts on Gowanus Heights, a ridgeline running east to west across Long Island. Greene's original plan envisioned a stiff but temporary stand on Gowanus Heights, then a retreat to the main defensive perimeter, which consisted of four forts on Brooklyn Heights, where he presumed the heaviest fighting would occur. It was a collapsible network of defensive positions that took maximum advantage of the terrain and allowed the American troops to fight behind cover rather than engage the British on open ground, where the superior discipline and experience of British soldiers would be likely to prevail.[13]

Sullivan's first, and last, act as a commander was to revise Greene's plan by enlarging the garrison on Gowanus Heights to 3,000 men, nearly half his force. As events were to demonstrate, this was a costly mistake, making Gowanus Heights the focus of the battle, where the American force would be outnumbered seven to one.

Then, on August 24, Washington had second thoughts about Sullivan and appointed Israel Putnam as overall commander on Long Island, with Sullivan restricted to command of the troops on Gowanus Heights. "Old Put" had the torso of a bull, the head of a cannonball, and the mentality of a natural warrior. A veteran of Bunker Hill and a legendary Indian fighter in the French and Indian War—he had once escaped while being roasted by Indians over a fire—Putnam had requested the command once it became clearer that the main British attack would come on Long Island. "The brave old man was quite miserable at being kept here," Joseph Reed wrote from the headquarters on Manhattan. While Washington's change of mind conveyed a certain indecisiveness, putting his most battle-tested leader in charge also reflected his recognition, at last, that Long Island was the British objective. Despite that recognition, he kept over half his troops on Manhattan, thereby covering his bases, but at the cost of ensuring that the British would enjoy a vastly superior force at the point of attack.[14]

William Howe was reputed to be the finest student of light infantry tactics in the British Army. And his experience at Bunker Hill meant that he was perhaps the last British officer in America to mount a frontal assault against Greene's formidable network of defenses. But the more he studied the maps, the more Greene's defensive scheme seemed to defy evasion, making a battle with high British casualties unavoidable.

Then Henry Clinton came up with a bold, if stunningly simple, solution. He had also been studying the maps. Far to the east, about seven miles from the center of the American defenses, was a little-used road called Jamaica Pass. Local loyalists reported that the Americans regarded it as too far away to justify anything more than a token force of defenders. But it was, Clinton claimed, the key to the battle for Long Island, because it would allow Howe to outflank Greene's layered entrenchments.

Clinton proposed a flanking maneuver up Jamaica Pass that would place British troops behind the American lines on Gowanus Heights, cutting off their retreat to the forts on Brooklyn Heights. He also proposed that British and Hessian units engage the right and center of the American defensive front in order to compel their attention until they found themselves surrounded. It was a brilliant plan, the obvious answer to Howe's tactical dilemma, but it was burdened by the awkward liability of coming from the obnoxious Clinton.[15]

Clinton later acknowledged that he was his own worst enemy during tactical debates with Howe. "My zeal may perhaps on these occasions," he recalled, "have carried me so far as to at times be thought troublesome." In this case, however, Clinton had the good sense to delegate the presentation of his plan to a subordinate. On August 26, Howe embraced it, invoking the commander's prerogative to claim it as his own.[16]

A group of loyalists then volunteered to guide British troops up Jamaica Pass in a night march. It was telling that no Long Island residents exposed the British plan to anyone in the Continental Army. This was perhaps the one place in America that was so predominantly loyalist in sentiment that the British enjoyed a significant advantage in intelligence, a rare occasion that Howe exploited fully.

· · ·

John Adams orchestrated the argument for American independence in the Continental Congress in the spring and summer of 1776, then served as the de facto secretary of war during the first two years of the conflict.
Harvard Art Museums/Fogg Museum, Harvard University Portrait Collection, Bequest of Ward Nicholas Boylston to Harvard College, 1828, H74

John Dickinson led the moderate faction in the Continental Congress, believing that war against the British army and navy was suicidal.
Independence National Historical Park

Benjamin Franklin was a latecomer to the cause of American independence, but once converted, he brought his enormous prestige to bear as the most famous American of the era. Franklin insisted that the British cause was both misguided and hopeless.
The Metropolitan Museum of Art

Thomas Paine, author of *Common Sense,* severed the last remaining link with the British Empire by condemning George III and monarchy in general as vestiges of the Dark Ages.
Courtesy of the Library of Congress

Thomas Jefferson became the poet of the American Revolution in the summer of 1776, drafting the words that have continued to echo through the ages. *The Metropolitan Museum of Art*

The Committee of Five—John Adams, Benjamin Franklin, Thomas Jefferson, Robert Livingston, and Roger Sherman—presents the draft of the Declaration of Independence to John Hancock on June 28, 1776, a scene often mistaken for having taken place on July 4. *Yale University Art Gallery, Trumbull Collection*

Above: After learning that independence had been declared, on July 9, 1776, New Yorkers celebrated by pulling down the massive statue of George III at Bowling Green in Lower Manhattan. *Lafayette College Art Collections, Easton, Pennsylvania*

Left: George Washington made the elemental strategic mistake of trying to defend New York against a vastly superior British army and navy. The debacle that resulted nearly lost the war at the very start. *U.S. Senate Collection*

George Germaine was the British secretary of state who orchestrated the naval and ground assault at New York, designed to quash the American rebellion with one massive blow.
Crown copyright

Above: Nathanael Greene was Washington's ablest and most trusted lieutenant. It was Greene who persuaded Washington to abandon the defense of New York and remove the Continental Army from the threat of total destruction.
Independence National Historical Park

Left: William Howe was the British commander in chief who adopted a measured and cautious strategy on the mistaken assumption that American support for the war was skin-deep.
Anne S. K. Brown Military Collection, Brown University Library

Richard Howe was generally regarded as the finest officer in the Royal Navy, but his fondest hope was to broker a political settlement of the American rebellion that kept the American colonies in the British Empire.
National Maritime Museum, Greenwich, London

Henry Clinton went to his grave believing that if he had been commander of British forces in the Battle of New York, the American Revolution would have ended in the summer of 1776. *Courtesy of the Council of the National Army Museum, London*

Drawing by a British naval officer depicting the arrival of Lord Howe's fleet at Staten Island on July 12, 1776. *Spencer Collection, The New York Public Library, Astor, Lenox and Tilden Foundations*

The Billopp House on Staten Island, also called the Conference House in recognition of the meeting held there on September 11, 1776, when the American delegation rejected Lord Richard Howe's plea for reconciliation. *Courtesy of the Library of Congress*

Lord Stirling leading American troops against the British line in a suicidal charge that successfully covered the retreat of the main American army to Brooklyn Heights. *Wikimedia Commons*

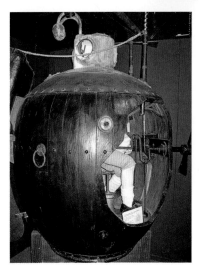

A replica of the primitive submarine, the *Turtle,* which sank in the Hudson after a vain attempt to destroy Admiral Howe 's flagship, the *Eagle,* in early September 1776. *Wikimedia Commons*

The Morris-Jumel Mansion, which served as Washington's headquarters during the fighting on Manhattan. *Courtesy Tom Stoelker*

A depiction of the Great Fire that destroyed one-third of New York City during the evening of September 20, 1776. *Eno Collection, Miriam and Ira D. Wallach Division of Art, Prints and Photographs, The New York Public Library, Astor, Lenox and Tilden Foundations*

AT NIGHTFALL ON August 26, Clinton led the vanguard of 10,000 British and Hessian troops on a looping seven-mile march around the left flank of the American defenses, Howe and Cornwallis trailing with the main body. How Sullivan could have neglected to defend Jamaica Pass invited criticism at the time and speculation ever since. He was aware that the pass existed, since he dispatched five horsemen to guard it, all of whom were quickly and easily captured. How a British force so large, hacking and sawing its way through underbrush, could move undetected has also seemed strange. In fact, two American officers, Samuel Miles and David Brodhead, later testified that they *did* spot the British column. "I was convinced . . . that General Howe would fall into the Jamaica road," Miles recalled, "and I hoped there were troops there to watch them." But there were not. Sullivan subsequently attempted to excuse his blunder by claiming, rather lamely, "I had no foot [i.e., soldiers] for the purpose."[17]

Meanwhile, up on Gowanus Heights, Clinton's plan was working perfectly. A formidable British force of 5,000 infantry and 2,000 marines commanded by General James Grant engaged Stirling's brigade on the right flank. Sullivan apprised Putnam that the main British attack had begun, and Putnam in turn urged Washington to cross the river and join him on Brooklyn Heights to oversee the battle. In truth, Grant's attack was only a diversion, designed to engage the American troops while the force under Clinton and Howe came around from the rear.[18]

Grant nevertheless used the occasion to bombard Stirling's men from a distance for two hours. "Both the balls and shells flew very fast," one soldier reported, "now and then taking off a head." Stirling had ordered his men to stand in formation rather than take cover, a way of exhibiting military discipline and embracing the code of honor still alive and well in the eighteenth century. "Our men stood it amazingly well," one soldier proudly declared, "not even one showed a disposition to shrink." A Hessian force under General Leopold von Heister, another 4,000 troops, gathered to the right of Grant's men as together they braced themselves to become the anvil to the Clinton-Howe hammer, the Continental Army in between.[19]

The hammer came down at nine o'clock on the morning of August 27, when 10,000 British soldiers emerged behind the American lines, producing panic among new recruits, who were simultaneously surrounded and outnumbered. In most units, discipline dissolved immediately as soldiers attempted to flee to the forts on Brooklyn Heights. Joseph Plumb Martin, then only fifteen years old, remembered that a young American lieutenant broke down, sobbing uncontrollably, begging forgiveness from his men as they ran past him to the rear. He also remembered officers removing the cockades from their hats so they could not be recognized as officers if captured. He witnessed a massacre at Gowanus Creek as retreating American soldiers either drowned or were gunned down by British infantry from the bank, the dead bodies floating over the entire surface of the water.[20]

In certain pockets of action, captured American troops were summarily executed. "The Hessians and our brave Highlanders gave no quarter," recalled one British officer. "And it was a fine sight to see with what alacrity they dispatched the rebels with their bayonets, after we had surrounded them so they could not resist." Other witnesses described Hessians pinning American prisoners to trees with their bayonets. Such atrocities were the exception rather than the rule, but they later became standard features in American newspaper accounts of the battle that depicted the Hessians as barbaric mercenaries.[21]

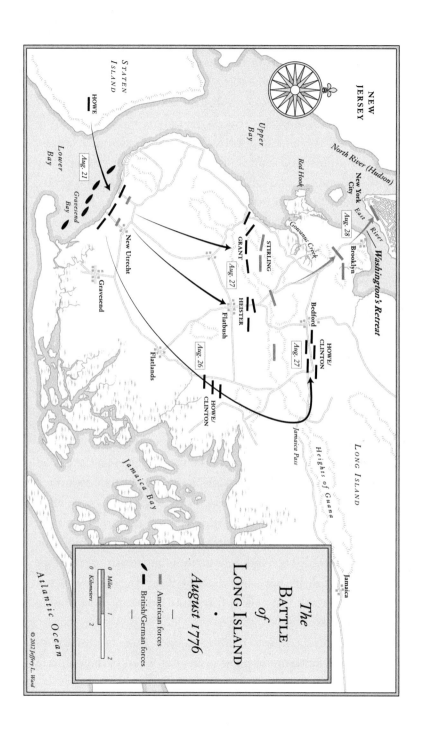

The
BATTLE
of
LONG ISLAND
·
August 1776

— American forces

— British/German forces

0 Miles 1 2
0 Kilometers 1 2

© 2012 Jeffrey L. Ward

While the dominant response of the American troops was fear and flight, in some sectors of the battlefield they fought with a ferocity that even the British acknowledged as impressive. This was especially true on the right flank, where Stirling commanded veteran regiments from Maryland and Delaware. Stirling himself was an unlikely combat leader, described by his biographer as "an overweight, rheumatic, vain, pompous, gluttonous inebriate." But in this intense time of testing, he was magnificent, several observers agreeing that he "fought like a wolf." In order to buy time for his other troops to escape, Stirling led his Marylanders on seven suicidal attacks against British regulars—400 against 2,000—suffering a 90 percent casualty rate in the process of inflicting heavy losses on the British. Observing the action from Brooklyn Heights through his spyglass, Washington was heard to remark, "Good God! What brave fellows I must this day lose."[22]

It was all over before noon. Both armies reported inflated casualty rates for the other side, Howe rather preposterously claiming more killed, wounded, or captured Americans than were engaged in the fighting on Gowanus Heights. The best estimate is that both sides suffered between 300 and 400 dead and wounded, the Americans more dead than wounded because of the Hessian massacres. But the best measure of the British victory was the number of Americans captured, nearly 1,000, most of whom were fated to die miserable deaths from disease and malnutrition on British prison ships in New York harbor supervised by Betsy Loring's husband. Two American generals, Stirling and Sullivan, were among the prisoners.[23]

Ironically, because so many inexperienced American troops fled so precipitously, simply ignoring the efforts of their officers to stand and fight, about 2,000 made it back to the forts to fight another day. Veteran British troops would have obeyed their officers and ended up casualties or prisoners.

Beyond the sheer calculus of casualties and captured, however, the will of the Continental Army had been broken and any semblance of military discipline destroyed. The psychological momentum on the battlefield had swung entirely in the British direction, so much so that British and Hessian troops had to be restrained from pursuing the fleeing Continentals into the forts on Brooklyn Heights.

Several witnesses, including Howe himself, believed that the forts and the entire American army on Long Island would have been taken if the British attack had continued. "Had they been permitted to go on," he later acknowledged, "it is my opinion that they would have carried the redoubts." Looking down from Brooklyn Heights, Putnam observed that "General Howe is either our friend or no general." In Putnam's judgment, Howe "had our whole army in his power.... Had he instantly followed up his victory the consequences to the cause of liberty must have been dreadful." And Clinton, true to form, believed that Howe had missed the chance to end the war in a single stroke. "Complete success would most likely have been the consequence of an immediate attack," he recorded in his memoirs, "for there is no saying to what extent the effect resulting from the entire loss of the army might have been ... or where it would have stopped." Clinton held to his conviction that the destruction of the Continental Army would have generated traumatic shock waves that in turn would have destroyed the will of the American people to continue the war.[24]

William Howe thought differently, though his thought process at this stage had become as layered as the American defenses on Long Island, and any attempt to do it justice requires the kind of analytical skills customarily associated with psychoanalysis.

As we know, Howe had once entertained serious hopes of negotiating a peaceful end to the rebellion, which he tended to regard as an unfortunate misunderstanding that had somehow escalated to the current bloodletting because of radical leaders in Philadelphia and ill-informed officials in London and Whitehall. His fondest dream, shared by his brother, was to go home not as a conquering hero but as a statesman who had successfully brokered a peaceful reconciliation with his former American brethren.

This dream was dashed in July, when his brother's entreaties were dismissed as wholly inadequate by both Washington and the Continental Congress. Having crossed the line toward independence just before the Howes arrived, the rebels were not disposed to retrace their steps. By August, then, Howe had become convinced that only a decisive military defeat could bring the Americans to their senses by exposing the utter futility of their fight against a vastly superior British army and navy. And he was fully prepared to deliver that defeat on Long Island, which is what by late August he was in the process of doing.[25]

Nevertheless, the dashed dream of a negotiated settlement never died. Howe had only put it aside to administer a proper thrashing to Washington's amateur army, after which the rebels would be more disposed to recognize the hopelessness of their cause. And for this reason, he conducted the war on the assumption that a careful and calibrated demonstration of British military supremacy was sufficient for the task at hand. Unlike Clinton, who believed that the war must be won quickly with a massive blow that destroyed the Continental Army so that it did not evolve into a protracted conflict of dubious conclusion, Howe thought British victory was inevitable, which in turn meant that a more limited strategy was wholly adequate. Unlike the British campaigns against the Irish and the Scots, which were savage, genocidal conflicts that left residues of resentment for centuries, Howe wanted his American campaign to be a more measured affair, permitting a postwar resumption of the prewar mutual affection that he remembered so well.[26]

Howe's preference for a strategy of limited war had a British component as well. He was obsessed with keeping his own casualties low, which was the consideration he subsequently cited in defense of his decision to halt the attack on Brooklyn Heights. "I would not risk the loss," he explained, "that might have been sustained in the assault." Bunker Hill still haunted him, to be sure, but so did a keen sense that he was managing resources that were expensive, finite, and not easily replaced.[27]

The American and British sides of the Howe equation, then, were perfectly balanced. On both sides, he preferred to keep damage to a minimum. In the case of those forts on Brooklyn Heights, that meant conducting a siege while the British navy bombarded them from offshore. In a matter of days, Washington would have no choice but to surrender, a delay of small consequence when compared to the losses on both sides that would be entailed with an immediate frontal attack. After all, if you were sure of the outcome, there was no need to hurry, a posture that also suited Howe's laid-back style.

Washington was too beleaguered to affect anything like a style. For two days, he wore himself out riding up and down the line on Brooklyn Heights, exhorting the dispirited troops. Exhausted, still dazed by the ruinous defeat, the man who would one day earn a well-deserved reputation for decisiveness did not know what to do. And as he stared into the abyss, a heavy rain filled the trenches so that sentries were standing waist-deep in water, many of their muskets useless because their powder was wet. Meanwhile, Howe's engineers were digging their own trenches, angling up toward the forts in zigzag formations that afforded cover in a classic siege tactic. It was now clear that Washington's decision to order another 1,200 troops over from Manhattan, enlarging the garrison on Brooklyn Heights to 9,500, had been a mistake, since it only put more American troops in the British trap. Given the forces arrayed against him, Washington had only three options: surrender, face annihilation, or attempt an escape across the East River to Manhattan.[28]

Joseph Reed had been pressing Washington to make the only plausible choice, but for several reasons he could not bring himself to order a retreat. He had, after all, been lecturing his men to stand fast against the British attack for months. How could he reverse himself now without appearing foolish?[29] More elementally, Washington was an honor-driven man in the eighteenth-century mode. He understood completely why Stirling had ordered his men to stand at attention while British artillery rounds and grapeshot (i.e., chain links and iron pellets) were lopping off heads and disemboweling his troops. Though it sounds irrational to our modern mentality, Washington believed that his personal honor, meaning the core of his character as an officer and a gentlemen, obliged him to suffer death rather than the dishonor of retreat. His apparent paralysis was the result of balancing two imperatives: his reputation against the survival of the Continental Army.[30]

The resolution of his dilemma came on August 29 in the form of General Thomas Mifflin, who had done a reconnaissance of the American perimeter and reported that troop morale was low, with several units actually talking about surrendering to the British. Mifflin was a wealthy Philadelphia merchant of Quaker background who had rejected his pacifist principles to become Pennsylvania's preeminent soldier. Washington agreed to call a council of war that afternoon if Mifflin himself proposed the retreat, which preserved Washington's honor because the request would come from someone else. Mifflin concurred, but with one provision, namely that he command the last troops to evacuate and therefore run the greatest risk of being killed or captured, a gesture that also preserved his own sense of honor.[31]

The council of war met at Four Chimneys, the baronial summer home of Philip Livingston, which offered a panoramic view of the escape route the Continental Army would take, near the modern-day Brooklyn Bridge. The conclusion was unanimous, thereby forcing Washington to embrace a course chosen by his generals rather than himself, allowing him to preserve the pretense that he preferred to go down fighting. All that remained was to plan and carry out the evacuation of nearly 10,000 men without alerting the British Army of their departure over a body of water that was controlled by the British navy. One young Connecticut officer, Major Benjamin Tallmadge, put the matter succinctly: "To move so large a body, across a river full a mile wide, with a rapid current, in face of a victorious well disciplined army nearly three times as numerous as his own and a fleet capable of stopping the navigation, so that not one boat could have passed over, seemed to present most formidable obstacles."[32]

At least the wind was blowing the Americans' way. A northeastern storm restricted the movement of British warships up the East River, though it also posed navigation problems for American boats trying to get across. Although he had no other choice, Washington now needed to perform one of the most brilliant tactical withdrawals in the annals of military history.

.   .   .

DECEPTION WAS THE essential ingredient in the evacuation plan. Washington issued a General Order to assemble all ships and flat-bottomed boats on Manhattan and Long Island, purportedly to ferry additional troops over from New Jersey. This allowed Colonel John Glover and his Massachusetts regiment of Marblehead fishermen and seamen to gather the fleet to evacuate Long Island under the pretense of reinforcing it. The very sight of Glover and his colorfully attired troops, all moving with the disciplined precision acquired from years of experience aboard ships at sea, made an immediate impression: "These were the lads," noted one young officer from Pennsylvania, "that might do something." What they were in fact about to do was show this army of amateur soldiers how a regiment of seasoned seamen staged a rescue operation at night.[33]

Only a few of the officers and none of the enlisted men knew that an evacuation was under way. In some units, when ordered to go "under arms with packs," the troops assumed they were about to attack the British trenches and proceeded to make out their wills in anticipation of certain death. Joseph Plumb Martin remembered the sudden code of silence: "We were strictly enjoined not to speak, or even cough. All orders were given from officer to officer, and communicated to men in whispers." Tench Tilghman, a young lieutenant soon to become one of Washington's most trusted aides, reported that whole regiments moved to the rear without knowing their destination: "The thing was conducted with so much secrecy that neither subalterns nor privates knew that the whole army was to cross back again to New York."[34]

The tactical retreat of an entire army currently engaged with a larger enemy force is so difficult to orchestrate because units have to be removed piecemeal, in staggered fashion, leaving a sufficient complement of troops to hold the perimeter. Timing, therefore, has to be precise, and the remaining troops need to spread out to replace those just evacuated. A nearly fatal blunder occurred on Brooklyn Heights midway through the evacuation, when Mifflin received an order to withdraw all his troops. The order was a mistake, since Mifflin's men were supposed to leave last and their withdrawal would leave the American front fully exposed. Mifflin questioned the order but reluctantly obeyed it.

As he led his troops back toward the ferry, Washington rode up and demanded to know what Mifflin was doing. "Good God! General Mifflin, I am afraid you have ruined us," he shouted. Mifflin, understandably exasperated and confused, explained the communication error, then led his troops back to the trenches. Though the American position had been undefended for over an hour, the British never noticed.[35]

This piece of good fortune was more than matched when the northeastern storm subsided and the winds shifted to the southeast, which greatly facilitated the movement of Glover's boats across the East River. The weather change should have prompted the appearance of British warships on the water, which would have transformed the American evacuation into a full-scale massacre, since the overloaded rowboats were defenseless. But Lord Howe, uncharacteristically, never noticed the wind shift and never brought the British fleet into play.

He was preoccupied with dinner conversation aboard the

Eagle, his flagship, where the two captured American generals, Stirling and Sullivan, were his guests, and Lord Richard was fixated on discovering whether the recent humiliation of the Continental Army might have changed their minds about his proposals for a peaceful end to the rebellion. Like his brother, if not more so, Richard Howe's fondest hope was for diplomatic reconciliation rather than military victory, and at this fateful moment that was where his fullest attentions were focused.

The gods smiled on the American escape one final time on the morning of August 30. The last troops to evacuate were most at risk, in part because no one remained in the rear to cover their retreat, in part because they would have to sneak out in broad daylight. Major Tallmadge remembered it well many years later:

> As the dawn of the next day approached, those of us who remained in the trenches became very anxious for our own safety. . . . At this time a very dense fog began to rise, and it seemed to settle in a peculiar manner over both encampments. I recollect this peculiar providential occurrence perfectly well; and so very dense was the atmosphere that I could scarcely discern a man at six yards' distance. . . . In the history of warfare I do not recollect a more fortunate retreat.[36]

As Tallmadge was being rowed across, he looked back to see Washington stepping into the last boat to leave Long Island. It was the stuff of legend. In all nearly 10,000 men were safely ferried to Manhattan with only three stragglers lost. The planning had to be precise, the officers and men needed to behave with uncommon courage, the winds and river currents had to be properly aligned, the Royal Navy had to be negligent, and, finally, a dense fog had to make a providential appearance at the end. And all these ingredients had to come together in the proper sequence. Although successful retreats seldom win wars, in this instance the evacuation of Long Island meant that the Continental Army would live to fight another day. One could be forgiven for believing that "The Cause" could never die.

The initial response on the British side was utter disbelief that Washington had somehow managed to extract his entire army without being noticed. The Americans, so it seemed to several British officers, had shown themselves to be wholly inadequate on the field of battle, but brilliant in their talent at running away.

The prevailing British impression, beyond astonishment, was that the spirit of the Continental Army had been broken on Long Island, the utter futility of confronting the British army and navy had been convincingly demonstrated, and it had been achieved with relatively few British casualties. In short, all of General Howe's campaign goals had been met. As one British general, Lord Hugh Percy, put it: "I may venture to assert that they will never again stand before us in the field. Everything seems to be over with them, and I flatter myself that this campaign will put a total end to the war."[37]

There were, however, dissenting voices. Captain George Collier, commander of the warship *Rainbow,* thought that each of the Howe brothers had missed an opportunity to destroy or capture the entire American army on Long Island. General Howe's decision to halt the British assault on the forts at Brooklyn Heights looked less convincing now that Washington had escaped the trap. And Admiral Howe's failure to throw the British fleet into the East River, which Collier claimed "we have been in constant expectation of being ordered to do," struck Collier as inexplicable, since only a few British frigates would have meant that "not a man would have escaped from Long Island." Whether such opportunities would come again no one could say. "Now, I foresee," Collier lamented, "they [the Americans] will give us trouble enough, and protract the war, Heaven knows how long."[38]

· · ·

NEWS OF THE American defeat slowly dribbled into the Continental Congress, in part because Washington was too exhausted to file a report. "For Forty Eight Hours," he explained to Hancock, "I had hardly been off my Horse and never closed my Eyes, so that I was quite unfit to write or dictate." His eventual report emphasized the successful evacuation from Long Island, played down the debacle on Gowanus Heights, and provided an inflated estimate of British casualties, thereby conveniently obscuring the full scope of the military disaster and the dispirited condition of the Continental Army. Gossip mills at Washington's headquarters on Manhattan began to circulate the opinion that Greene's unfortunate absence was the primary cause of the defeat: that if Greene had been commanding on Long Island, the whole battle would have gone differently.[39]

The General Orders for August 31 sustained the same patriotic rhetoric as before the battle, suggesting that nothing had really changed: "From the justice of our cause, America can only expect success," it read. "Now is the time for every man to exert himself, and make our Country glorious, or it will become contemptible." In order to set an example, Washington deliberately chose to expose himself to British artillery fire from the Long Island shore. After two rounds missed overhead, and having made his point, Washington allowed his staff to lead him away.[40]

By any detached measure, the Continental Army had suffered a humiliating defeat. And according to General Howe's strategic calibrations, the political and psychological consequences of that crushing experience should have shocked the leadership of the American rebellion into the realization that their glorious cause was, in truth, a hopeless waste of blood and treasure. Washington's initial management of the after-action reports undercut Howe's strategy by concealing the depth of the disaster, a justifiable distortion from his perspective in order to reduce the sudden impact that the military debacle might have on popular opinion. If he had failed to control the movement of his troops on the battlefield, he would attempt to control the perception of the battle's consequences in that larger battle for popular opinion.

Down in Philadelphia, Adams was having similar thoughts. He had originally intended to return to Braintree and his family. But a premonition that the news from New York might be bad convinced him to remain at his station: "Indeed, if the Decision should be unfortunate . . . , perhaps I may be as well calculated to Sustain such a Shock, as Some others." He worried most about the psychological effect of Howe's victory on the faint of heart in the congress and on the so-called half-Tories out there in the countryside. "The Panic may seize whom it will," he confided to Abigail, "it shall not seize me. I will stay here until the public Countenance is better, or much worse. It must and will be better."[41]

Adams's first instinct was to minimize the damage by claiming that matters could have been much worse. If the Howe brothers had failed in New York, he argued somewhat dubiously, they would have attacked Boston, and its loss would have been more devastating. Then he argued that the very enormity of the British victory would prove to be a military liability. "If they get Possession of New York, Long Island, and Staten Island," he observed, "these are more Territory than their whole Army can defend." According to this line of thought, which was at best counterintuitive, every British military victory only increased the burden of occupation, implying that the best way to win the war was to lose every battle. Arguments like this suggest that Adams could not acknowledge any possibility of an American military defeat leading to British victory in the war.

The truth was that the amateur status of the Continental Army had been exposed in no uncertain terms on Long Island, and all the platitudinous incantations about the moral superiority of the American cause had fallen victim to the military superiority of a professional army. These were uncomfortable facts that Adams, like Washington, needed to obscure, even to himself.[42]

If all Americans were like his beloved Abigail, Adams would not have faced a political problem. Like her husband, Abigail was resolute. "We seem to be kept in total Ignorance of affairs at [New] York," she observed, insisting that "if our Army is in ever so critical a state, I wish to know it, and the worst of it." She was prepared to know the unvarnished truth because she was beyond compromise. "But if we should be defeated," she insisted, "I think we shall not be conquered." In response to her request for a candid assessment of the American performance on Long Island, Adams was elegantly succinct: "In general, our Generals were out generalled."[43]

Adams was particularly attuned to gauging sudden shifts in the political weather. The preceding spring, he had watched with a combination of admiration and amazement as popular opinion shifted quite dramatically toward independence in response to George III's decision to impose a military solution on the American rebellion. Now he sensed a shift in the other direction in response to the disaster on Long Island: "The Successes of Howe have given a strange Spring of Toryism," as another delegate put it. "Men who have hitherto lurked in silence and neutrality seem willing to take a side in opposition to the liberties of their Country." Washington had even been heard to predict that more American volunteers in New York and New Jersey were likely to join Howe than enlist in the Continental Army.[44]

The correspondence of other delegates to the Continental Congress suggests that Adams was not alone in attempting to manage the political momentum. Although Benjamin Rush confessed to his wife that the setback in New York had transformed the political climate and that matters were likely to get worse rather than better, in letters to others he put the best face on the current crisis. "I can therefore from authority assure you," he wrote a French friend, "that a fixed determination still prevails in that body [the Continental Army] to establish the liberties of America or to perish in their ruins. No difficulties discourage us, no losses depress us."[45]

Franklin joined the chorus, though in his case there was no need to stretch the truth, since he remained confident that Howe's victory was merely a minor setback, a brief chapter in the eventual and inevitable story of American triumph. He acknowledged that British troops "have been rather too Strong for our people to cope with, and consequently have succeeded in their interprizes, which have not been of the importance that they will probably seem to the World." Franklin held firm to his elemental conviction that the British military mission in

America was impossible, and nothing about the recent British success had changed his mind: "For what have they done?" he asked rhetorically. "They have got possession of three small islands on the coast of America . . . , and yet if every Acre of American territory is contested in the same Proportion, the Conquest would ruin all Europe."[46]

In the spectrum of political opinion within the Continental Congress, Adams and Franklin were among the most resolute in believing that, having crossed the line toward independence, there could be no turning back, regardless of what happened to Washington's army in New York. Then, in the first week of September, a dramatic event galvanized opinion among the other delegates within the congress around a nonnegotiable strategy.[47]

The event was General John Sullivan's arrival in Philadelphia. Recall that Sullivan, along with Stirling, had dined with Lord Howe on board the *Eagle* the night that Washington's army escaped across the East River. During the dinner, Lord Richard managed to persuade the earnest Sullivan that his peace commission empowered him to offer generous terms that would allow the Americans to end this senseless and unnecessary war with their honor intact. Howe had then offered to send Sullivan on parole to apprise the congress of these terms.

In his report, Sullivan described Lord Howe's utter sincerity. Then he argued that by sending him to Philadelphia, Howe was implicitly recognizing the authority and legitimacy of the Continental Congress. More substantially, Howe had made clear his personal opinion "that Parliament had no right to tax America or meddle with her internal Polity," and he was confident that George III and his ministers were now open to such an arrangement once hostilities ceased.[48]

Sullivan's report provoked a vigorous debate. Rush subsequently remembered that Adams leaned over during the debate "and whispered to me a wish that the first ball that had been fired on the day of the defeat of our army [on Long Island] had gone through his [Sullivan's] head." Adams then rose to protest the proceedings, calling Sullivan "a decoy duck whom Lord Howe has sent among us to seduce us into renunciation of our independence."[49]

The following day, September 5, John Witherspoon of New Jersey delivered the major speech denouncing Lord Howe's proposals, and no one rose to challenge his conclusions. "It is plain," Witherspoon argued, "that absolute submission is what they require us to agree to," so that despite the appearance of generosity, Lord Howe "has uniformly avoided any circumstance that can imply that we are anything else but subjects of the king of Great Britain, in rebellion." Once framed in that fashion, only an outright loyalist could embrace Howe's terms, and no such creature could be found in the Continental Congress. Those delegates who had been shaken by events in New York and were harboring doubts had nowhere else to go.[50]

The only controversy arose over how to reply to Lord Howe, if at all. Trusting Sullivan to deliver their answer was unacceptable, since his reputation, already tarnished by his conduct on Gowanus Heights, was now in deeper decline for his having been duped by Howe. But failure to respond might be perceived by lukewarm patriots as excessively defiant. Best not to risk losing them and to err on the side of diplomacy.

Howe had offered to receive a delegation from the congress, but only in their capacity as private citizens, since his instructions prohibited him from recognizing the legitimacy of the Continental Congress. The delegates tossed this diplomatic problem back in his face with the following resolution: "Resolved that this body cannot with propriety send any of its members to confer with His Lordship in their private characters." On the other hand, "ever desirous of establishing peace on reasonable terms, they will send a Committee of their body, to know whether he has any Authority to meet with persons authorized by Congress for that purpose in behalf of America." Given his instructions, Howe either could refuse to meet with the American delegation, thereby assuming responsibility for the diplomatic impasse, or he could meet with but then acknowledge that he had no authority to negotiate with representatives of an American government. In either case, the peace initiative would be exposed as a diplomatic mirage.[51]

.   .   .

THE FOLLOWING DAY, September 6, the congress chose Adams, Franklin, and Edward Rutledge of South Carolina to meet with Lord Howe on Staten Island. The selection of Adams and Franklin ensured an interesting conversation that would end in failure, since Adams was high on the list of prominent American rebels scheduled for public hanging for treason if and when Howe's peace terms were accepted. And Franklin, Howe's former friend, had recently advised him that his military mission was hopeless and that continued service in this ill-fated cause would destroy his reputation forever.

Even though the conclusion was foreordained, the meeting on September 11 was a dramatic occasion. Clearly, Howe held out the hope that the recent American catastrophe on Long Island might have generated second thoughts among the Americans about the prospects for an easy exit from the British Empire. Just as clearly, the American delegation came to the conference determined to dash that hope. Not quite so clearly, but most probably, a poll of the American population would have revealed a citizenry more politically divided and receptive to Howe's terms than the Continental Congress or its diplomatic representatives. Unfortunately for Howe, polls were not possible.

Diplomatic etiquette on both sides was almost excessively correct. Howe had arranged to leave a British officer as a hostage at Perth Amboy, where the Americans disembarked, as a guarantee of their safety once in British hands. Adams insisted that no hostage was necessary, since Lord Howe's word was a more-than-sufficient guarantee. "You make me a very high Compliment," Howe observed, "and you may depend on it, I will consider it the most sacred of things." An honor guard of resplendent British grenadiers ushered the Americans into the meeting place with all the ceremonial trappings. Inside, Howe had laid out a sumptuous spread of "good Claret, good Bread, Cold Ham, Tongues and Mutton." The civilities were assiduously observed.[52]

Howe began by pleading his sincerity as a famous friend of America. He explained that he had delayed his voyage for several weeks in order to acquire instructions as a peace commissioner, but that very delay had meant that he arrived just after passage of the Declaration of Independence. "Is there no way of treading back this step of Independence," he asked, "and opening the door to a full discussion?"[53]

Adams and Franklin led the American response, which was polite but wholly negative. If the British ministry had recognized American sovereignty over taxation and its own domestic affairs a year earlier, the conflict could almost certainly have been avoided. But that was then and this was now. Adams spelled out the British transgressions since the outbreak of hostilities at Lexington and Concord, culminating in the very invasion force that Lord Howe now co-commanded.

In response to this long string of abuses, the American states had voted unanimously for independence, and the Continental Congress had ratified that vote, which could not be undone. In fact, the American delegation was just as powerless to reverse that verdict as Howe was to recognize them as American citizens rather than as British subjects. When Howe explained that he preferred to regard his guests as fellow gentlemen, Adams replied that his Lordship was free to meet with them in any capacity he wished, "except that of British subjects."[54]

The unspoken item on the agenda, which Howe thought awkward to address directly, was the recent action on Long Island, which surely cast at least a shadow of doubt over American prospects for success against the vastly superior British army and navy. Howe's more elliptical way of raising the issue was to express his deep affection for America, then add that "if America should fall, he should feel and lament it like the loss of a brother." Years later Adams still remembered with relish Franklin's deft response: "Dr. Franklin, with an easy air and a collected countenance, a bow, a smile and all the Naïveté which sometimes appeared in his conversation . . . replied 'My Lord, we will do our utmost to save your Lordship that mortification.' "[55]

Rutledge then proposed that since American independence was a nonnegotiable fact, perhaps Howe could persuade his friends back in London to embrace it and then make an economic alliance with the United States with all its attendant commercial advantages for both parties. Howe expressed his doubts that any of his superiors in London would find that idea acceptable; nor was it what he had in mind.[56]

There was really nothing more to say. Despite the military setback on Long Island, not to mention the highly precarious status of the Continental Army on Manhattan, nothing had changed in the American political posture. Ambrose Serle, Howe's snobbish secretary, was furious. His summation of the proceedings, recorded in his journal that night, was terse and vitriolic: "They met, they talked, they parted. And now nothing remains but to fight it out against a Set of the most determined Hypocrites & Demagogues compiled by the refuse of the Colonies that ever were permitted by Providence to be the Scourge of a Country."[57]

Adams went back to Philadelphia equally angry. He told Sam Adams that "the whole Affair . . . appears to me, as it ever did, to be a bubble, an Ambuscade, a mere insidious Maneuver, calculated only to decoy and deceive." His only explanation, which contained more than a kernel of truth, was that "they must have a wretched opinion of our Generalship to suppose that we can fall into it."[58]

7

Hearts and Minds

I give it as my opinion that a General And Speedy
Retreat is absolutely Necessary, and that the honor and
Interest of America require it.

—NATHANAEL GREENE TO GEORGE WASHINGTON,

September 5, 1776

According to the calibrated strategy of the Howe brothers, the humiliation of the Continental Army on Long
Island was supposed to generate shock waves that would shake
the foundation of the American rebellion. But the conference
with Lord Howe on Staten Island seemed to expose the flaw in
that strategy, since the American delegation refused to regard
the debacle on Long Island as anything more than a temporary setback of minor significance. Adams and Franklin even
harbored the conviction that the annihilation or surrender of
the entire Continental Army would have made no difference,
except perhaps to prolong the inevitable American victory. The
Howe brothers were trying to use their superior army and navy
as instruments of a not-so-gentle persuasion, but the leaders
of the Continental Congress, having committed to American
independence, were beyond persuasion, in a zone where any
prospect of reconciliation with their British betters was now
unimaginable.

The Continental Army, on the other hand, was experiencing precisely the sense of shock that the Howe brothers had intended to deliver. Favorable winds, shifting river currents, then a providential fog, had allowed Washington's troops to make a near-miraculous escape across the East River, but their spirit had been broken. "Our situation is truly distressing," Washington reported to Hancock. "The Militia, instead of calling forth their utmost efforts . . . are dismayed, Intractable, and Impatient to return [home]. Great numbers of them have gone off, in some cases by whole Regiments." As the troops arrived on Manhattan, one witness described them as "sickly, emaciated, cast down. . . . In general everything seemed to be in confusion."[1]

Exact numbers are impossible to know, since Washington himself could not keep track of the deserters. But the best estimate is that about 10,000 militia walked away during the first two weeks of September. Washington issued an order to stop the deserters at King's Bridge on the northern end of Manhattan, but quickly rescinded the order on the grounds that the militia had proven worse than worthless, and their very presence fed an epidemic of fear and defeatism. Their departure meant that Washington commanded an army of 18,000, of whom only about 13,000 were "fit for duty," which meant that he was now outnumbered more than two to one.[2]

Even those troops who were categorized as "fit for duty" were dazed and demoralized, "constantly rambling about," as Washington described them, "at such distances from their respective quarters and encampments, as not to be able to oppose the enemy in any sudden approach." Fortunately for them and the American cause, William Howe did not launch an invasion of Manhattan to follow up his triumph on Long Island. This delay seemed inexplicable to several British officers, since it was clear that the Continental Army was wholly vulnerable, while the British Army was poised to end it all in one final battle. "For many succeeding days did our brave veterans . . . stand on the banks of the East River," remembered Captain George Collier, "like Moses on Mount Piszak, looking at their promised land less than half a mile away."[3]

Howe's apparent lack of initiative was, in fact, wholly in keeping with his strategic priorities. He was waiting to hear about the results of his brother's conference with the rebels on Staten Island. There was no point in launching another military action if a diplomatic resolution of the conflict was imminent. Besides, the rebel army, if indeed it still could be described as an army, had escaped from one trap on Long Island to another on Manhattan. There was no need to hurry, since Washington's dispirited troops had nowhere else to go.

British spies reported that American soldiers were busy plundering all the homes in the city, apparently justifying their thievery on the grounds that otherwise the booty would fall into the hands of the British Army, which could occupy the city whenever it chose to do so. Just as Howe had hoped, their near-death experience on Long Island forced them to face the fact that the defense of New York was, and always had been, misguided.

Indeed, from the British perspective, the American rebellion had already been quashed, and what remained was merely a mopping-up operation. Back in London, news of the Long Island victory prompted Lord Germain to initiate the paperwork for William Howe's elevation to a knighthood as a reward for his services in preserving Great Britain's empire in North America. "The leaders of the rebellion have acted as I could have wished," Germain wrote to Admiral Howe, meaning taken a stand at New York. "I trust that the deluded people will soon have recourse to your lordship for mercy and protection, leaving their chiefs to receive the punishment they deserve." This presumably meant that Washington, Adams, and Franklin, among others, would go to the gallows.[4]

．．．

WASHINGTON REMAINED IN his quarters during the early days of September, recovering from exhaustion. The deeper truth was that he was groping toward the realization that the decision to defend New York had been an elemental mistake, and now, caught in the consequences of that mistake, he did not know what to do.

The clearest recommendation came from Nathanael Greene, just released from the hospital after a near-death experience of his own: "The object under consideration is whether a General and speedy retreat from this Island is Necessary or not. To me it appears the only Eligible plan to oppose the Enemy successfully and secure ourselves from disgrace. I think we have no Object on this side of King Bridge. . . . I would burn the City and suburbs." In Greene's calculus, the survival of the Continental Army counted more than the defense of any piece of ground. "I give it as my opinion," he reiterated, "that a General And Speedy Retreat is absolutely Necessary and that the honor and Interest of America require it."[5]

Greene was asking Washington to embrace two unpalatable and intractable realities: first, that the decision to defend New York had been a mistake, and the time had come to recognize that fact and cut American losses; and second, that Washington needed to subordinate his honor-driven instinct to stand and fight to larger political imperatives, which in this case meant the survival of the Continental Army. It was clear that Greene, unlike Adams and Franklin, believed that the destruction of the Continental Army put the movement for American independence at risk.

Greene's diagnosis of Washington's temperament was just as sharp as his assessment of the strategic options facing the Continental Army. He recognized that Washington harbored a deeply ingrained sense of personal honor in which the failure of the Continental Army cast a shadow over his own reputation. He tended to equate retreat with defeat, and defeat with a permanent stain on his own character. Within this code, a strategic retreat was dishonorable behavior, like refusing an invitation to duel. Greene's point was that Washington's highest priority must be the principled cause for which they were fighting, and there was nothing principled or honorable about ordering the demise of the Continental Army.

Nevertheless, Washington's first instinct was to reject Greene's advice. His correspondence with Hancock at this moment was uncharacteristically unfocused and meandering, perhaps a symptom of residual fatigue, or an aftershock from the trauma of the Long Island disaster. (He regarded Hancock, as president of the Continental Congress, as his civilian superior, not Adams, even though Adams was better informed on military matters as head of the Board of War and Ordnance.) Despite the desperate situation of the Continental Army, he was uncomfortable with the decision to surrender New York without a fight, telling Hancock that "it would have the tendency to dispirit the Troops and enfeeble the Cause." It might also have serious political consequences throughout the colonies, "where the Common cause may be affected by the discouragement it may throw over the minds of many . . . , especially after our

Loss upon Long Island." Whether the crucial consideration was his own personal sense of honor, or the need to recover the confidence of the army, or the fear that abandoning New York would generate doubts in the minds of lukewarm patriots everywhere, he felt the need to deliver "a brilliant stroke" against the British on Manhattan, even if that meant running the risk of losing everything, including his own life, in the process.[6]

One intriguing attempt at "a brilliant stroke" involved the deployment of a one-man submarine. As we have seen, Franklin had approached Washington several weeks earlier about the prospect of an underwater vessel that might sink British warships by cruising beneath them and attaching a delayed-reaction bomb to their hulls. On September 6, Washington gave his approval to a pioneering effort at underwater warfare. Despite difficulty with river currents, the experimental submarine, named the *Turtle,* managed to get beneath Admiral Howe's flagship, the *Eagle*, with a 150-pound bomb but could not manage to attach it to the copper-covered keel. If successful, the *Turtle* might have significantly reduced the tactical advantage enjoyed by the British navy on the rivers surrounding Manhattan. But soon after its maiden voyage, the *Turtle* sank in the Hudson while being transported upstream for another trial run. It would take more than a century for submarine warfare to become technologically feasible.[7]

On September 7, Washington convened a council of war that voted to endorse his preference for a stand—perhaps a last stand—on Manhattan. It was a confusing debate because Washington had received orders from the Continental Congress not to burn New York City, which some officers interpreted as an order to defend it at all costs. Washington seemed to endorse that interpretation by reminding his fellow officers that the principle of civilian control of the military must be respected, even though it was clear that the Continental Congress did not fathom the truly desperate situation confronting its army.

Once the big decision to defend Manhattan had been made, the council of war voted to divide its forces, placing 5,000 troops at the southern end of the island to defend the city; 9,000 men at the northern end, where the British attack was most likely; and 4,000 of the newest recruits in the middle, where an attack was least likely. Because the British retained the initiative, they would enjoy a significant numerical advantage wherever they chose to launch their assault.[8]

Washington wanted Hancock to understand that Manhattan was all but lost. "It is our Interest & wish," he explained, "to prolong it as much as possible." As Joseph Reed explained to his wife, the goal was to inflict heavy losses on the British before surrendering, "and if a sacrifice of us can save the cause of America, there will be time to collect another army before spring, and the country will be preserved." This fatalistic formulation almost surely reflected Washington's thinking—or what passed for thinking—at this tense and crowded moment. Washington was preparing to make himself into a martyr.[9]

It is also possible that he believed he had no other choice but to sacrifice himself and the Continental Army because, outnumbered and isolated as they were, they had no realistic prospect of escaping from Manhattan. General Howe would have to be a blithering idiot not to block the one avenue of escape at King's Bridge, and the American commander there, William Heath, apprised Washington that he lacked the troops to stop Howe from sealing the trap. An engineering officer, Rufus Putnam, scouted the terrain and confirmed Heath's assessment that there was no way of preventing Howe from putting the Continental Army in "a Bad Box."[10]

Writing from the relative security of Fishkill, the delegates of the provisional government of New York confirmed the strategic diagnosis: "We are so fully satisfied of the Enemies Design to land above New York, and of the Mischiefs that will result thereupon . . . we have Reason to dread the Consequences." All concurred that British naval supremacy on the Hudson and East rivers, plus British superiority on the ground at the northern end of Manhattan, meant that Washington was marooned. Since surrender was not an option, the only choice was to fight.[11]

During the second week of September, three new developments combined to change Washington's mind. First, the Continental Congress clarified its earlier order not to burn the city of New York, leaving the decision to defend it to Washington's discretion. His judgment, not theirs, was more fully informed by the facts on the ground and enjoyed their support. Second, still waiting on word from his brother about the peace initiatives, General Howe showed no inclination to mass his army around King's Bridge. He preferred to prepare for his occupation of the city and port of New York. Third, Greene lobbied his fellow generals for another council of war to reconsider the decision to defend Manhattan, arguing that its defense was untenable and the survival of the Continental Army was synonymous with the survival of American independence. "The present Case is of such Magnitude and big with such Consequences to all America," Greene insisted, "that a reconsideration of the earlier decision is imperative."[12]

The day after the failed peace conference on Staten Island, on September 12, the general officers voted 10–3 to reverse their decision of the preceding week. They would now abandon any defense of the city of New York and consolidate their force at King's Bridge to resist the anticipated British attack there rather than spread the Continental Army the entire length of Manhattan. For the time being, they would leave 2,000 troops at Fort Washington, near the present-day George Washington Bridge, to contest British naval supremacy on the Hudson. The new goal was to block Howe's likely invasion at the northern tip of Manhattan, then evacuate the entire Continental Army off the island. The new priority was the preservation of the army at all costs, including the loss of New York.[13]

Washington embraced the new strategy reluctantly. It violated all his primal instincts, his honor-driven temperament, and the military assumption he had been harboring for the last four months about making New York a more lethal version of Bunker Hill. In explaining the new plan to Hancock, he was almost apologetic. He wanted Hancock to know that he had fully intended to defend New York, because he recognized its strategic importance. "But I am fully convinced that it cannot be done," he pleaded, "and that an attempt for that purpose if preserved, might and most certainly would be attended with consequences the most fatal and alarming in their nature."[14]

By "fatal" he almost surely meant the destruction of the Continental Army. Whether he agreed with Greene that the end of the army meant the end of American independence is not so clear. He had been regarding the American cause as invincible for so long that it was psychologically difficult for him to give it up. But if the destruction of the Continental Army did put American independence at risk, then it was not a risk worth running. He was fully prepared to surrender his own life on this ground, and he wanted that fact to be known to all his officers. But matters larger than his own honor were at stake, and he needed to subordinate his own instincts to that larger purpose.

. . .

REPORTS FROM THE field began to gather on Adams's desk in Philadelphia after his return from Staten Island. His position as head of the Board of War and Ordnance made him privy to the alarming desertion rates, the dispirited condition of the remaining troops, and what Henry Knox described as "the sense of Panic" that had gripped the entire Continental Army in the wake of the Long Island ordeal. "I despise that Panic and those who have been infected with it," he apprised Knox and half seriously urged that "the good old Roman fashion of Decimation should be Introduced," meaning that every tenth man in a demoralized regiment should be executed as a lesson to the others. Meanwhile, his job was to prevent the infection from spreading to the Continental Congress, which, even more than the army, was the center that had to hold.[15]

William Hooper of North Carolina reported conversations with former moderates on the independence question, who were now whispering "I told you so" in the corridors. But in the full-scale debate over Lord Howe's peace initiative, it had become clear that any chastened second thoughts generated by Howe's victory in New York were regarded as inadmissible; American independence remained nonnegotiable. The leadership in the congress effectively enforced a silence on the troubling fact that they were losing the war.[16]

This in turn meant that the political agenda should proceed apace, undistracted by unwelcome news from New York. On September 9, for example, the delegates finally got around to revising the style manual for all official correspondence, so that it replaced "United Colonies" with "United States." On September 17, they adopted the final draft of Adams's Plan of Treaties, designed to forge a diplomatic alliance with France, subsequently choosing Jefferson to join Silas Deane in Paris to negotiate the treaty. (Jefferson declined for personal reasons, chiefly the fragile health of his wife.) On September 20, they approved another Adams draft, the Articles of War, which standardized regulations for promotions, procedures, and punishments within the Continental Army and which Adams freely acknowledged "were copied from the British Articles of War, *totidem verbis*."[17]

The underlying presumption remained that regardless of what happened on the battlegrounds of New York, the American Revolution was going forward. If Adams needed any boost to his revolutionary confidence—and he did not—he received it from his indomitable Abigail. If all the men in Washington's army were killed or captured, she declared, the Howe brothers would have to contend with "a race of Amazons in America."[18]

While the British had convinced themselves that the war was all but over, the leaders in the congress wanted to make a clear statement that it had barely begun. For months, Washington had been warning that an American army of short-termers supplemented with militia could not compete on an equal basis against British regulars. Now the fiasco on Long Island and the demoralized and deteriorating condition of the troops on Manhattan had proven his point. "We are now, as it were, upon the eve of another dissolution of our Army," he warned Hancock, meaning that desertions were increasing and enlistments were about to expire, "and unless some speedy and effectual measures are adopted by Congress, our cause will be lost."[19]

Greene chimed in with a rant against the illusory prowess of militia, now deserting in droves. "The policy of Congress has been the most absurd and ridiculous imaginable," he wrote his brother, "pouring in militia who come and go every month.

A military force established on such principles defeats itself." Washington seconded the verdict, observing that if the battle of Long Island taught anything, it was that "to place any dependence on Militia is, assuredly, resting upon a broken staff."[20]

Unknown to Washington and Greene, the Continental Congress had already voted to give them everything they were asking for and more. On September 16, the delegates ordered the creation of 88 new battalions, another 60,000 men. Enlistments would be encouraged by signing bonuses of $20, and enlistments "for the duration" by the promise of 100 acres of western land at the end of the war.[21]

In order to implement this order, troop quotas were established for each state according to population. (Interestingly, although the delegates could not agree on whether representation in the new government should be by state or proportional according to population, they easily agreed that big states like Virginia and Massachusetts should bear a larger burden militarily.) Hancock wrote to the governors of all the states, urging them to "bend all your Attention to raise your Quota of the American Army."[22]

This new initiative reflected the recognition that events in New York had dashed all hopes for a short war. As Washington put it, the winning of independence "is not likely to be the Work of a day." Moreover, in the kind of prolonged struggle they now faced, reliance on patriotic zeal, much like reliance on militia, would no longer suffice. "When men are irritated & the Passions inflamed, they fly hastily and cheerfully to Arms," Washington intoned in his most realistic mode. But those heady days were now over, and the war was entering a new phase in which discipline and endurance replaced patriotic virtue as the ingredients essential for victory. "To expect among such People as compose the bulk of the Army that they are influenced by any other Principles than those of Interest," Washington warned, "is to look for what never did, & I fear never will happen."[23]

The decision by the Continental Congress represented a collective commitment to provide Washington with the kind of permanent standing army he believed necessary to win the war. It also represented a symbolic statement of political resolve that, no matter what happened to Washington's army on Manhattan, the pool of manpower available to the American cause was virtually inexhaustible, a message calculated to generate tremors in the corridors of Whitehall.

But the decision was also symbolic in another sense, for its implementation depended upon compliance by all the state legislatures, which were predisposed to fund militias within their own borders rather than recruits for the Continental Army. And since a mandatory draft defied the republican principles that they were all purportedly fighting for, the order was really a request, and compliance was wholly voluntary, which meant that a new 60,000-man army was never going to happen. Washington might well have argued that republican principles were meaningless if America lost the war, and the leadership of the Continental Congress obviously agreed. But the political reality was that the delegates in Philadelphia were making a promise they could not keep.

To be sure, all the state governments remained resolute on the question of American independence. (The Howes had expected some defections after Long Island.) But when it came to providing money and men for the Continental Army, each state government made the protection of its own citizenry the highest priority. They were no more willing to cede authority to the Continental Congress than they were to recognize the sovereign authority of Parliament. They were united on the question of independence, but only as long as each state was permitted to pursue that goal as it saw fit.

. . .

IT IS DIFFICULT to generalize about the bulk of the American citizenry. No question, these were the most important hearts and minds of all and therefore the ultimate target of the Howe strategy, which intended the humiliation of the Continental Army to serve as a demonstration of British military superiority. Something akin to a referendum on independence had occurred in May and June, with decisive results. Would the results be equally decisive or dangerously divisive if a referendum occurred in September?

No such referendum occurred, of course, but even if it had, no major change would have been likely, because most of the population remained ignorant that the Continental Army had suffered any kind of defeat at all. And the simple reason for the widespread ignorance was that American newspapers did not report it. Abigail Adams was reading the newspapers as intensively as anyone, and she complained about the lack of coverage: "We seem to be kept in a total Ignorance of affairs at [New] York. . . . Who fell, who [were] wounded, who made prisoner or their Numbers is as undetermined as it was the day after the Battle. If our army is in ever so critical a state, I wish to know it, and the worst of it."[24]

In fact, one of the Boston newspapers Abigail was reading, *The New England Chronicle,* reported a glorious American victory on Long Island.

The ministerial army attacked our lines on Long Island at three different places, with their utmost force; but the intrepidity of the soldiers of the United States, joined with that vigor becoming to a free people, repulsed them; that they were obliged to retreat precipitously, with great loss, the particulars of which we have not yet been able to learn.

The *Chronicle* also reported, prominently but inaccurately, the death of General James Grant, the British officer who had previously predicted that he could subdue the American rebellion in a matter of weeks with 5,000 British regulars. Several other newspapers picked up this story, which had great patriotic appeal given Grant's disdain for the fighting prowess of American troops.[25]

The *Connecticut Courant* accurately described the size of the British and Hessian invasion force and the encirclement of American troops on Gowanus Heights, but then reported that the beleaguered Americans "bravely fought their way through the enemy, killing great numbers of them and brought off many prisoners." The *Pennsylvania Packet* repeated this version of the battle almost word for word, but then added the first-hand description, wholly fabricated, of "the glorious death of General Stirling from a witness who was close to him when he fell."

The *Newport Mercury* printed an account by a Rhode Island soldier that accurately described the heavy American losses and Stirling's bravery as well as his capture but emphasized the steadfast courage and eventual victory of the American troops, despite being outnumbered. The *Virginia Gazette* emphasized the "high spirits" of the Continental Army on the eve of the battle, but then offered no coverage of the battle itself. A later story erroneously reported that "General Howe had his leg dangerously shattered by a ball" and that an epidemic had broken out among the Hessian troops, who were purportedly on the verge of mutiny.[26]

Virtually all of the newspapers provided extensive and accurate coverage of the meeting with Lord Howe on Staten Island and the subsequent rejection of his peace initiative by the Continental Congress, a decision that received editorial accolades from all quarters as the proper statement of American defiance. Only a few papers mentioned the charmed and desperate escape at night over the East River to Manhattan, presumably because it did not square with earlier accounts of American victory on Long Island.[27]

The press, in short, did not provide an unbiased version of the Battle of Long Island or the glaring problems within the Continental Army. In this highly charged and vulnerable moment, loyalty to "The Cause" trumped all conventional definitions of the truth so completely that journalistic integrity became almost treasonable. As a result, there was little discernible wavering in the commitment to American independence in any province beyond the New York theater, where loyalists were volunteering in droves to join the British Army. The partisan American press had concealed the full extent of the demoralized condition of the Continental Army. Few Americans knew they were losing the war.

. . .

ON SEPTEMBER 12, GENERAL HOWE LEARNED that his brother's efforts at negotiation had failed. This was the same day that the council of war decided to abandon the defense of Manhattan. From Howe's perspective, this meant that the city and port of New York had to be taken. The irascible Clinton questioned this decision, proposing a diversion toward lower Manhattan, followed by the main attack at King's Bridge, thereby "corking the bottle" and sealing the entire Continental Army on the island. "Had this been done without loss of time," Clinton later claimed in his *Memoirs*, "while the rebel army lay broken in separate corps . . . each part of it [must have] fallen into our power one after the other."[28]

Hindsight is not required to recognize the strategic wisdom of Clinton's proposal. All of Washington's general officers realized that the Howe brothers had it in their power to entrap them on Manhattan, which Reed described as "this tongue of land, where we ought never have been." Indeed, this was precisely the reason why they voted to move the entire army to the northern end of Manhattan, where they would then try to fight their way off the island.[29]

The only dissenters happened to be the two commanders in chief. Washington reluctantly accepted that the city and port of New York could not be defended once the British occupied Brooklyn Heights, but he was still searching for a way to engage the British Army on Manhattan before escaping to the mainland. The Long Island humiliation had to be redeemed, the officers and men of the Continental Army needed to have their confidence restored, and "The Cause" needed a victory of some sort, no matter how token.

Both of the Howe brothers detested Clinton and would have rejected his strategic advice even if it had come with endorsements from the gods. But more significantly, it was now abundantly clear that they did not want to trap and destroy the Continental Army on Manhattan. Despite the disappointing results of Lord Howe's conference on Staten Island, they retained the conviction that support for the rebellion was

skin-deep, and they regarded their role as peace commissioners as more important than their role as military commanders. They wanted to limit the carnage on both sides until the
Americans came to their senses. Intriguingly, both Washington and the Howes were subordinating military strategy to the
larger battle for hearts and minds.

. . .

AFTER EXPLORING SEVERAL options on the east side of Manhattan for their attack, the Howes chose Kip's Bay, between
what is now Thirty-second and Thirty-eighth streets. On the
morning of September 15, 4,000 British and Hessian troops
were transported across the East River, preceded by five warships that had anchored in the bay that night, poised to lay
down an artillery barrage before the invasion. Ironically, the
American evacuation of Manhattan was already under way, so
if the British had waited another day, they would have landed
unopposed.[30]

Instead, the shoreline at Kip's Bay was defended by about
800 Connecticut militiamen and recent recruits to the Continental Army, including Joseph Plumb Martin. These were
the most inexperienced troops under Washington's command.
Their defensive position consisted of a shallow trench topped
off by mounds of dirt. Many had only spears for weapons.
No orders had been issued about how to respond to an attack,
except to hold their position. At daylight, Martin remembered
looking out at the British warships and the upward of eighty
cannons leveled at his ditch, wondering what he was supposed
to do.

The answer to that question became obvious as soon as the

naval barrage began. All five ships let loose at once, producing a display of firepower that several British naval officers described as more intense than any they had ever witnessed. Within minutes the American defensive line was blown away, and Martin, as he put it, "began to consider which part of my carcass was to go first." The bombardment lasted for a full hour, during which time one British ship, the *Orpheus,* expended over 5,000 pounds of gunpowder. By that time Martin and his fellow soldiers, quite understandably, had long since decided to flee the killing zone as quickly as possible. The British and Hessian troops landed unopposed, without a single casualty. The few American soldiers who remained in the trench were summarily executed when they tried to surrender. It was Long Island all over again.[31]

Clinton led the invasion force, and he was under orders to seize the beachhead, then await the arrival of the second wave of 9,000 British troops led by Howe. Since he was unopposed, Clinton could have moved across Manhattan and thereby cut off the 5,000 American troops under Putnam coming up from the south. But Clinton obeyed his orders, against his own better judgment, which allowed "Old Put" to squeeze past the British and Hessian force on what is now Riverside Drive. His precocious young aide, Aaron Burr, had identified the escape route.

What happened next was one of the low points for the American side in the war. The panic that seized the troops fleeing the bombardment at Kip's Bay was a plausible response to the overwhelming firepower of the British navy. But as they fled north, their fear proved contagious, creating an epidemic of shock that caused whole regiments of Connecticut militia and levies to toss aside their muskets and knapsacks when confronted by only token British opposition. "The demons of fear and disorder seemed to take full possession of all and everything that day," Martin remembered. The retreat became a rout.[32]

Washington encountered the frantic troops in full flight while riding south from his headquarters to the sound of gunfire. He made a futile effort to establish order by instructing officers to make a stand behind a stone wall, but the men just ran past him. One witness reported that "he struck several officers [with his riding crop] in their flight, three times dashed his hatt to the ground, and at last exclaimed, 'Good God, have I got such Troops as these?' " The approaching British infantry came within fifty yards, but his staff could not persuade their commander to leave the field. Eventually Joseph Reed grabbed the reins of his horse and led Washington to safety, cursing all the way. The next day, Greene recalled the scene, claiming that Washington was "so vext that he sought Death rather than life."[33]

The man of almost preternatural control lost it all in that terrifying moment and was fortunate to escape death or capture. For Washington, it was the nadir, the conclusive demonstration that all his hopes for the fighting prowess of the Continental Army had been delusional. And since he regarded the army as a projection of himself, the events of the day spread a stain over his own reputation that he found intolerable, in his honor-driven world worse than death itself. When word of the debacle reached Adams two days later, he too was stunned, though he did not take the humiliation personally. "I am so outraged by the infamous cowardice of the New England troops," he observed, "that I am ashamed of my Country."[34]

But even cowardice had an upside, since the headlong flight of the troops meant that most of them made it safely to the American lines at Harlem Heights. The number of killed, wounded, or captured was only a fraction of the losses on Long Island, even though the sting of the defeat was more painful for Washington.

Meanwhile, the Howe brothers could be excused for basking in the reflected glow of their triumph. With only negligible casualties, they had captured their primary objective, the city and port of New York, and had delivered another devastating blow to the military pretensions of the Continental Army along the way. All was going according to plan.

Lord Howe sensed that this second thrashing might have cracked the will of the rebels, much as the naval barrage at Kip's Bay had broken the spirit of the helpless defenders in their pitiful ditch. On September 19, he issued a proclamation to "the American people," thereby bypassing the delegates in the Continental Congress, who had shown themselves to be beyond redemption or rational recognition of their predicament, and appealed to the populace at large.

He urged them "to judge for themselves whether it be more consistent with their honor and happiness to offer up their lives as a sacrifice to the unjust and precarious cause in which they are engaged." (After Kip's Bay, that cause was presumably even more precarious.) If they would only abandon their pretense of independence and "return to their old allegiance," the unnecessary bloodletting would stop, and they would enjoy "the blessings of peace . . . and the full enjoyment of their liberty and property." Whether or not this message was more credible in the wake of the Kip's Bay disaster can never be known, since only the loyalist press in New York and New Jersey saw fit to publish it. Washington dismissed Lord Howe's appeal as old wine in old bottles, in effect requiring total submission "after which His Majesty would consider whether or who should be hung."[35]

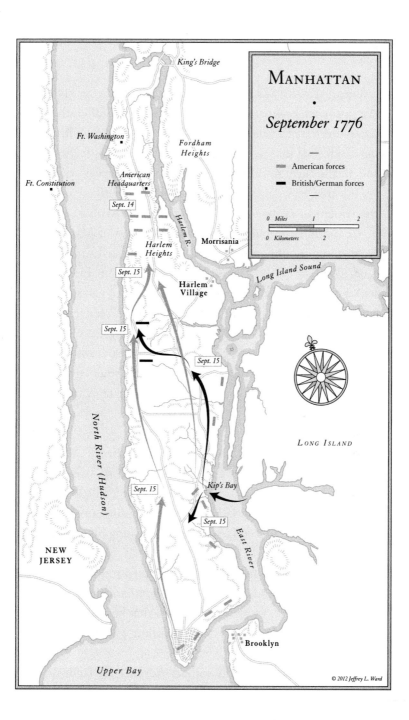

MANHATTAN

•

September 1776

—

American forces

British/German forces

—

King's Bridge

Fordham Heights

Ft. Washington

American Headquarters

Ft. Constitution

Sept. 14

Harlem Heights

Harlem R.

Morrisania

Sept. 15

Long Island Sound

Sept. 15

Harlem Village

Sept. 15

Sept. 15

LONG ISLAND

North River (Hudson)

Sept. 15

Kip's Bay

Sept. 15

East River

NEW JERSEY

Brooklyn

Upper Bay

© 2012 Jeffrey L. Ward

· · ·

HARLEM HEIGHTS WAS A rocky plateau running across Manhattan just north of what is now 125th Street. Its southern border was protected by a line of steep bluffs, some sixty feet tall, creating a ridgeline that resembled a natural fortress. If there was a rough equivalent to Bunker Hill on the island, this was it.[36]

For that very reason, it was selected as the rallying point in the American evacuation, as the Continental Army moved all its troops and equipment to the northern end of Manhattan. By the evening of September 15, the traumatized survivors of Kip's Bay had reached the safe haven of Harlem Heights, as had the exhausted troops under "Old Put," who had somehow eluded the British on their forced march up the western side of Manhattan.

It had not been a good day for the American cause. About 60 troops had been killed or wounded, another 300 taken prisoner. As on Long Island, the only conspicuous talent the Continental Army had demonstrated was its impressive skill at running away.

From his new headquarters (now the Jumel Mansion, on the brink of Coogan's Bluff at 161st Street), Washington enjoyed a panoramic view of the entire island. His focus was south, where he presumed Howe was preparing an attack on Harlem Heights. In fact, Howe was establishing his own headquarters in New York City, where the bulk of the residents were greeting the British Army as liberators. Indeed, a frontal assault on the formidable defenses at Harlem Heights never occurred to Howe, for the same reason that he had refused to attack Brooklyn Heights. He was unwilling to risk the casualties.

Washington's mood was somber, verging on fatalistic. A

letter to Lund Washington, his cousin and manager at Mount Vernon, conveyed his sense that the end was near:

> In short, such is my situation that if I were to wish the bit-
> terest curse to an enemy on this side of the grave, I should
> put him in my stead with my feelings. . . . In confidence I
> will tell you that I was never in such an unhappy, divided
> state since I was born. . . . If I fall, it may not be amiss that
> these circumstances be known, and declaration made to the
> justice of my character. And if the men will stand by me
> (which by the by I despair of), I am resolved not to be forced
> from this ground while I have life.[37]

In preparation for what he seemed to regard as Washington's last stand, he ordered the bulk of the troops to begin
digging trenches and constructing redoubts. But in order to
discover the disposition of British troops to the south, he also
ordered a reconnaissance by a recently organized elite unit of
Connecticut rangers led by Colonel Thomas Knowlton.

Knowlton was a thirty-six-year-old veteran of the French
and Indian War whose heroics at Bunker Hill had already
become legendary. (John Trumbull saw fit to make Knowlton
the central figure in his depiction of the battle, which currently
hangs in the Museum of Fine Arts in Boston.) In the post-
mortem after the Kip's Bay fiasco, there was a consensus that
a lack of leadership within the officer corps had been a major
source of the failure, but Knowlton embodied the highest combat leadership standard in the Continental Army. Aaron Burr
had been heard to remark that "it was impossible to promote
such a man too rapidly."[38]

About a half mile south of Harlem Heights (near the present juncture of 107th Street and Riverside Drive), Knowlton's

120 men encountered a British infantry regiment of 400 regulars. A fierce skirmish ensued, with the Americans firing to excellent effect from behind a stone wall. But then a regiment of Scottish Highlanders, the renowned Black Watch, appeared, and Knowlton, now badly outnumbered, retreated toward Harlem Heights. The British were so accustomed to seeing American troops in flight that a bugler sounded the signal used in foxhunts at the end of the chase when the fox is trapped.

This enraged Washington and his staff, who also recognized that the roughly 1,000 British and Scottish troops, in their exuberance, had overextended themselves and were walking into a trap, enveloped by an American force ten times their size. Washington sent Joseph Reed to the scene with orders for Knowlton, reinforced by Virginia Continentals under the command of Major Andrew Leitch, to flank the British and get behind them while several American regiments came down from Harlem Heights to engage them at the front. This envelopment tactic failed when the Virginia troops fired on the British before they were behind them. In the firefight that ensued, both sides took heavy casualties, including Leitch and Knowlton, who was hit in the lower back while exhorting his men from an exposed ledge. His purported last words, duly reported within weeks in most American newspapers, were the stuff of martyrdom: "I do not value my life if we do but get this day."[39]

Both sides then threw more men into the action, transforming a skirmish into the Battle of Harlem Heights. The British made a stand in a wheat field just south of the present Grant's Tomb and, after two hours of ferocious fighting, were forced to withdraw, having suffered 270 killed or wounded to 60 for the Americans, who had to be restrained from pursuing the fleeing redcoats. It was the first occasion in the battle for New

York in which the British Army experienced defeat. Although it was not a major battle—at its high point, about 2,000 troops were engaged on each side—Harlem Heights had a significant psychological impact on the morale of the Continental Army, which until then had good reason to doubt its ability to hold its own against British professionals.[40]

In his General Orders for the following day, Washington saw fit to underline that very point: "The Behavior of Yesterday was such a Contrast to that of some Troops before, as must show what may be done, when Officers & soldiers will exert themselves." He had been searching for a way, as he put it, "to strike some stroke" that would not only bolster the confidence of his troops but also send a signal to the American population as a whole that "The Cause" was alive and well. The latter goal was reinforced by coverage in most American newspapers, which neglected to mention the Kip's Bay disaster but featured Harlem Heights as a glorious American victory and Thomas Knowlton as the newest American martyr-hero. Though the strategic predicament facing the Continental Army had not really changed, at least for the moment, the defeatist mood had subsided. It remained to be seen, however, whether the army could get off the island.[41]

8

A Long War

Give me leave to say, Sir, that your Affairs are in a more
unpromising way than you seem to apprehend.
— GEORGE WASHINGTON TO JOHN HANCOCK,
October 4, 1776

One might have thought that the victory at Harlem
Heights, small though it was, would serve as the stroke
that Washington had been hoping to deliver. Having scored
that important point, he was now free to evacuate the Continental Army off Manhattan, honor intact, before General
Howe could block his exit.

But instead he ordered his troops to dig more trenches, in
anticipation of a major British assault from the south. He had
finally found the ideal defensive position that perfectly embodied his entire strategic plan for defending New York, and he
intended to use the rocky elevation at Harlem Heights to inflict
maximum casualties on the British Army before beating his
retreat. It was a bold but dangerous decision, since he was putting the survival of the Continental Army at risk in order to
deliver one more telling blow in behalf of "The Cause."[1]

On the evening of September 20, as he scanned the sky to
the south, looking for Howe's approaching army, the horizon

became ablaze from the fires consuming more than one-third of New York City. The Continental Congress had given strict orders not to torch the city upon evacuation, reasoning that one day it would be recaptured—a palpable measure of the confidence still dominating the deliberations in Philadelphia.[2]

What came to be called the "Great Fire" was probably the work of arsonists, most likely self-styled American patriots who were now a beleaguered minority in the city. Two suspects were summarily dispatched, one thrown into the flames, the other hanged on a lamppost. Washington apprised Hancock that the fire was not his doing and was probably an accident. But privately he confided to Lund Washington that "Providence, or some good honest fellow, has done more for us than we can do for ourselves." Whatever the cause, for the remainder of the war the occupying British Army lived among the ashes of all the homes, churches, and buildings west of Broadway.[3]

. . .

MEANWHILE, AS WASHINGTON awaited Howe's frontal assault of Harlem Heights, which never materialized, the Continental Congress was attempting to digest the full implications of the Kip's Bay disaster. Unlike the American populace as a whole, the delegates in Philadelphia were fully apprised of the humiliation.

Caesar Rodney, for example, provided his fellow delegates from Delaware with a full narrative of the debacle, taking care to absolve Washington of any responsibility and casting blame on "the beardless boys" he commanded. "I have wrote on the Subject till I am in ill Humour," Rodney concluded, "and the only Comfort is that by the time you have read it you'll be as

Angry as I am." William Hooper of North Carolina believed it was time to take off the patriotic blinders. "It becomes our duty to see things as they really are[,] divested of all disguise," he urged, "and when the happiness of the present age and Millions yet unborn depends upon a reformation of them, we ought to spare no pains to effect so desirable a purpose." Washington, in fact, had been trying to tell Hancock for several weeks that the Continental Congress did not seem to fathom the deplorable condition of the army. After Kip's Bay, the delegates finally got the message and voted to send a three-man committee to confer with Washington and his staff at Harlem Heights. They met for five days, from September 20 to September 24.[4]

No record of the deliberations was kept, but the problems addressed and solutions proposed were clearly outlined in the committee's report to the Continental Congress two weeks later. The underlying conclusion was that the Continental Army was really not much of an army at all. To the extent that a quick victory was no longer tenable and that therefore success in the war for American independence depended on a fighting force that could compete on equal terms with the British Army, there needed to be a "New Model" or "New Establishment." In effect, the committee recommended all the reforms that the congress had already tried and failed to implement a month earlier, this time with a greater sense of urgency and comprehension.

First, the Continental Army needed to expand to at least 60,000 troops, with a majority committed to serving "for the duration." This would eliminate the need for militia, since the New York campaign had demonstrated that dependence on "Minutemen" had proved to be one of those glorious presumptions that produce only inglorious consequences. And one-year enlistments had proven equivalently problematic, since the troops were scheduled to rotate out of the army just when they had begun to internalize the discipline of military service and became reliable soldiers.

Second, the organizational infrastructure of an effective army did not exist. The quartermaster corps, the commissary, and the hospital units were all fly-by-night improvisations. The troops were poorly clothed, poorly fed, and poorly cared for if wounded or incapacitated by disease. The prevailing assumption that it was going to be a short war had allowed the Continental Army to function in this ad hoc fashion. Now that the assumption had changed—it was clearly going to be a protracted conflict—organizational reforms had to be institutionalized along lines modeled on the British Army, precisely what Washington had been urging for months.

Third, the officer corps at both the senior and the junior levels was woefully inadequate. After-action reports on the collapse of discipline at Gowanus Heights and Kip's Bay placed the blame on inexperienced officers. Poorly led troops became mere gangs. On the other hand, when a natural leader like Lord Stirling or Thomas Knowlton was commanding, the troops fought well. Nathanael Greene even thought that, properly led, American troops were a match for British regulars. "If the officers were as good as the men," Greene claimed, "America might bid defiance to the whole world."[5]

The visiting committee endorsed all the reforms that Washington and his staff suggested. The New York campaign had been a painful learning experience, so the only sensible thing to do was to fix the glaring problems in order to make the Continental Army an effective fighting force worthy of its name. The problems were clear, so the solutions were obvious—in fact, the solutions had been bandied about in the congress for several weeks. Now, with greater resolve, the full congress embraced all the recommendations for a "New Establishment" during the first week of October.[6]

But it was one thing to endorse the recommendations, another to implement them. Once again it became clear that the Continental Congress lacked the authority to enforce troop levies in the states, so the proposed enlargement of the Continental Army to 60,000 was a political, economic, and logistical impossibility, which in turn meant that Washington would remain dependent on the militias for the foreseeable future. Even offering enhanced incentives for volunteers who signed up "for the duration" made little appreciable difference. One-year enlistments remained the norm. Only a mandatory draft could have solved the problem, and that was out of the question. The manpower for a much enlarged Continental Army was undoubtedly available, and the political will to draw on it was present in the Continental Congress, but that will did not extend to the state legislatures, whose vision remained local rather than national.

Moreover, the necessary organizational reform could not be effected merely by drafting new procedural guidelines for the different branches of the army. The regulations had to be enforced up and down the chain of command by men with little or no military experience, then internalized until routinized. This was not a natural act for the kind of men in the Continental Army. The truth was that a "New Establishment" could not be created overnight except on paper. The fact that the war was going to be long meant that the army would have time, on a trial-and-error basis, to work out the all-important details. The Continental Army, it would seem, was destined to be a permanent work in progress. And that more limited projection of a national army was all that could be justified within a republican framework.

The recommendation for an improved officers corps caught John Adams's attention, in part because it confirmed battlefield reports from New York, in part because he had been reading histories of the Roman army in order to educate himself as head of the Board of War and Ordnance. He discovered that Polybius had concluded that most Roman defeats were not the fault of troops but "always the Fault of the officers." This same failure of leadership haunted the Continental Army, but Adams believed there was no swift cure for the problem: "The true Cause of the want of good officers in the army is because . . . such officers in sufficient Numbers are not in America. Without Materials the best Workman can do nothing. Time, Study, and Experience alone must make a sufficient Number of officers."[7]

What he meant was that America lacked the kind of British aristocracy that encouraged military careers in the manner of the Howe brothers. And lacking such a tradition, the Continental Army would have to manufacture officers the republican way, by recognizing and promoting merit on the battlefield. (Henry Knox, Nathanael Greene, and the much-missed Thomas Knowlton were all excellent examples of this slow but sure process, and a young artillery captain named Alexander Hamilton was a looming discovery.) In the long run, America needed a military academy to produce competent officers, and Adams was prepared to recommend such an institution after the war was won. For now, however, demand vastly exceeded supply, and since there was no immediate solution, the very act of talking about the problem only advertised a congenital weakness in the Continental Army. "Concealing it is the way to cure it," Adams concluded, "not publishing it," meaning that the unsolvable problem should be conveniently obscured.[8]

As the summer turned to fall, then, two conclusions were clear: first, on all matters related to the war effort, the Continental Congress continued to function as a provisional national government prepared to give Washington everything he asked for; and second, while there was the will, there was no way to translate that rhetorical support into reality, in part because the congress lacked authority over the state legislatures, in part because many of the ills affecting the Continental Army had no immediate cure.

Washington fully grasped this unpleasant but intractable reality. In a long letter to Hancock on October 4, he expressed his appreciation for the endorsement of all his recommendations by the visiting committee but added that "there is a natural difference between voting for Battalions and raising of Men." For the foreseeable future, he would command an army of unqualified officers, wholly undependable militia, and short-term enlisted troops. As his newest aide, Tench Tilghman, put it, it would take a miracle to "stop the career of Monsi Howe with the finest army that ever appeared in America," while Washington commanded "as bad a one as ever appeared in any part of the Globe."[9]

At bottom, Washington concluded, what was militarily essential was politically impossible. Nothing less than a permanent standing army on the British model could win the war, but there was "such a distrust & jealousy of Military power, that the Commander in Chief has not an opportunity . . . to give the least assurance of success." To be sure, "The Cause" was glorious, but the Continental Army, as currently constituted, was an inherently problematic improvisation.[10]

Indeed, the deplorable situation was sufficiently obvious to his own troops that some deserters were already going over to the British Army. One British officer, Frederick MacKenzie, claimed that they were arriving at the rate of eighty a day. And as Washington predicted, loyalists from Long Island and lower Manhattan were volunteering in company-size units to join Howe's army. Meanwhile, over in New Jersey, a civil war seemed to be brewing, as nearly three thousand citizens, including one signer of the Declaration of Independence, took up Lord Howe's offer of amnesty and signed an oath of allegiance to George III.[11]

These defections could plausibly be regarded as the first cracks in the edifice of American independence and therefore as early indications that the Howe strategy was working. Several British officers expressed confusion when General Howe let weeks pass without taking any action against Harlem Heights. They presumed, as Captain MacKenzie put it, that "the grand point in view is certainly to beat and disperse this principal army, which, if once effected, little more will remain to be done." But Howe, in fact, did not share that presumption. Having delivered a series of devastating blows to the Continental Army, he was waiting for the aftershock to take effect. He felt no need to destroy the Continental Army, since he believed it was going to disintegrate on its own. And no less a witness than Washington himself feared that, as he had told Hancock, his army "is upon the eve of its political dissolution."[12]

. . .

IN ORDER FOR the Howe strategy to succeed, the epidemic of fear and disillusionment had to spread beyond New York and New Jersey. Pro-American press coverage limited the contagion, but Washington worried that deserting troops would carry the infection back to their respective states and the unattractive reality would begin to settle in; namely, that it was going to be a long war, and that the Continental Army as currently constituted was ill equipped to fight it.

The leadership in the Continental Congress had demonstrated its wholehearted support for Washington and provided a united front on the nonnegotiable status of American independence. Even though they could not deliver on their promises about a "New Establishment," the political gesture itself was important as a statement of commitment during this vulnerable moment. The delegates in Philadelphia had to demonstrate that they were immune to the infection.

Adams, for example, used his position as head of the Board of War and Ordnance to reassure officers who were having doubts about the dispirited condition of the Continental Army. "I am extremely sorry to learn that the troops have been disheartened," he wrote to one officer. "But the despondency of spirit was the natural Effect of the Retreats you have made one after the other." After the defeats on Long Island and at Kip's Bay, Adams observed, "the finest Army in the world would have been seized, in similar circumstances, with more or less of a Panick. But your Men will soon recover their Spirits in a short Time."[13]

Franklin took a different tack, preferring in his ever-agile way to use the deplorable condition of the Continental Army as leverage to extract money and supplies from the French. In his instructions to Silas Deane, the new American minister to France, he urged complete candor about the sad state of the army: "Upon the whole our Army near New York are not sufficiently strong to Cope with General Howe in the open Field. . . . They want better Arms, better Tents and more Clothing than they now have, or is in our power now to Supply them with, consequently we cannot recruit or increase that Army under these discouragements." Nothing less than immediate French assistance could save the day.[14]

Among several delegates, at yet another, somewhat deeper level, the need to immunize themselves from doubt prompted a variety of ingenious and often counterintuitive arguments, all designed to serve as flying buttresses that reinforced the interior architecture of their revolutionary confidence. Like Thomas Aquinas's five proofs of God's existence, these were rational attempts to justify a belief that ultimately rested on faith, which in this case was the conviction that the military defeats in New York were meaningless because the American cause was destiny's child.

Benjamin Rush, who would later be celebrated as the founder of American psychiatry, told his wife that the recent British victories were, in truth, a godsend. "I think we stood in need of a frown from heaven," he wrote. "It is, you know, through difficulties & trials that states as well as individuals are trained up to glory & happiness. My faith is now stronger than ever." Indeed, Rush claimed that "for a long time I not only expected, but wished that General Howe might gain possession of New York." For now all the loyalists from adjacent states would flee to New York, "where they will ripen as the Tories of Boston did for banishment & destruction." The rest of the country would then "be purged of those rascals whose idleness or perfidy have brought most of our calamities upon us." All of America's rotten eggs would now be gathered into one basket.[15]

William Williams, a delegate from Connecticut, took a

more theological route to reach a similar conclusion. His preferred interpretive framework was the Puritan jeremiad, which
transformed the British victories on Long Island and Kip's
Bay into acts of divine retribution for a sinful American people. "God has blunted the weapons of our warfare," Williams
intoned, "and made us flee before our Enemies, and given them
possession of our strongholds." In Williams's moral universe,
the issue was not the relative weakness of the Continental
Army but the depravity of the entire American population:
"A thorough Repentance & Reformation . . . will appease the
Anger of a holy & just God, avert these amazing Calamities,
secure Liberty & Happiness to this and all succeeding Ages &
eternal Felicity & Glory to all the Subjects of it." The obvious
solution was not better officers, better equipment, or aid from
France. All those items would be forthcoming after American
patriots fasted, did penance, and prayed for their providential
redemption.[16]

Adams discovered assurance in Greek and Roman history,
chiefly the lessons learned in the Peloponnesian and Punic
wars. When Henry Knox expressed concern about the impact
of the series of defeats on the morale of the Continental Army,
Adams told him to stop worrying: "It is very true that a Silly
Panic has been spread in your Army, and from there come to
Philadelphia." But Hannibal had inflicted an equivalent panic
on the Roman army yet could never manage to take advantage
of it and eventually lost the war. Howe was likely to prove the
Hannibal of the American Revolution.[17]

For, like Hannibal, Howe would discover that winning
battles was not synonymous with winning wars: "Conquests
were easily made, because We atchieve them with our whole
force—they are retained with difficulty because We defend

them with only a part of our forces." In Howe's case, the occupation of Long Island and Manhattan would stretch his resources to the breaking point. "After such a division and distribution of his forces," Adams predicted, "I think he has nearly reached the end of his tether for this Year." The greater Howe's victories, the greater his difficulties. Howe was destined to win his way to defeat.[18]

Moreover, Adams explained, the Americans had the example of Thebes in the Peloponnesian War to guide them. After some initial defeats akin to the American losses in New York, the Thebans realized that they could not win a conventional war against Sparta and adopted a defensive strategy that rendered it "rash to hazard a decisive Battle against the best troops in Greece." Instead, they chose "to harass the Spartans with frequent Skirmishes . . . whilst they gained Experience, Confidence, and Courage by daily Encounters." The humiliations in New York were really a marvelous learning experience that taught the Americans the lessons the Thebans had learned two thousand years before. For the British, like the Spartans, had to win the war. And the Americans, like the Thebans, had only not to lose it. That seminal insight had been learned the hard way in New York but would now guide the American side to ultimate victory.[19]

The Adams analysis would prove prescient as the war dragged on, though it would take a herculean effort on Washington's part to embrace a defensive, or Theban, strategy, partly because of his own aggressive instincts, partly because he was worried that superior British financial resources would win out in a protracted war. But in the crucible of that moment, what stands out is the multiple arguments the leading members of the Continental Congress were able to construct in order to dismiss the military disasters at New York. Whether it was demographically, divinely, or historically sanctioned, they regarded the fate of American independence as foreordained. Even if the specific arguments were specious, the underlying faith on which they rested was unshakable. The Howes had badly miscalculated the depth of that faith.

. . .

BY EARLY OCTOBER, Washington had come to the realization that General Howe was not going to take him up on his invitation to attack the fortress at Harlem Heights. About the same time, Howe was coming to the realization that the campaign season was drawing to a close and that he needed to stage another evocative demonstration of British military supremacy—in effect, to deliver another shock to the dazed and dwindling Continental Army.

Howe's tactic of choice was almost always a flanking movement, so after consulting his brother about navigation options and obstacles in the East River, he chose to launch an invasion at Throg's Neck (also called Frog's Neck), nine miles northeast of Harlem Heights, near present-day Fort Schuyler in the Bronx.

In keeping with his measured strategy, Howe's objective was not to block Washington's escape from Manhattan but, just the opposite, to threaten encirclement in order to force the Continental Army to evacuate the island, then fight an open-field battle in which the superiority of the British Army would once again prove decisive. As he later put it to Germain, his goal was not to trap Washington on Manhattan but to draw him out of his Harlem Heights fortress "and if possible to bring him to action."[20]

The movement of British ships and men up the East River immediately caught Washington's attention. "I have reason to believe," he wrote Hancock on October 11, "that the greatest part of their Army has moved upward, or is about to do it, pursuing their original plan of getting in our rear & cutting off our communications with the Country." Washington plausibly presumed that Howe intended to seal the trap, when in fact he intended to open the door.[21]

Washington conducted a personal survey of the shore-line northeast of Manhattan, including the terrain at Throg's Neck. It revealed that the isthmus was really an island at high tide, connected to the mainland by a causeway and bridge. He ordered an undersize regiment of Pennsylvania Continentals to block this prospective landing spot. Under the command of Colonel Edward Hand, the exit off the island was destroyed, and when the advance wave of 4,000 British troops under Henry Clinton landed on October 12, they found themselves marooned in a mosquito-infested swamp. Throg's Neck, it turned out, was the worst possible place to launch an invasion.[22]

Events then moved at lightning speed on both sides. Washington convened a council of war on October 16 that voted almost unanimously—there was one dissenter—to evacuate Manhattan and move the army eighteen miles to the high ground of White Plains, which would provide a natural defensive refuge akin to Harlem Heights. The goal was to get there before Howe blocked the route.

The council of war also voted to leave 2,000 troops at Fort Washington. This made no strategic sense, since leaving "a castle in the rear" violated every conventional principle of warfare and since it was already abundantly clear that British warships could sail up the Hudson past Fort Washington with impunity, which undermined the core mission of the garrison. But the commitment made perfect sense psychologically, as a statement of American resolve to defend New York, even as Washington was ordering an evacuation. It was simultaneously an indefensible military decision, a heartfelt act of honor, and Washington's worst tactical blunder of the entire war.[23]

Present for the council of war was none other than Charles Lee, recently arrived from his victorious campaign in South Carolina. Despite his irreverent and erratic mannerisms, his beaked nose, disheveled appearance, and ever-present pack of dogs, Lee was second-in-command only to Washington. His presence bolstered the confidence of several officers, including Joseph Reed, who had been murmuring about Washington's apparent confusion and indecisiveness ever since the brilliant escape from Long Island.

One can detect the early symptoms of rivalry between the two commanders, most glaringly when Lee suggested that Washington offer his resignation to the Continental Congress for the recent failures on the battlefield, an offer allegedly designed to extract a vote of confidence from his civilian superiors. Washington ignored the suggestion; further, he did not interpret Lee's advice as a hostile act. Indeed, he renamed Fort Constitution, on the New Jersey side of the Hudson, Fort Lee to commemorate Lee's return. And the decision to evacuate Manhattan was an implicit endorsement of Lee's judgment, since he had always thought that New York was indefensible.[24]

On October 18, the same day that the Continental Army began its evacuation, the Howe brothers transported Clinton's troops off Throg's Neck, added two regiments of recently arrived Hessians to the invasion force, and landed at Pell's Point, a few miles up Long Island Sound in present-day Pelham. The complicated amphibious maneuvers went like clock-

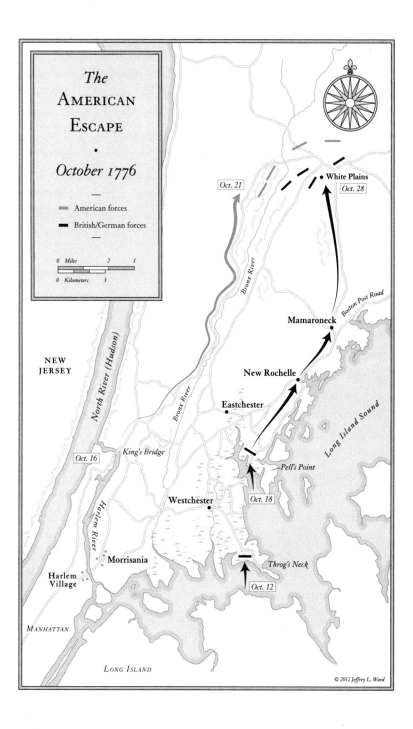

The
AMERICAN
ESCAPE

•

October 1776

—

▰▰ American forces

▬▬ British/German forces

—

0   Miles   2   3

0   Kilometers   3

NEW
JERSEY

White Plains
Oct. 28

Oct. 21

Boston Post Road

Mamaroneck

New Rochelle

Eastchester

Oct. 16

King's Bridge

Long Island Sound

Pell's Point

Oct. 18

Westchester

Bronx River

North River (Hudson)

Morrisania

Harlem
Village

Harlem River

Oct. 12

Throg's Neck

MANHATTAN

LONG ISLAND

© 2012 Jeffrey L. Ward

work, the landing site was on the mainland rather than on a quasi-island, and the landing was initially unopposed.

But unluckily for the Howes, they had chosen a location that was guarded by John Glover and his Marblehead regiment, perhaps the most disciplined troops in the Continental Army. Glover later remembered looking through his telescope and seeing two hundred British ships approaching his position: "Oh! The anxiety of mind I was in then for the fate of the day. . . . I would have given a thousand worlds to have had General Lee . . . present to direct or at least approve what I had done."[25]

Acting on his own initiative, Glover moved his 750 men into position behind a series of stone walls and, though outnumbered more than five to one, invited an attack. As the British advanced, one row of Glover's troops rose up to fire, then retreated, and as the British charged forward with bayonets at the ready, the next row rose up to deliver another withering salvo, and so on from wall to wall. In a little more than a hour, the British lost more men at Pell's Point than they had in the entire Long Island campaign. (Glover later claimed that his men remained as calm throughout the engagement "as if shooting ducks.") By one estimate, the British suffered over 300 dead and wounded, the Americans only 20.[26]

Howe was sufficiently stunned by the unexpected fighting prowess of American troops to order a halt in the British advance. The next day he moved cautiously inland toward New Rochelle, where he decided to wait for 8,000 newly arrived Hessians to come up from Long Island. Glover's troops had, in fact, retreated to join Washington's army, so there were only a handful of militia to contest Howe's march toward White Plains. But Howe did not move.

The Continental Army did move, though ever so slowly, advancing less than three miles a day. Fully a quarter of the 13,000 troops were sick or wounded; there were not enough horses to pull the wagons and cannons, which had to be hauled by hand; and food supplies were nonexistent, forcing troops to scavenge whatever they could find along the route. Joseph Plumb Martin remembered, with irony, that he was required to carry an iron cooking kettle, which was never used because there was nothing to cook. The troops were in no condition to fight, but that was not necessary, because Howe made no effort to block their path. It was almost as if he wished them to escape.[27]

Whatever Howe's motives, the final stragglers in the Continental Army reached the safety of the hills at White Plains on October 24, at last out of the trap. The strategic decision to defend New York had always been a fundamental mistake that created the potential for an American catastrophe; now, thanks to the diplomatic priorities of the Howes, it had been averted. True to form, William Howe waited four more days to launch an attack on White Plains, enough time for Washington to prepare his defenses.

• • •

IT WAS THE END of the beginning for the American side, meaning that its army had managed to survive what proved to be the most vulnerable moment of the war. Washington, from lessons learned at New York, would never again allow the survival of the Continental Army to be put at risk. Though it ran counter to all his instincts, he now realized that his goal was not to win the war but rather not to lose it.

It was the beginning of the end for the British side, meaning that the Howe brothers, despite their tactical brilliance, had failed to deliver the decisive blow that killed the rebellion at its moment of birth. Indeed, they had deliberately decided not to do so. What might have happened if they had acted otherwise will always remain one of the most intriguing and unanswerable questions in American history.

But several other intriguing questions had, in fact, been answered during America's revolutionary summer, and the answers largely defined the parameters of the war that would ensue. They cut in two different directions, one making the prospects for a British victory remote in the extreme, the other making any outright American military triumph equally unlikely. Taken together, they defined the terms of the protracted conflict that would play out over the next five years and end with the British decision after Yorktown that the war was unwinnable.

On the one hand, it was now clear that the Continental Congress was immune to any British proposal for reconciliation. Commitment to "The Cause" was creedal in character, impervious to the calamities on Long Island and Manhattan, which were dismissed as temporary setbacks and then folded into the providential sense of American independence. This was not a wholly rational mentality, for it ruled as inadmissible any evidence that challenged that core conviction. It turned out that Jefferson's lyrical rendering of the revolutionary pledge—"our Lives, our Fortunes, and our sacred honor"—was much more than a rhetorical gesture. It accurately reflected the bottomless level of commitment in the Continental Congress, which had now been tested to the limit and never wavered. The central assumption on which the Howes had based their military strategy, namely that support for the rebellion was soft and shallow, was exposed as misguided. Whatever subsequent disappointments and disasters might befall "The Cause" out there in the vast American theater, the center would always hold.

On the other hand, it was equally clear that the consensus on independence did not translate into a consensus on American union. And because local, state, and regional allegiances remained supreme, all prospects for a fully empowered Continental Army were impossible. Americans regarded both a national government and a potent Continental Army as embodiments of consolidated political and military power that ran against the grain of the very values the American Revolution claimed to stand for.

This, in turn, meant that the Continental Army would forever remain a kind of awkward orphan, indispensable but suspect, always on the verge of dissolution. Its persistence was obviously essential, but its marginal status constituted a more essential statement about the hostility toward standing armies in the fledging American republic. There was no way that such an army could win the war.

Taken together, these two products of the revolutionary summer virtually ensured a long conflict that the British could not win for political reasons and the Americans could not win for military reasons. Many fateful decisions and challenges remained ahead—Washington's inspired bravado at Trenton, Howe's bizarre decision to capture Philadelphia rather than seal the Hudson corridor, the endurance test at Valley Forge, the crucial French entry into the war—but they all played out within the strategic framework created in the summer of 1776.

9

Postscript: Necessary Fictions

The ink on the Treaty of Paris (1783) was barely dry when Washington predicted that the true story of the improbable American victory would never get into the history books:

> If Historiographers should be hardy enough to fill the pages of History with the advantages that have been gained with unequal numbers (on the part of America) in the course of this contest, and attempt to relate the distressing circumstances under which they have been obtained, it is more than probable that posterity will bestow on their labors the epithet and marks of fiction; for it will not be believed that such a force as Great Britain has employed for eight years in this Country could be baffled . . . by numbers infinitely less, composed of men oftentimes half starved, always in Rags, without pay, and experiencing, at times, every species of distress which human nature is capable of undergoing.[1]

Washington was calling attention to the persistence of the Continental Army—the embodiment of "The Cause" for eight long years—as the essential ingredient in the ultimate American triumph. As Henry Clinton had realized from the start but the Howe brothers had not, the strategic center of the rebellion was not a place—not New York, not Philadelphia, not the Hudson corridor—but the Continental Army itself.

Within this narrative framework, the New York campaign of 1776 loomed large, for this was the most vulnerable moment, when the Continental Army nearly ceased to exist. Indeed, a history of the war from the perspective that survival was the key to success featured the near-miraculous escape across the East River in August 1776 and the endurance of the Continental Army at Valley Forge in the winter of 1777, even more than the dramatic victories at Saratoga and Yorktown, as the decisive events.

Washington's own cast of mind about the course of the conflict assumed a providential character based on recollections of the summer of '76. For he realized, more than most, that the decision to defend New York had been a monumental blunder, rescued from catastrophe only by some combination of sheer luck and the inexplicable reticence of the Howes. This was what he meant when he described the American victory as "a standing miracle" that came about because of "a concatenation of causes, which in all probability at no time, or under any circumstances, will combine again." Though Washington was not a deeply religious man, the early months of the war made him a believer in providence, which meant that on some occasions the gods took matters into their own hands.[2]

He was convinced throughout the remainder of the war that New York was the divinely ordained place where he would return to redeem his earlier mistakes and deliver the decisive blow that ended all pretensions of the British Empire in North America. He was obsessed with New York as the place where the climactic battle would occur, because New York was the place where "The Cause" had nearly died, so it stood to reason it should be the place where it would ultimately triumph. He was completely surprised when the fates, and the French fleet, chose an obscure location on the Tidewater peninsula instead.

His description of the Continental Army—"half starved, always in Rags, without pay"—was intended as a tribute to the long-suffering troops who had stayed the course. But it was also a caustic comment on a political pattern that had first congealed in the summer of '76, and then only deepened and darkened over the ensuing years of the war: namely, that the Continental Army was kept on life support but was never provided the money and men Washington requested, even though the resources for a larger and better-equipped army were readily available.[3]

From the start, as we have seen, the respective states preferred to support the manpower needs of their own militias rather than meet the allocations recommended by the congress for the Continental Army, primarily because local and state allegiances outweighed any collective or national ethos. As the war dragged on, these centrifugal forces only accelerated, and each request for money and men was more deeply resented by the state legislatures. Nor was it merely a matter of state versus national loyalty. The very idea of a robust Continental Army was generally regarded as an American version of the British Army, which had the menacing look of a domestic leviathan that threatened the republican principles that the war was purportedly being fought to defend. In that sense, Washington's interpretation of the American victory focused attention on the gritty and stubborn persistence of an institution that a majority of Americans regarded as somewhat embarrassing.

The urge to airbrush the Continental Army out of the patriotic picture became palpable when the matter of pensions came up in the wake of the Treaty of Paris. A promise had been made during the course of the war, chiefly for recruitment purposes, to include pensions of half pay for life for officers. As it became increasingly clear that this promise was not going to be kept because the states would refuse to raise the taxes to fund it, an alternative proposal called "commutation" was put forward, whereby retired officers would receive full pay for five years.[4]

The popular response to the commutation scheme, most especially in letters and editorials in the New England press, was overwhelmingly negative, verging on scatological. Veteran officers were described as indolent nobodies, flushed with their sense of significance, feeding at the public trough like "ravenous harpies with whetted beaks and piercing eyes." If they were truly virtuous men, as they claimed, then virtue should suffice as their only reward. One retired Connecticut officer complained that reports of his pension made him a pariah among his neighbors: "I became obnoxious to the mass of people. . . . When I had any severe sickness they hoped I would die. One noisy man said he hoped I would die and they would take my skin for a drum head to drum other officers out of town."[5]

The antiveteran sentiment then coalesced around the creation of a fraternal organization of retired officers called the Society of the Cincinnati, which seemed to embody all the values ordinary Americans loathed. Henry Knox had been the main proponent for the preservation of the "band of brothers" who had suffered and sacrificed together to win American independence. But once it became known that membership in the society was hereditary on the male side of the family line, it was stigmatized as an aristocratic institution that threatened republican values. The widespread hostility to the Society of the Cincinnati stunned Washington, who regarded it as an abiding reminder of the countless personal sacrifices that had made American independence possible. But as it turned out, the crucial role of the Continental Army was just about the last thing most Americans wished to remember.[6]

· · ·

FIRSTHAND MEMORIES HAD nearly evaporated by the time Joseph Plumb Martin got around to publishing his memoirs in 1830. Writing from his farm in Maine when he was seventy years old, Martin recalled his first experience of combat on Long Island and Manhattan as a fifteen-year-old boy brimming over with patriotic confidence, wholly bereft of military experience, the poster child for an army of amateurs. His major theme echoed Washington's emphasis on sheer persistence, his own and the Continental Army's capacity to survive despite hardships that subsequent generations could not possibly comprehend and apparently preferred to forget.[7]

There was nothing glorious about the episodes in Martin's account, which focused on the mundane, day-by-day challenges of staying alive that often took the form of finding food to eat. He made no effort to assess the larger strategic implications of the battles on Long Island and Manhattan, since his vantage point, like the shallow ditch at Kip's Bay, hardly afforded a panoramic perspective. But in his own unassuming way, Martin provided what we might call a Tolstoyan view of war, meaning a recovery of the authentic emotional experience of an ordinary soldier. In the end, his message was simple but profound: both he and the Continental Army had been survivors, and that was how the war was won, or perhaps not lost.

By the time he wrote, the enforced amnesia about the essential role of the Continental Army had established itself as received wisdom, and what Martin called "the myth of the militia" had emerged in the folklore to explain the improbable American victory, which was allegedly won by "Minutemen" rather than regulars like Martin. As one of the few veterans of the Continental Army still alive, he felt a special obligation to challenge this misguided version of history:

> It has been said by some . . . that the Revolutionary army was needless; that the Militia were competent for all that the crisis required. . . . But I still insist that they would not have answered the end so well as regular soldiers, who were there, and there obliged to be . . . and could not go away when we pleased without exposing ourselves to military punishment.[8]

Americans needed to believe that they had enjoyed an Immaculate Conception, that they had given birth to an independent American republic without resorting to a standing army of regular soldiers. Martin's memoir was a poignant plea for the regulars like him who had been written out of the patriotic script because they did not fit the republican stereotype of the citizen-soldier. Washington had warned from the start that the story of America's successful war for independence might have the look of fiction, but he had no way of knowing that the fictional version would portray the militia as the stars of the story.

· · ·

EXPLAINING A DEFEAT is always a more difficult assignment than explaining a victory. But the publication of the Treaty of Paris created an impossible dilemma for Great Britain, since its terms revealed that the British Empire in North America was lost forever. All the blood and treasure—40,000 casualties and 50 million pounds—had been for nothing. As the improbability and totality of the defeat sank in, a collective silence settled like a cloud over the subject, as if it were an unwelcome guest at a dinner party that, if ignored, would eventually go away. John Adams, who had the misfortune to serve as America's first minister to the Court of St. James's in 1785, reported that members of the British court averted their eyes whenever he entered the room, since he was such a painful reminder of an unattractive reality they preferred to deny. Abigail claimed that vast sectors of the London press, influenced by the delusional stories of the loyalists-in-exile, were reporting that a majority of Americans were having second thoughts about independence, and that Benjamin Franklin, upon his return from Paris, had nearly been stoned to death by Philadelphia artisans angry with him for leading them astray.[9]

Denial was vastly preferable to a candid appraisal of the debacle, for that would have required the British government to face some extremely unpleasant facts that, taken together, undermined the core presumption on which the entire British imperial agenda rested. For the unattractive truth was that several British ministries, starting in 1763, had badly miscalculated the depth and range of American opposition to the extension of Parliament's authority over the colonies. These ministries had arrogantly assumed that the imposition of British military power in 1774 would coerce the colonists into submission. They had consistently misread the level of resistance within the American population. And they had incorrectly presumed that the superiority of British arms would produce a quick end to the rebellion in 1776.

On all counts, history had proven them wrong. The American colonists had provided them with multiple opportunities to alter their course, on several occasions offering glimpses of a reconfigured British Empire based on the principle of shared sovereignty and mutual consent. The British had rejected all such suggestions, on the constitutional ground that sovereignty was indivisible and must reside in one place, which was Parliament, but also for deeper psychological reasons rooted in the need to ensure control over their colonial subjects. This imperious conviction was, they believed, the nonnegotiable principle that defined an empire. It transcended political and constitutional niceties and came down to an entrenched sense of superiority that rendered their American cousins as inferior creatures. But the resulting war had demonstrated quite conclusively that the British could not control the outcome; their sense of superiority was an illusion. It is probably apocryphal, but it made historical sense that the defeated British army that marched out of Yorktown played "The World Turned Upside Down."

An alternative narrative had begun to cushion the pain of defeat even before the full implications of that defeat were felt. In the spring of 1779, from late March to late June, the House of Commons put itself into committee-of-the-whole format in order to debate what it called "The Conduct of the American War." This highly unusual inquiry had been requested by William Howe, recently recalled from America, now to be addressed as Sir William, the knighthood a reward for his services as commander of His Majesty's troops in the American theater. But despite the honorific title, upon his return Howe had encountered widespread criticism of his conduct of the war in the London press, essentially accusing him of making military decisions almost designed to protract rather than end the rebellion. Howe used his status as a member of Parliament to request, in lieu of a trial or court-martial, a special session of the House of Commons to answer his critics and clear his name.[10]

In response to those critics who accused him of excessive

caution throughout the New York campaign, Howe offered a blanket explanation: "The most essential duty I had to observe was not wanting to commit his Majesty's troops where the object was inadequate. I knew fully well that any considerable loss sustained by the army could not speedily or easily be repaired." Howe did not acknowledge that he and his brother had had aspirations as diplomats, and were hopeful of negotiating a peaceful end to the conflict. He took refuge, instead, in his judgment as an officer in the British Army who, in fact, had achieved his stated objective of capturing the city and port of New York with a minimum of British casualties.[11]

His most ardent critics had focused their fire on his failure to follow up his victory on Long Island by attacking the fleeing American troops on Brooklyn Heights, which might very well have resulted in the surrender of the entire Continental Army. Howe acknowledged that the blood of his troops had been up and that, if allowed, they could have taken the forts on Brooklyn Heights. But he insisted that such a victory would have come at the cost of massive British casualties, which he judged to be unnecessary. He had no way of knowing that Washington would find a way to evacuate his defeated army across the East River, a quite miraculous extraction that defied all the conventional tactics of modern warfare. His critics, he implied, were second-guessing a battlefield decision that had been made for sound tactical reasons in the crucible of the moment—that is, without the benefit of their hindsight wisdom.[12]

Thus far Howe's defense rested on his narrow definition of the accusations made against him, justifying his tactical caution in several actions on Long Island and Manhattan on strictly military grounds that civilians and politicians lacked the competence to criticize. But the argument expanded exponentially when several British officers were called to testify on Howe's behalf. They confirmed his claim that his decision to delay a frontal assault on the forts on Brooklyn Heights had been tactically correct, indeed that such an attack would have been "an act of desperate rashness." But then they went on to describe the larger strategic dilemma that Howe had faced:

> That the force sent to America was at no time equal to the subjugations of the country—That this proceeded from the general enmity and hostility of the people, who were almost unanimous in their aversion to the government of Great Britain; and also from the nature of the country, which was most difficult and impracticable with respect to military operations than could possibly be conceived . . . , which rendered it impossible for the army to carry on its operations at any distance from the fleet.[13]

This testimony caught the immediate attention of two prominent critics of the war, Charles Fox and Edmund Burke, good Whigs who from the start had opposed the coercive policy of George III and his ministers that culminated in Germain's decision to invade New York in the summer of 1776. Fox was particularly outspoken in defending Howe, who was being made a scapegoat, he claimed, in order to deflect criticism from the real culprits in the British government: "We have lost 25,000 men. We have spent upwards of 30 million [pounds] by this accursed American war. Who has been the cause of this miscarriage? Is that not the question? Who led us into this war?" Since blaming the king would have verged on treason and violated the unspoken code of conduct for debates in Parliament, Fox fixed his sight on a safer target. It was not

Howe who was on trial but Germain. Burke chimed in with his expression of profuse thanks to Howe, an honorable officer, who had had the misfortune to be appointed commander in chief in a war that was both unnecessary and unwinnable.[14]

No one, including Howe, had anticipated this turn of events, and even those members of the House who harbored serious doubts about his management of His Majesty's troops now called for an end to the deliberations, which had become a freewheeling critique of the British government. But Howe insisted on continuing the proceedings, arguing that nothing less than his reputation was at stake, and he did not yet feel fully vindicated. Fox, who was having a field day at the expense of Germain's reputation, heartily concurred that, by all means, the debate should continue, for Sir William had become the agent for the emergence of truth in the House of Commons after years of obfuscation and denial.

Germain had said nothing up to this point, but he now felt obliged to respond to those criticizing his conduct of the war. He was at pains to express his abiding respect for Howe and his deep disapproval of the way Sir William's reputation had been bandied about by "runners and whisperers, and coffee house politicians." But he was also resolute in his conviction that he had provided the Howe brothers with overwhelming military superiority. He had no doubts or second thoughts about this: "The force sent out from this country was fully competent to the attainment of its objective, by the total reduction of the rebellion and the consequent recovery of the colonies." Germain did not say it outright, but the clear implication of his remarks was that for whatever reason, the Howes had failed to accomplish their mission.[15]

He was especially distressed to hear Howe and other British officers misrepresent the level of popular support for the rebellion as "almost unanimous." His own sources, mostly loyalists-in-exile, assured him that only between one-fourth and one-third of the colonists were committed rebels; the rest were either loyalists or neutrals. To document his case, Germain presented evidence that there were "more Americans regimented in our service than were to be found under the rebel commander in chief." He also cited the recruitment problems afflicting the Continental Army, "which wanted 60,000 but had never been able to muster more than 20,000 in one army."[16]

Howe requested the opportunity to contest Germain's figures but was blocked when the House voted to end the proceedings on June 29. It is clear in retrospect that Germain's estimate of loyalist sentiment was vastly inflated. We now know that approximately 20 percent of the American populace was loyalist, but the claim of Howe's supporters that almost the entire American population embraced the rebellion was also an exaggeration.

From Howe's point of view, the results of the inquiry were equivocal. On the one hand, his critics had been answered, and no one had suggested that he be stripped of his knighthood or receive any official reprimand. On the other hand, his conduct had become a political prize in a larger argument about the wisdom and winnability of the war. And his defenders had rallied behind him on the grounds that he had been given an impossible mission that no display of military competence could have overcome. For long-standing opponents of the war in Parliament, he was a victim. For supporters of an imperial agenda toward the American colonies, he was the convenient one-word answer to the awkward question: How could we possibly have lost the war?

· · ·

WHAT WE MIGHT CALL the Howe interpretation of the British defeat never received official status. For that matter, the British government never saw fit to conduct an official inquiry into the reasons for the rather monumental debacle, preferring instead to draw a curtain of silence around the entire episode, treating it like a wound that would heal itself over time.

One exception to this policy of enforced amnesia was Henry Clinton, who saw fit to begin writing his own memoirs soon after returning from America in 1782. Clinton had inherited command of the British Army from Howe in 1778, so his primary motive was to justify his own decisions during the latter stages of the war, arguing that once the French entered the conflict, he faced insuperable obstacles and that the surrender of Cornwallis's army at Yorktown was not his fault. But in the early pages of his memoir, Clinton went back to the New York campaign and, after bowing to Howe's status as commander in chief, proceeded to tell a story that insinuated that Howe had missed a golden opportunity to win the war at its very inception.[17]

Clinton described three occasions when Howe had rejected his advice. Claiming that he was motivated "by no other principle than to contribute my utmost toward the speedy extinction of the rebellion," he had initially proposed an attack on the northern tip of Manhattan, which would have sealed the Continental Army on the New York archipelago without hope of escape. He had also argued for pursuing the Continentals at Brooklyn Heights, when they had still been reeling from the defeat on Gowanus Heights. And he had recommended an assault at King's Bridge rather than Kip's Bay, which would have trapped the Continental Army on Manhattan. In each instance, Howe had rejected his advice, and although Clinton went out of his way to defend Howe's authority as commander in chief, he nevertheless created the distinct impression that the Continental Army could have been destroyed several times over in the New York campaign, and if that had happened, the war might very well have ended then and there.[18]

Clinton's memoirs probably reflected the critical appraisal of Howe's decisions within certain segments of the officer corps of the British Army, but they had no impact on the ongoing if surreptitious debate about who to blame for the British defeat, because Clinton died before completing them, and they were not published until the middle of the twentieth century. It does seem clear, however, that Clinton went to his maker believing that the American war for independence might very well have ended differently if he, rather than Howe, had been in command in New York.

Clinton's account was obviously self-serving, but it was reinforced by the first comprehensive history of the war from the British side, published in two volumes in 1794. Its author was Charles Stedman, a British staff officer throughout the war who wanted to strike an upbeat note despite the British defeat. "Although the issue of the war was unfortunate," Stedman explained, "neither martial ardor was wanting, among our countrymen, nor patriotic zeal." Stedman's main argument was that the British Army had done its duty, fought bravely, and should not suffer criticisms or blame for the eventual outcome of the war.[19]

The only exception was William Howe. Stedman's account of the New York campaign followed the same line as Clinton's critique, describing Howe's decisions on Long Island and Manhattan as "inexplicable." Since Stedman had served on Richard Howe's staff, he was surely aware that the military decisions of both Howe brothers were considerably influenced by their hopes for a peaceful reconciliation, but he did not mention that fact, preferring instead to characterize Howe's decisions as "tactical blunders." He was especially critical of Howe's failure to pursue Washington's depleted troops as they retreated through New Jersey in November 1776, citing that as the final and most opportune occasion to destroy the Continental Army.[20]

According to Stedman's account, once that vulnerable moment passed, the likelihood of a British victory diminished for three reasons: first, Washington adopted a more defensive strategy, what was called "a war of posts," that made decisive engagement highly improbable; second, the Continental Army got better with experience, especially in the development of a more professional officer corps; and third, the Franco-American treaty of 1778 threw money and men into the American side. Taken together, these developments made the war unwinnable for the British, despite heroic efforts by the army and navy.[21]

Stedman's version of history provided an attractive story line for both the British government and the British Army, as it contradicted the claim of opposition leaders like Burke, Fox, and Pitt that the war had been, from the start, a misguided venture. But it had to be won quickly, with one smashing blow, which was precisely what Germain had proposed and orchestrated in the summer of 1776. When that effort failed, the British military had performed heroically in support of what had become a lost cause.

The beauty of this interpretation was that it sidestepped the question of whether the policies of the British ministry that had caused the war were sensible, which they clearly were not, and it located the source of the British failure in one discreet moment, the summer of 1776, and one British officer, William Howe, who missed the chance to destroy the Continental Army. This meant that fundamental questions about the core assumptions underlying Britain's imperial agenda need not be raised. It assumed that if the Howes had acted more aggressively, the Continental Army would have ceased to exist, which is almost certainly correct, but also that the destruction of the Continental Army would have ended the war. While we can never know for sure, the balance of historical scholarship over the last forty years has made that a highly problematic assumption.[22]

ACKNOWLEDGMENTS

The chronological terrain over which this story moves is highly contested ground, littered with the dead bodies of historians who have preceded me. My effort to offer a fresh interpretation that brings together the political and military sides of the story has been aided by several distinguished historians who have scouted the same terrain and laid down their markers on the trail.

Five historians read all or most of the book in manuscript form and saved me from multiple blunders, but they are in no sense responsible for those that remain: Edmund S. Morgan, the acknowledged dean of early American historians, my mentor and friend for nearly fifty years; Gordon Wood, the reigning scholarly expert on the American Revolution and early republic; Pauline Maier, the leading scholar on the drafting of the Declaration of Independence, whose marginal comments (e.g., "Joe, you can't say that!") could not be ignored; Edward Lengel, editor in chief of the *Washington Papers* and ranking expert on Washington as commander in chief; and Robert Dalzell, that wise man of Williams College, who moves across great patches of the American past with such easy erudition.

Stephen Smith, editor of the *Washington Examiner,* is my long-standing critical eye in that crucial junction where substance meets style, a genius at noticing where a phrase, sentence, or paragraph does not quite say what it wants to say.

Dan Frank of Random House came aboard as editor of this book and ushered it through the corridors of power with an impressive combination of wisdom and grace. His able assistant, Jill Verrillo, never put my calls on hold.

Paul Staiti, my colleague at Mount Holyoke and one of the leading historians of the art and architecture of revolutionary America, helped with the selection of illustrations. Jeffrey Ward did a masterful job of making the maps both depict the battles and fit the text.

Ike Williams, my agent, handled all the contractual niceties, made sure the people at Knopf were paying attention, and routinely brought me back from the eighteenth century with gossip about the Celtics, Patriots, and Red Sox.

Linda Chesky Fernandes, my assistant, did not do any of the research, but she did just about everything else, to include deciphering my scrawl, compensating for my technological incompetence, balancing my mood swings, and kissing me on the cheek.

My wife, Ellen Wilkins Ellis, did not edit my writing, but she did edit my psyche. I have a strong suspicion that this made a huge difference.

Most of the writing was done in longhand in my study at Amherst, surrounded by a feisty Jack Russell terrier, an earnest Labradoodle, and a very brave cat.

This book is dedicated to Ashbel Green, my editor at Knopf for twenty years and six books. Ash passed away just as I was finishing the manuscript. We always argued over adverbs, semicolons, and subtitles, conversations that invariably drifted to the pathetic state of his beloved Cleveland Indians. Ash was a legend in his own time at Knopf, the essence of editorial integrity, a dour Presbyterian with an aristocratic sense of honor. We shall not see his likes again.

JOSEPH J. ELLIS
Amherst, Massachusetts

NOTES

KEY TO ABBREVIATIONS

Titles

AA   Peter Force, ed., *American Archives,* 9 vols. (Washington, D.C., 1833–53)

AFC   Lyman H. Butterfield et al., eds., *Adams Family Correspondence,* 9 vols. to date (Cambridge, Mass., 1963–)

AP   Robert J. Taylor et al., eds., *The Papers of John Adams,* 11 vols. to date (Cambridge, Mass., 1983–)

DA   Lyman H. Butterfield et al., eds., *The Diary and Autobiography of John Adams,* 4 vols. (Cambridge, Mass., 1961)

FP   William B. Willcox et al., eds., *The Papers of Benjamin Franklin,* 28 vols. to date (New Haven, 1959–)

GP   Richard K. Showman et al., eds., *The Papers of General Nathanael Greene,* 7 vols. to date (Chapel Hill, 1976–)

JCC   Worthington C. Ford, ed., *The Journals of the Continental Congress, 1774–1789,* 34 vols. (Washington, D.C. 1904–37)

JP   Julian Boyd et al., eds., *The Papers of Thomas Jefferson,* 28 vols. to date (Princeton, 1950–)

LA   Library of America, *The American Revolution: Writings from the War of Independence* (New York, 2001), selections and notes by John Rhodehamel

LDC   Paul H. Smith et al., eds., *Letters of Delegates to Congress, 1774–1789,* 26 vols. (Washington, D.C., 1976–2000)

PH   T. C. Hammond, ed., *The Parliamentary History of England,* 30 vols. (London, 1806–20)

PWR   W. W. Abbott, Dorothy Twohig, and Philander Chase, eds.,
      The Papers of George Washington: Revolutionary War Series,
      12 vols. to date (Charlottesville, 1985–)
WMQ   *William and Mary Quarterly,* 3rd series

Persons

AA   Abigail Adams
BF   Benjamin Franklin
GW   George Washington
JA   John Adams
NG   Nathanael Greene
TJ   Thomas Jefferson

PREFACE

1. See my *American Creation: Triumphs and Tragedies at the Founding of the Republic* (New York, 2007), 38–44, for the argument that delaying the full promise of republican principles was essential in achieving independence.

2. See Don Higginbotham, *War and Society in Revolutionary America: The Wider Dimensions of the Conflict* (Columbia, 1988), 153–73, for the impact of the Vietnam War on our understanding of the dilemma facing the British Army in 1776.

I. PRUDENCE DICTATES

1. This synthesis of the early months of the war is taken from multiple accounts, especially from the following: Ron Chernow, *Washington: A Life* (New York, 2010), 181–205; Joseph J. Ellis, *His Excellency: George Washington* (New York, 2004), 73–92; David McCullough, *1776* (New York, 2005), 3–92; and Michael Stephenson, *Patriot Battles: How the War of Independence Was Fought* (New York, 2007), 211–29. The quotation is from AA to JA, 16 March 1776, *AFC* 1:358.

2. Jack N. Rakove, *The Beginnings of National Politics: An Interpretive History of the Continental Congress* (New York, 1979), 91–92.

3. Merrill D. Peterson, ed., *The Portable Jefferson* (New York, 1977), 235–36.

4. GW to John Augustine Washington, 31 May 1776, *PWR* 4:412–13.

5. William Blackstone, *Commentaries on the Laws of England* (Oxford, 1765), 1:49. For a synthesis of the constitutional argument, see

Gordon S. Wood, "The Problem of Sovereignty," *WMQ* 68 (October 2011), 572–77.

6. *PH* 18:149–59, for Pitt's speech on 20 January 1775.

7. Ibid., 18:233, 263, 304, 335.

8. The best analysis of the moderate mentality in the middle colonies is Jack Rakove, *Revolutionaries: A New History of the Invention of America* (Boston and New York, 2010), 71–111.

9. On Dickinson's life and thoughts, see Jane Calvert, *Quaker Constitutionalism and the Political Thought of John Dickinson* (New York, 2009).

10. John Dickinson, Notes for a Speech in Congress, 23–25 May 1775, *LDC* 1:378.

11. The clearest expression of the Dickinsonian solution came in an address that Dickinson coauthored with Thomas Jefferson in the summer of 1775 titled *Declaration of the Causes and Necessity for Taking Up Arms,* available in *JP* 1:213–19.

12. See, for example, Robert G. Parkinson, "War and the Imperative of Union," *WMQ* 68 (October 2011), 631–34.

13. JA to James Warren, 24 July 1775, *AP* 3:89–93.

14. For Adams's latter-day recollections on who deserved credit for producing the break with the British Empire, see Joseph J. Ellis, *Passionate Sage: The Character and Legacy of John Adams* (New York, 1993), 53–83.

15. McCullough, *1776,* 3–12; JA to John Trumbull, 13 February 1776, *AP* 4:22. For George III's crucial role in forcing a military response to the American protests, see Alexander Jackson O'Shaughnessy, " 'If Others Will Not Be Active, I Must Drive': George III and the American Revolution," *Early American Studies* 3 (Spring 2004), 1–46.

16. Eric Foner, *Tom Paine and Revolutionary America* (New York, 1976). See also Harvey J. Kaye, *Thomas Paine and the Promise of America* (New York, 2005).

17. The authoritative biography of Paine is John Keane, *Tom Paine: A Political Life* (Boston, 1995). The Adams quotation is from JA to William Tudor, 12 April 1776, *AP* 4:118.

18. JA to AA, 19 March 1776, *AFC* 1:363.

19. For the "raging bulls" reference, see *DA* 1:33. I am drawing here and below on my own work on Adams, chiefly *Passionate Sage: The Character and Legacy of John Adams* (New York, 1993) and *First Family: Abigail and John Adams* (New York, 2010). There are also four distinguished biographies: Page Smith, *John Adams,* 2 vols. (New York, 1962); Peter Shaw, *The Character of John Adams: A Life* (Chapel Hill, 1976); John Fer-

ling, *John Adams: A Life* (Knoxville, 1995); and David McCullough, *John Adams* (New York, 2001).

20. See editorial note, *AFC* 1:136–37.

21. For the Ciceronian pose, see *DA* 1:63, 95.

22. JA to James Warren, 18 May 1776, *AP* 4:192; JA to Moses Gill, 10 June 1775, *AP* 3:21; JA to AA, 17 June 1775, *AFC* 1:216.

23. JA to James Warren, 22 April 1776, *AP* 4:135.

24. JA to Mercy Otis Warren, 16 April 1776, *AP* 4:124.

25. AA to JA, 27 November 1775, *AFC* 1:310.

26. JA to John Winthrop, 12 May 1776, *AP* 4:183–84.

27. See editorial note, *AP* 4:65–73.

28. My interpretation of *Thoughts* has been shaped by Edmund S. Morgan, *Inventing the People: The Rise of Popular Sovereignty in England and America* (New York, 1988).

29. JA to James Warren, 15 May 1776, *AP* 4:186.

30. Ibid., 4:185.

31. JA to AA, 17 May 1776, *AFC* 1:410. See as well *AP* 4:93, from the preface to *Thoughts,* where Adams also dramatizes the historical significance of his role.

32. JA to Horatio Gates, 23 March 1776, *AP* 4:58–60, for Adams's conviction that George III had, in effect, declared war on the American colonies.

33. Adams believed, correctly it turned out, that the resolution of May 15 was an implicit call for a referendum on independence. What he feared was that the debates in the colonial legislatures would not be confined to that core question but would spin out of control and in the process undermine the consensus he considered crucial.

34. Unknown to JA, 9 June 1775, *AP* 3:18–19; "Humanity" to JA, 23 January 1776, *AP* 3:411.

35. AA to JA, 31 March 1776, *AFC* 1:370.

36. JA to AA, 14 April 1776, *AFC* 1:382; AA to JA, 7 May 1776, *AFC* 1:402. In the effort to find some kind of common ground, they eventually agreed that women should be better educated in the new American republic, in order to instruct the next generation of American leaders. See AA to JA, 14 August 1776; JA to AA, 25 August 1776, *AFC* 2:94, 108.

37. *Pennsylvania Evening Post,* 14 March 1776. On the role of Philadelphia artisans and mechanics in Pennsylvania politics at this propitious moment, see Richard Alan Ryerson, *The Revolution Is Now Begun: The Radical Committees of Philadelphia, 1765–1776* (Philadelphia, 1778).

38. James Sullivan to JA, 12 April 1776, *AP* 4:212–13.

39. JA to James Sullivan, 26 May 1776, *AP* 4:208–12.

2. OF ARMS AND MEN

1. For a succinct but stirring account of the battle, including Warren's fall, see Michael Stephenson, *Patriot Battles: How the War of Independence Was Fought* (New York, 2007), 211–21. The most recent and comprehensive study of Bunker Hill is Paul Lockhart, *The Whites of Their Eyes: Bunker Hill, the First American Army, and the Emergence of George Washington* (New York, 2011). For the desecration of Warren's body, see Benjamin Hichborn to JA, 25 November 1775, *AP* 3:323.

2. A lengthier analysis of Washington's selection as commander in chief of the Continental Army is in Joseph J. Ellis, *His Excellency: George Washington* (New York, 2004), 68–72. Adams was joking about the relevance of Washington's height, but the joke contained a kernel of truth. First impressions of Washington were almost always responses to his physical impressiveness.

3. John Hancock to GW, 2 April 1776, *PWR* 4:16–17; for the Harvard degree, *PWR* 4:23; for the medal, *JCC* 4:248–49; for the same kind of lavish praise from the Massachusetts General Court, *PWR* 3:555–57.

4. The best study of Washington's capacity to embody multiple versions of the American Revolution is Barry Schwartz, *George Washington: The Making of an American Symbol* (New York, 1987). My understanding of Washington is based on a reading of the *Washington Papers* and additional research for *His Excellency.* Among the multiple biographies, three stand out: Marcus Cunliffe, *George Washington: Man and Monument* (Boston, 1958); Peter R. Henriques, *Realistic Visionary: A Portrait of George Washington* (Charlottesville, 2006); and Ron Chernow, *Washington: A Life* (New York, 2010).

5. GW to John Hancock, 9 February 1776, *PWR* 3:275.

6. The seminal work on the Continental Army is Charles Royster, *A Revolutionary People at War: The Continental Army and the American Character* (Chapel Hill, 1979). See also Robert K. Wright, *The Continental Army* (Washington, D.C., 1983).

7. T. H. Breen, *American Insurgents, American Patriots: The Revolution of the People* (New York, 2010).

8. GW to Joseph Reed, 14 January 1776, *PWR* 3:89.

9. GW to Joseph Reed, 1 February 1776, *PWR* 3:237–38.

10. General Orders, 12 November 1775, *PWR* 2:353.

11. On the dying "spirit of '76," see Joseph J. Ellis, *American Creation* (New York, 2007), 20–57. On the "Norman Rockwell moments," see Stephenson, *Patriot Battles,* 15.

12. John R. Alden, *General Charles Lee: Traitor or Patriot?* (Baton Rouge, 1951), remains the standard biography. Lee's letters to Washington during the Boston Siege, which are sprinkled throughout *PWR* 3, contain multiple examples of his colorful eccentricities, as well as a less formal attitude toward Washington, whom he usually addressed as "my dear general."

13. Terry Golway, *Washington's General: Nathanael Greene and the Triumph of the American Revolution* (New York, 2005).

14. Mark Puls, *Henry Knox: Visionary General of the American Revolution* (New York, 2008).

15. JA to GW, January 1776, *PWR* 3:36–37; Charles Lee to GW, 5 January 1776, *PWR* 3:30; Charles Lee to GW, 16 February 1776, *PWR* 4:339–41.

16. Barnet Schecter, *The Battle for New York: The City at the Heart of the American Revolution* (New York, 2002), 82–87, for the tactical problems posed by New York. See also the little classic by Bruce Bliven, *Battle for Manhattan* (New York, 1955), 9–12.

17. Stephenson, *Patriotic Battles,* 231–32, for the most recent estimate of the British invasion force; see also Schecter, *Battle for New York,* chap. 5, for a more detailed description of how the men and ships were assembled.

18. Quoted in Piers Mackesy, *The War for America, 1775–1783* (Cambridge, Mass., 1964), 55.

19. Ibid., 50–55; see also Gerald S. Brown, *The American Secretary: The Colonial Policy of Lord George Germain, 1775–1778* (Ann Arbor, 1963), and Stanley Weintraub, *Iron Tears: America's Battle for Freedom, Britain's Quagmire, 1775–1783* (New York, 2005), 26–44.

20. Mackesy, *War for America,* 56–70. David Hackett Fischer, *Washington's Crossing* (New York, 2004), 73–78, also provides a succinct overview of Germain's Hudson-corridor strategy. This strategy failed spectacularly a year later because Howe, for reasons that will forever remain mysterious, chose to attack Philadelphia rather than move up the Hudson, and Burgoyne's army, coming down from Ticonderoga, was forced to surrender at Saratoga.

21. Ira D. Gruber, *The Howe Brothers and the American Revolution* (New York, 1972), remains the authoritative source. See also Troyer S.

Anderson, *The Command of the Howe Brothers During the American Revolution* (New York, 1936), and Kevin Phillips, *The Cousins' War* (New York, 1999), which emphasizes the American sympathies of the Howe brothers.

22. This sketch is heavily indebted to the above-mentioned works by Gruber and Anderson; see also the thoughtful essay by Maldwyn Jones in George A. Billias, ed., *George Washington's Opponents: British Generals and Admirals in the American Revolution* (New York, 1969), 39–72. On the seductive charms of Elizabeth Loring, see the long note in Schecter, *Battle for New York,* 403–4, and the reliably savvy account in Fischer, *Washington's Crossing,* 72–73. On the lasting influence of Bunker Hill on Howe's thinking, see Henry Lee, *Memoirs of the War in the Southern Department,* 2 vols. (Philadelphia, 1812), 1:55, where Charles Lee recalls that "the sad and impressive experience of this murderous day [Bunker Hill] sunk deep into the mind of Sir William Howe; and it seems to have had its influence upon all his subsequent operations with decisive control."

23. William Howe to Lord George Germain, 26 April 1776, quoted in Anderson, *Command of the Howe Brothers,* 120; see also William Howe to Lord George Germain, 23 April 1776, ibid., 118–20, where Howe worries that his biggest challenge will be to lure Washington into a fight.

24. See Ellis, *His Excellency,* 89–93, for my summary of the strategic options discussed by the senior officers outside Boston during the siege.

25. GW to John Hancock, 5 May 1776, *PWR* 4:210.

26. See General Orders, 22 May 1776, *PWR* 4:396, for the official description of the fortifications. Lee's original plan made no mention of Bunker Hill, but my point here is that his defensive scheme implicitly acknowledged that actually preventing the capture of New York was tactically impossible.

27. On Alexander, or Lord Stirling, see *GP* 1:216; on Greene's feverish effort to fortify Brooklyn Heights, see *GP* 1:231, which provides a good map.

28. NG to Christopher Green, 7 June 1776, *GP* 1:232–33.

29. General Orders, 14 April 1776, *PWR* 4:59.

30. For a description of the numerous prostitutes, see Edward Bangs, ed., *Journal of Lt. Isaac Bangs* (New York, 1890; reprint, 1968). See also General Orders, 27 April 1776, *PWR* 4:140–42, for the public punishment of the regiment that pulled down the houses.

31. GW to John Hancock, 25–26 April 1776, *PWR* 4:128. The Canadian drain left Washington with 10,192 rank and file, 596 officers, 78

staff officers, and 881 noncommissioned officers, of whom nearly 20 percent were not fit for duty, mostly because of dysentery as a consequence of contaminated water. He estimated that this was about half of what he needed to oppose Howe successfully. And his estimate of Howe's invasion force proved low by more than 10,000 troops.

32. GW to John Augustine Washington, 31 May–4 June 1776, *PWR* 6:413.

33. See John Hancock to GW, 21 May 1776, *PWR* 4:352–53, for Martha's inoculation, which occurred in Thomas Jefferson's lodgings on Chestnut Street. See Philip Schuyler to GW, 13 May 1776, *PWR* 4:291–92, for news of the Quebec defeat. See Message from the Six Nations, 16 May 1776, *PWR* 4:319–20, requesting "a Dram [of liquor] in the Morning & in the Eveng."

34. Pauline Maier, *American Scripture: Making the Declaration of Independence* (New York, 1997), 37–41, is the best account of the process leading up to the drafting of the document.

35. GW to John Augustine Washington, 31 May–4 June 1776, *PWR* 4:412.

36. See John Hancock to GW, 14 June 1776, *PWR* 4:525–26, for the creation of the Board of War and Ordnance. See JA to NG, 22 June 1776, *GP* 238–40, for Adams's expression of incompetence.

37. NG to JA, 2 June 1776, *GP* 226.

38. GW to John Hancock, 10 July 1776, *PWR* 5:260.

39. See John Hancock to GW, 11 June 1776, *PWR* 4:499, for the additional militia deployments. See General Order, 3 June 1776, *GP* 1:227–28, for a special unit of 200 officers and men to round up the loyalists on Long Island. See *JCC* 4:406–7, for the new obstacles in the Hudson and East rivers.

40. General Orders, 6 June 1776, *PWR* 4:445.

3. DOGS THAT DID NOT BARK

1. The ships and troops represent my distillation from Bruce Bliven, *Under the Guns: New York, 1775–1776* (New York, 1972), 328; Ira D. Gruber, *The Howe Brothers and the American Revolution* (New York, 1972), 72–88; and Barnet Schecter, *The Battle for New York: The City at the Heart of the American Revolution* (New York, 2002), 95–111.

2. Quoted in Pauline Maier, *American Scripture: Making the Declaration of Independence* (New York, 1997), 59. Maier was the first modern historian to call attention to "the other declarations," by which she

means the resolutions and petitions generated throughout the colonies in response to the May 15 resolution by the Continental Congress. See ibid., 47–96.

3. An excellent synthesis of the petition tradition in English history, which began with Magna Carta, is ibid., 50–55.

4. Ashby, Middlesex County, 1 July 1776, *AA* 6:706

5. Town of Boston, 23 May 1776, *AA* 6:556–57.

6. Topsfield, Essex County, 21 June 1776, *AA* 6:703–4.

7. Town of Malden, 27 May 1776, *AA* 6:602–3. The only Massachusetts town to reject independence was Barnstable, though the dissenters were barely outvoted and their minority opinion was much longer and more passionate. See *AA* 6:706.

8. Virginia in Convention, 15 May 1776, *AA* 6:461–62.

9. See, for example, the resolution from Buckingham County, 21 May 1776, *AA* 5:1206–8.

10. Maier, *American Scripture,* 64–68, gives a clear account of the political contexts in Pennsylvania and New York.

11. Memorial, City of Philadelphia, 25 May 1776, *AA* 6:560–61; Proceedings of the Provincial Conference . . . of Philadelphia, 18–25 June 1776, *AA* 6:951–57. For the role of the radical mechanics in Philadelphia politics, see Richard A. Ryerson, *The Revolution Is Now Begun: The Radical Committees of Philadelphia* (Philadelphia, 1978).

12. See "The Humble Address of the General Committee of Mechanics," 29 May 1776, *AA* 6:614–15, which also includes the reply from the provincial congress. See John Hazelton, *The Declaration of Independence: Its History* (New York, 1906), 181–86, for the tardy New York vote.

13. Topsfield, Essex County, 21 June 1776, *AA* 6:704.

14. JA to John Hughes, 4 June 1776, *AP* 4:238–39.

15. JA to Patrick Henry, 3 June 1776, *AP* 4:234–35.

16. JA to AA, 2 June 1776, *AFC* 2:3.

17. JA to William Cushing, 9 June 1776, *AP* 4:245.

18. See, for example, Adams's work on the Board of War and Ordnance, *AP* 4:253–59, and the Plan of Treaties, *AP* 4:260–78. More on this in Chapter 5.

19. See *JCC* 5:428–29, for the delay of a vote until 1 July. See editorial note, *AP* 4:341–44, for the creation of the draft committee.

20. Maier, *American Scripture,* 41–46, is the most comprehensive and recent account. But this is sacred ground, and several generations of historians have told the story of the Declaration with considerable dis-

tinction and influenced my account here and below. See especially Carl Becker, *The Declaration of Independence: A Study in the History of Political Ideas* (New York, 1922); Julian Boyd, *The Declaration of Independence: The Evolution of the Text* (Princeton, 1945); and Gary Wills, *Inventing America: Jefferson's Declaration of Independence* (New York, 1968). My own earlier effort is in *American Sphinx: The Character of Thomas Jefferson* (New York, 1998), 46–59. I have also edited an anthology of the different interpretations, *What Did the Declaration Declare?* (Boston and New York, 1999).

21. TJ to Thomas Nelson, 16 May 1776, *JP* 1:292.

22. Ellis, *American Sphinx,* 24–26.

23. Ibid., 29–36.

24. TJ to James Madison, 30 August 1823, TJ to Henry Lee, 8 May 1825, quoted in editorial note, *JP* 1:415. See *JP* 1:413–33, for Julian Boyd's long note on the multiple drafts of the document. Maier, *American Scripture,* 99–105, is also excellent on this score.

25. Edmund Pendleton to TJ, 22 July 1776, *JP* 1:471.

26. See *DA* 3:336, for the Adams recollection.

27. See *DA* 3:396–97, for Adams's autobiographical account of the speeches on 1 July 1776.

28. Maier, *American Scripture,* 97–153, makes the longest and strongest case for seeing the delegates as coauthors of the Declaration based on their extensive revisions.

29. Ibid., 236–41, reproduces the revised Jefferson draft in which all the revisions and deletions are shown. All quotations are taken from this accessible version of the text. A slightly different version that also italicizes the deleted sections of Jefferson's draft is conveniently available in Merrill Peterson, ed., *The Portable Jefferson* (New York, 1977), 235–41.

30. See H. Trevor Colbourn, *The Lamp of Experience: Whig History and the Intellectual Origins of the American Revolution* (Chapel Hill, 1965), 158–84, for Jefferson's "expatriation" and the Saxon myth.

31. See Ellis, *American Sphinx,* 52–53, for my treatment of this sentimental passage, which despite its deletion accurately captured the mood of many ordinary Americans. There was a potent sentimental streak in Jefferson, and the historian who has best captured it is Andrew Burstein, *The Inner Jefferson: Portrait of a Grieving Optimist* (Charlottesville, 2000).

32. Maier, *American Scripture,* 236.

33. Lincoln quoted in Ellis, *American Sphinx,* 54.

34. For the rest of his long life, Jefferson was obsessed with preserv-

ing his original draft of the Declaration, convinced that it was vastly superior to the official version edited by the congress. See Richard Henry Lee to TJ, 21 July 1776, *JP* 1:471, for Lee's attempt to empathize with Jefferson, wishing that "the Manuscript had not been mangled as it is."

35. Bliven, *Under the Guns,* 318–19.

36. General Orders, 2 July 1776, *PWR* 5:180.

4. ETC., ETC., ETC.

1. See Sylvia R. Frey, *The British Soldier in America: A Social History of Military Life in the Revolutionary Period* (Austin, 1981), 37–38, for the casualty rate during the voyage; and Elizabeth A. Fenn, *Pox Americana: The Great Smallpox Epidemic of 1775–1782* (New York, 2001).

2. Journal of Ambrose Serle, 12–23 July 1776, *LA* 147–48.

3. See Stanley Weintraub, *Iron Tears: America's Battle for Freedom, Britain's Quagmire, 1775–1783* (New York, 2005), 65, for the quotation.

4. See David McCullough, *1776* (New York, 2005), 142, for the quotation.

5. Frey, *British Soldier in America,* 20–26.

6. NG to Jacob Greene, 28 September 1776, *GP* 1:303–4. See also Matthew H. Spring, *With Zeal and with Bayonets Only: The British Army on Campaign in North America* (Norman, 2008), which argues that most of Howe's army had only limited combat experience.

7. John Hancock to GW, 6 July 1776, *PWR* 5:219.

8. See editorial note, *PWR* 5:247; Journal of Isaac Bangs, 10 July 1776, *LA* 132–33, for the reading of the Declaration. See Weintraub, *Iron Tears,* 70–71, for the "melted majesty" quotation. See General Orders, 10 July 1776, *PWR* 5:256, for Washington's reprimand.

9. NG to GW, 5 July 1776, *PWR* 5:212.

10. GW to John Hancock, 4 July 1776, *PWR* 5:200.

11. See *PWR* 5:350–62, for the multiple letters on the northern campaign.

12. Council of War, 12 July 1776, *PWR* 5:280.

13. GW to John Hancock, 12 July 1776, *PWR* 5:283–85; NG to GW, 14 July 1776, *GP* 1:253–56.

14. Joseph Plumb Martin, *A Narrative of a Revolutionary Soldier* (New York, 2001), 17–18.

15. General Orders, 13 July 1776, *PWR* 5:290.

16. Pennsylvania Committee of Safety to GW, 11 July 1776, *PWR*

5:271–73; editorial note, *PWR* 5:569 and Thomas Mifflin to GW, 6 August 1776, *PWR* 5:580–81, for the sunken ships; Benjamin Franklin to GW, 22 July 1776, *PWR* 5:421–22, for the submarine proposal.

17. See NG to GW, 27 June 1776, *GP* 1:243, for the livestock matter. Six letters were subsequently exchanged on this issue, which was not resolved until 12 August 1776.

18. For the correspondence on the loyalists, see *GP* 1:241, 276–78, and *PWR* 5:252, 327–28.

19. John F. Roche, *Joseph Reed: A Moderate in the American Revolution* (New York, 1957), 84–85.

20. See the correspondence in *PWR* 5:232, 235, 439, 490–93, and *GP* 1:284–86.

21. GW to John Augustine Washington, 28 July 1776, *PWR* 5:428–30.

22. Lord Richard Howe to GW, 13 July 1776, *PWR* 5:296–97.

23. GW to John Hancock, 14 July 1776, *PWR* 5:306.

24. Journal of Ambrose Serle, 14 July 1776, *LA* 145; GW to John Hancock, 14 July 1776, *PWR* 5:306.

25. GW to General Horatio Gates, 19 July 1776, *PWR* 5:380–81.

26. Joseph Reed, Memorandum of Meeting Between George Washington and James Patterson, 20 July 1776, *LA* 152–55. See also *PWR* 5:398–403 for the same documentation.

27. Among the many biographies of Franklin, four strike me as invaluable: Carl Van Doren, *Benjamin Franklin* (New York, 1938); Edmund S. Morgan, *Benjamin Franklin* (New Haven, 2002); Walter Isaacson, *Benjamin Franklin: An American Life* (New York, 2003); and Gordon Wood, *The Americanization of Benjamin Franklin* (New York, 2004). For Franklin's London years, see David Morgan, *The Devious Dr. Franklin: Benjamin Franklin's Years in London* (Macon, 1996). For a more critical view of Franklin's character, see Robert Middlekauf, *Benjamin Franklin and His Enemies* (Berkeley, 1996).

28. BF to Lord Howe, 20 July 1776, *FP* 22:518–21.

29. Lord Howe to Lord George Germain, 6 August 1776, *PWR* 5:402, editorial note.

30. GW to John Hancock, 22 July 1776, *PWR* 5:424–25.

31. Most historical accounts put the British invasion force at 32,000, but I am including the naval complement in my estimate because they were an integral part of the ensuing combat.

32. JA to AA, 20 July 1776, *AFC* 2:53.

33. GW to Colonel Adam Stephen, 20 July 1776, *PWR* 5:408–9; GW to Brigadier General Willliam Livingston, 8 August 1776, *PWR* 5:632.

34. GW to Militia Colonels in Western Connecticut, 7 August 1776, *PWR* 5:593–94; GW to Jonathan Trumbull, 7 August 1776, *PWR* 5:615–16.

35. JA to AA, 27 July 1776, *AFC* 2:63; JA to AA, 3–4 August 1776, *AFC* 2:75–76.

36. General Orders, 13 August 1776, *PWR* 6:1.

37. GW to John Hancock, 8–9 August 1776, *PWR* 5:627.

38. JA to AA, *AFC* 2:81.

5. AFTER VIRTUE

1. Two old but still valuable accounts are Merrill Jensen, *The Articles of Confederation: An Interpretation of the Social-Constitutional History of the American Revolution, 1774–1781* (Madison, 1940), and Edmund C. Burnett, *The Continental Congress* (New York, 1941). More recently, Herbert James Henderson, *Party Politics in the Continental Congress* (New York, 1974), and Jack N. Rakove, *The Beginnings of National Politics: An Interpretative History of the Continental Congress* (New York, 1979), see regional and sectional splits appearing in the summer of 1776 after the vote on independence. Rakove is best at suggesting the start of a new political chapter following over a year of improvised unity.

2. TJ to Francis Eppes, 15 July 1776, *JP* 1:458–60; TJ to John Page, 30 July 1776, *JP* 1:482–83.

3. See Anthony Wayne to BF, 31 July 1776, *FP* 22:539–40, for the rumor of 60,000 troops.

4. Elbridge Gerry to JA, 3 August 1776, *AP* 4:431–34.

5. BF to Anthony Wayne, 28 August 1776, *FP* 22:584.

6. See *LDC* 4:233–50, for the Dickinson Draft.

7. See *LDC* 4:251, note 1, for the quotations from Bartlett and Rutledge.

8. *LDC* 4:233–34.

9. *LDC* 4:239, 242–43.

10. *LDC* 4:338–39.

11. *DA* 2:245–46; *JP* 1:320–23.

12. *LDC* 4:242.

13. *FP* 22, 536–38, editorial note; *DA* 2:245.

14. *DA* 2:247.

15. *DA* 2:246; *JP* 1:323–27.

16. *DA* 2:241–43, 249–50.

17. Edward Pendleton to TJ, 15 July and 3 August 1776, *JP* 1:462–65, 484–85.

18. JA to Joseph Hawley, 25 August 1776, *LDC* 5:60–62.

19. See *AP* 4:260–78, for the full text of the Plan of Treaties, with an editorial note on the political context and diplomatic legacy.

20. *AP* 4:265.

21. *AP* 4:266. See *DA* 2:236, 3:337, for JA's earliest articulation of restricting a treaty with France to commerce.

22. *AP* 4:268.

23. See *AP* 4:290–92, for the Plan of Treaties as adopted.

24. TJ to Richard Henry Lee, 8 July 1776; Richard Henry Lee to TJ, 21 July 1776, *JP* 1:455–56, 471.

25. *JP* 1:21–28.

26. TJ to Edmund Pendleton, 30 June 1776, TJ to Richard Henry Lee, 29 July 1776, *JP* 1:408, 477.

27. TJ to Edmund Pendleton, 13 and 26 August 1776, *JP* 1:491–94, 503–6.

28. TJ to John Page, 5 August 1776, *JP* 1:485–86.

29. TJ to Edmund Pendleton, 26 August 1776, *JP* 1:505–6.

30. See *AP* 4:253–59, for JA's duties as chair of the Board of War and Ordnance, 12 June–27 August 1776.

31. Joseph Reed to JA, 4 July 1776, *AP* 4:358–60; Nathanael Greene to JA, 14 July 1776, *AP* 4:380–82.

32. JA to William Heath, 3 August 1776, *AP* 4:426–27.

33. Horatio Gates to JA, 17 July 1776, *AP* 4:388–89.

34. JA to Horatio Gates, 13 August 1776, *AP* 4:426–27.

35. AA to JA, 17 and 19 August 1776, *AFC* 2:98, 101.

36. JA to AA, 16 July and 28 August 1776, *AFC* 2:50–51, 111.

37. James Bowdoin to BF, 19 August 1776, *FP* 22:569–71.

38. Lord Howe to BF, 16 August 1776, *FP* 22:565–66; BF to Lord Howe, 20 August 1776, *FP* 22:575, which was not sent.

39. Editorial note, *FP* 22:551–52.

40. Editorial note, *FP* 22:537–38. On August 20 Franklin drafted a letter to protest state-based representation but decided not to send it. See *FP* 22:571–75.

41. See editorial note, *FP* 22:529–33, for Franklin's role in the Pennsylvania Convention.

42. George Ross to BF, 18 August 1776, *FP* 22:568; BF to Horatio Gates, 28 August 1776, *FP* 22:583–84.

6. THE FOG OF WAR

1. Ira D. Gruber, *The Howe Brothers and the American Revolution* (New York, 1972), 100–2.

2. GW to Lund Washington, 19 August 1776, *PWR* 6:82–86. The final size of the American force is an educated guess, based on rough calculations of the size of the late-arriving state militia units. Washington himself did not know how many troops he commanded when the battle began.

3. NG to GW, 15 August 1776, *GP* 1:287; Stirling quoted in Michael Stephenson, *Patriot Battles: How the War of Independence Was Fought* (New York, 2007), 231.

4. William Howe to GW, 1 August 1776, *PWR* 5:537.

5. GW to William Howe, 17 August 1776, *PWR* 5:537–38.

6. Editorial note, *PWR* 6:23–24; Hugh Mercer to GW, 19 August 1776, *PWR* 6:79; General Orders, 7 August 1776, *GP* 1:277; Barnet Schecter, *The Battle for New York: The City at the Heart of the American Revolution* (New York, 2002), 129.

7. William B. Willcox, *Portrait of a General: Sir Henry Clinton in the War for Independence* (New York, 1964), preface, 492–524, provides the deepest analysis of any British officer in the war, as well as the most sophisticated psychological analysis of any prominent figure on either side. See also William Willcox and Frederick Wyatt, "Sir Henry Clinton: A Psychological Exploration in History," *WMQ* 14 (January 1959), 3–26.

8. William B. Willcox, ed., *The American Rebellion: Sir Henry Clinton's Narrative of His Campaigns, 1775–1782* (New Haven, 1954), 40–41; Schecter, *Battle for New York,* 60–61.

9. Gruber, *Howe Brothers,* 106–7.

10. NG to GW, 15 August 1776, *PWR* 6:29–31; GW to John Hancock, 23 August 1776, *PWR* 6:111, for the appointment of Sullivan.

11. Ambrose Serle, *The American Journal of Ambrose Serle* (San Marino, 1940), 72–74; Stephenson, *Patriot Battles,* 232–33, for Washington's allocation of troops.

12. General Orders, 23 August 1776, *PWR* 6:109–10. Several secondary works on the ensuing battle, in addition to those already cited, have helped to shape my understanding of the story. On the British side, Piers Mackesy, *The War for America, 1775–1783* (Cambridge, Mass., 1964). On the American side, Bruce Bliven, *Under the Guns: New York, 1775–76* (New York, 1972); Thomas Fleming, *1776: Year of Illusions* (New York, 1975), 308–38; James Thomas Flexner, *George Washington: In the Ameri-*

can Revolution (Boston, 1967), 87–156; David Hackett Fischer, *Washington's Crossing* (New York, 2004), 81–114; and David McCullough, *1776* (New York, 2005), 115–200.

13. Editorial note, *GP* 1:291–93.

14. John Sullivan to GW, 23 August 1776; GW to John Hancock, 26 August 1776, *PWR* 6:115–16, 129–30; Schecter, *Battle for New York,* 131–32. See Ron Chernow, *Washington: A Life* (New York, 2010), 246, for background on Putnam, who has no modern biographer.

15. Willcox, *Sir Henry Clinton's Narrative,* 40–42; Schecter, *Battle for New York,* 135–37.

16. Willcox, *Sir Henry Clinton's Narrative,* 35.

17. All quotations from Schecter, *Battle for New York,* 132–34.

18. Ibid., 141–43.

19. Stephenson, *Patriotic Battles,* 237–38.

20. Joseph Plumb Martin, *A Narrative of a Revolutionary Soldier* (New York, 2001), 22–23.

21. E. J. Lowell, *The Hessians and the Other German Auxiliaries of Great Britain in the Revolutionary War* (New York, 1884), 65–67.

22. Schecter, *Battle for New York,* 149–54; Paul David Nelson, *William Alexander, Lord Stirling* (Tuscaloosa, 1987), 44; Lord Stirling to GW, 29 August 1776, *PWR* 6:159–62.

23. William Howe to Lord George Germain, 3 September 1776, in K. G. Davies, ed., *Documents of the American Revolution, 1770–1783* (Dublin, 1976), 12:217; Howard H. Peckham, ed., *The Toll of Independence: Engagements and Battle Casualties of the American Revolution* (Chicago, 1974), 22; editorial note, *PWR* 6:143.

24. William Howe to Lord George Germain, 3 September 1776, in Davies, *Documents of the American Revolution,* 12:218; Schecter, *Battle for New York,* 166–67; Willcox, *Sir Henry Clinton's Narrative,* 44.

25. This is the major argument made by Gruber, *Howe Brothers.*

26. Howe defended his conduct before Parliament soon after his return to England. See William Howe, *The Narrative of Lieutenant General William Howe . . .* (London, 1780). The earliest case that Howe's American sympathies lost the war for Great Britain came from a member of his own staff. See Charles Stedman, *The History of the Origin, Progress, and Termination of the American War* (Dublin, 1794). In my view, Howe's motives were psychologically intricate, but his chief mistake was to assume that British victory was assured, so he could afford to fight more cautiously. Like most British officers, he overestimated the level of

loyalist sentiment and underestimated the staying power of the Continental Army. His concern about British casualties, though misguided in retrospect, was wholly plausible at the time.

27. Davies, *Documents of the American Revolution,* 218.

28. Robert Hanson Harrison to John Hancock, 28 August 1776, *PWR* 6:142–43, provides Washington's initial and somewhat incoherent report on the battle for Gowanus Heights, which is the only direct evidence we have on Washington's somewhat dazed state of mind. Among Washington's biographers, Chernow, *Washington,* 247–49, is most astute on this score.

29. William Bradford Reed, *Life and Correspondence of Joseph Reed* (Philadelphia, 1847), 1:226–27.

30. This interpretation of Washington's thought process at this intense moment is based on my assessment of his personality in *His Excellency: George Washington* (New York, 2004).

31. This emphasis on Mifflin's influence was first argued in Fleming, *Year of Illusions,* 322–23.

32. Council of War, 29 August 1776, *PWR* 6:153–55; Tallmadge quoted in Henry P. Johnston, *The Campaign of 1776 Around New York and Brooklyn* (Brooklyn, 1878), 2:11; Schecter, *Battle for New York,* 155–67.

33. See Alexander Graydon, *A Memoir of His Own Time* (Philadelphia, 1846), 164, for the quotation. The standard work on Glover is George Billias, *General John Glover and His Marblehead Mariners* (New York, 1960).

34. See Graydon, *Memoir,* 166, for the making of wills; and Martin, *Narrative of a Revolutionary Soldier,* 26–27. The Tilghman quotation is in Johnston, *Campaign of 1776,* 2:85.

35. Graydon, *Memoir,* 168; George F. Scheer and Hugh Rankin, eds., *Rebels and Redcoats* (New York, 1957), 171. This incident was the beginning of bad blood between Mifflin and Washington.

36. Benjamin Tallmadge, *Memoir of Colonel Benjamin Tallmadge* (New York, 1858), 11.

37. Charles K. Bolton, ed., *Letters of Hugh Earl Percy from Boston and New York* (Boston, 1972), 69.

38. Sir George Collier, "Admiral Sir George Collier's Observations on the Battle of Long Island," *New-York Historical Society Quarterly* (October 1964), 304.

39. GW to John Hancock, 31 August 1776, *PWR* 6:177–78; editorial note, *GP* 1:293, for making Greene's absence the reason for the defeat.

40. General Orders, 31 August 1776, *PWR* 6:173.

41. JA to James Warren, 17 August 1776, JA to AA, 5 September 1776, *LDC* 5:12, 107.

42. JA to AA, 4 September 1776, JA to Samuel Cooper, 4 September 1776, *LDC* 5:101–2.

43. AA to JA, 7 September, 20 September, 29 September 1776, *AFC* 2:122, 129, 134–36; JA to AA, 8 October 1776, *AFC* 2:140.

44. William Hooper to Samuel Johnston, 26 September 1776, *LCD* 5:182–83.

45. Benjamin Rush to Julia Rush, 18–25 September 1776, Benjamin Rush to Jacques Barbeu-Dubourg, 16 September 1776, *LCD* 5:198–99.

46. BF to William Bingham, 21 September 1776, *FP* 22:617.

47. John F. Roche, *Joseph Reed: A Moderate in the American Revolution* (New York, 1957), 92.

48. Editorial note, *FP* 2:591–92.

49. Editorial note, *DA* 3:415.

50. John Witherspoon's Speech in Congress, 5 September 1776, *LDC* 5:108–13.

51. *DA* 3:416.

52. *DA* 3:419–20.

53. Report to Congress, 13 September 1776, *FP* 22:606–8.

54. Henry Strachey, Memorandum of Meeting Between Lord Howe and the American Commissioners, 11 September 1776, *LA* 186–91.

55. *DA* 3:422.

56. *DA* 3:422–23.

57. Journal of Ambrose Serle, 13 September 1776, *LA* 215.

58. JA to Samuel Adams, 14 September 1776, *DA* 3:428.

7. HEARTS AND MINDS

1. GW to John Hancock, 2 September 1776, *PWR* 6:199–201; *PWR* 6:163, editorial note.

2. GW to John Hancock, 4 September 1776, *PWR* 6:215–16; Barnet Schecter, *The Battle for New York: The City at the Heart of the American Revolution* (New York, 2002), 168.

3. General Orders, 4 September 1776, *PWR* 6:212–13; Collier quoted in Schecter, *Battle for New York*, 175.

4. George Germain to William Howe, October 1776, quoted in

Stanley Weintraub, *Iron Tears: America's Battle for Freedom, Britain's Quagmire, 1775–1783* (New York, 2005), 75.

5. NG to GW, 5 September 1776, *GP* 1:294–96.

6. GW to John Hancock, 8 September 1776, *PWR* 6:248–54.

7. Henry P. Johnston, "Sergeant Lee's Experience with Bushnell's Submarine Torpedo in 1776," *Magazine of History* 29 (1893), 262–66. This episode is nicely covered in Thomas Fleming, *1776: Year of Illusions* (New York, 1975), 338–41. See also the editorial note on the *Turtle* in *PWR* 6:528.

8. GW to John Hancock, 8 September 1776, *PWR* 6:248–52.

9. Joseph Reed to Esther Reed, 2 September 1776, quoted in John F. Roche, *Joseph Reed: A Moderate in the American Revolution* (New York, 1957), 92.

10. William Heath to GW, 31 August 1776, Rufus Putnam to GW, 3 September 1776, *PWR* 6:179–81, 210–11.

11. New York Committee of Safety to GW, 31 August 1776, *PWR* 6:185–86.

12. John Hancock to GW, 10 September 1776, *PWR* 6:273; *JCC* 5:749; Petition of Nathanael Greene and Others to General Washington, 11 September 1776, *GP* 1:297–98.

13. Council of War, 12 September 1776, *GP* 1:299–300; see also *PWR* 6:288–89.

14. GW to John Hancock, 14 September 1776, *PWR* 6:308–9.

15. JA to Henry Knox, 29 September 1776, *LDC* 5:260–61.

16. William Hooper to Samuel Johnston, 26 September 1776, *LDC* 5:245–49; *JCC* 5:762–63.

17. *LDC* 5:xiii; John Hancock to TJ, 30 September 1776, *LDC* 5:264–65; *DA* 3:409–10.

18. AA to JA, 20 September 1776, *AFC* 2:129.

19. GW to John Hancock, 25 September 1776, *PWR* 6:393–94.

20. GW to Jacob Greene, 28 September 1776, *GP* 1:303–4; GW to John Hancock, 25 September 1776, *PWR* 6:394–98.

21. *JCC* 5:762–63.

22. John Hancock to the States, 24 September 1776, *LDC* 5:228–30.

23. GW to John Hancock, 25 September 1776, *PWR* 6:304.

24. AA to JA, 29 September 1776, *AFC* 2:134–36.

25. *New England Chronicle,* 5 September 1776.

26. *Connecticut Courant,* 6 September 1776; *Pennsylvania Packet,* 10 September 1776; *Newport Mercury,* 16 September 1776; *Virginia*

Gazette, 6 September and 8 November 1776. I realize that this is only a geographically spread sampling, and other newspapers might have provided more accurate accounts of the Long Island debacle. But if so, they were the exception rather than the rule.

27. See, for example, *Virginia Gazette,* 4 October 1776; *Independent Chronicle,* 3 October 1776; *Newport Mercury,* 30 September 1776.

28. William B. Willcox, ed., *The American Rebellion: Sir Henry Clinton's Narrative of His Campaigns, 1775–1782* (New Haven, 1954), 44–45; Schecter, *Battle for New York,* 179–80.

29. Joseph Reed to Esther Reed, 2 September 1776, *New-York Historical Society.*

30. My account of the Kip's Bay engagement draws on the eyewitness reports of Philip Vickers Fithian and Benjamin Trumbull, both in *LA,* 219–24, and on the memoir of Joseph Plumb Martin, *A Narrative of a Revolutionary Soldier* (New York, 2001), 30–32. In addition, three secondary accounts were indispensable: David McCullough, *1776* (New York, 2007), 209–12; Schecter, *Battle for New York,* 184–87; and Michael Stephenson, *Patriotic Battles: How the War of Independence Was Fought* (New York, 2005), 244–46.

31. Martin, *Narrative of a Revolutionary Soldier,* 31.

32. Ibid., 32. GW to John Hancock, 16 September 1776, *PWR* 6:313–17, provides Washington's official report on the battle, plus editorial notes on troop strength, logistics, and the naval bombardment.

33. *PWR* 6:316–17; NG to Nicholas Cooke, 17 September 1776, *GP* 1:380.

34. JA to William Tudor, 20 September 1776, *LDC* 5:200.

35. Trevor Steele Anderson, *The Command of the Howe Brothers* (New York, 1936), 160; GW to Lund Washington, 6 October 1776, *PWR* 6:495.

36. My treatment of the action at Harlem Heights is indebted to McCullough, *1776,* 217–20; to Stephenson, *Patriotic Battles,* 246–47; and most especially to Bruce Bliven, *Battle for Manhattan* (New York, 1955), 65–107. The old but still reliable account by Henry P. Johnston, *The Battle of Harlem Heights* (New York, 1897), contains information not found elsewhere.

37. GW to Lund Washington, 30 September 1776, *PWR* 6:440–43.

38. Burr is quoted in Bliven, *Battle for Manhattan,* 84; Ashbel Woodward, *Memoir of Colonel Thomas Knowlton* (Boston, 1861).

39. See GW to John Hancock, 18 September 1776, *PWR* 6:331–37, for Washington's official report of the battle. See also Johnston, *Battle for*

Harlem Heights, 44–91. The Knowlton quotation is in Bliven, *Battle for Manhattan,* 94.

40. *GP* 1:301–2, editorial note, nicely synthesizes the secondary literature.

41. General Orders, 17 September 1776, *PWR* 6:320–21. See also GW to Philip Schuyler, 20 September 1776, *PWR* 6:356–58, noting that the victory at Harlem Heights "has inspired our troops prodigiously." For newspaper coverage, see *Virginia Gazette,* 4 October 1776; *Newport Mercury,* 7 October 1776; *Independent Chronicle,* 26 September 1776.

8. A LONG WAR

1. General Orders, 21 September 1776, *PWR* 6:359–60.

2. See John Hancock to GW, 3 September 1776, *PWR* 6:207, for the order not to burn the city. See Frederick MacKenzie, *Diary of Frederick MacKenzie,* 2 vols. (Cambridge, 1930), 1:59–60, for an eyewitness account of the fire. See David McCullough, *1776* (New York, 2007), 221–23, for an excellent secondary account.

3. GW to Lund Washington, 6 October 1776, *PWR* 6:495. John Shy, "The American Revolution: The Military Conflict Considered as a Revolutionary War," in Stephen G. Kurtz and James H. Hutson, eds., *Essays on the American Revolution* (Chapel Hill, 1973), 121–56, argues that American control of the countryside, in which militia served as a roving police force, proved decisive in determining the outcome of the war.

4. Caesar Rodney to Thomas McKean and George Read, 18 September 1776, *LDC* 5:197–98; William Hooper to Samuel Johnston, 26 September 1776, *LDC* 5:245–49.

5. NG to William Ellery, 4 October 1776, *GP* 1:307.

6. See editorial note, *GP* 1:244–45, for the recommendations of the visiting committee. See *JCC* 5:808, 810–11, 842–44, for the congressional vote on the recommendations. See John Hancock to GW, 21 September 1776, *JCC* 5:230–31, for Hancock's assurance that the Continental Congress will provide whatever he needs; John Hancock to GW, 9 October 1776, *PWR* 6:515–16 and *JCC* 5:853–56, for the final vote on all resolutions.

7. JA to Henry Knox, 29 September 1776, *LDC* 5:260–61.

8. JA to William Tudor, 26 September 1776, *LDC* 5:241–43.

9. GW to Hancock, 4 October 1776, *PWR* 6:463; Tilghman quoted in editorial note, *PWR* 7:105.

10. GW to Patrick Henry, 5 October 1776, *PWR* 6:479–82.

11. MacKenzie, *Diary,* 1:64; Leonard Lundin, *Cockpit of the Revolution: The War for Independence in New Jersey* (Princeton, 1940), 157.

12. Committee of Correspondence to Silas Deane, 1 October 1776, *LDC* 5:198–99.

13. JA to Daniel Hitchcock, 1 October 1776, *LDC* 5:271–72.

14. Committee of Correspondence to Silas Deane, 1 October 1776, *LDC* 5:277–81.

15. Benjamin Rush to Julia Rush, 18–25 September 1776, *LDC* 5:198–99.

16. William Williams to Jonathan Trumbull, Sr., 20 September 1776, *LDC* 5:208–11.

17. JA to Henry Knox, 29 September 1776, *LDC* 5:260–61.

18. JA to General Parsons, 2 October 1776, *DA* 2:444–46.

19. JA to William Tudor, 26 September 1776, *LDC* 5:242–43.

20. William Howe to George Germain, 30 November 1776, quoted in editorial note, *PWR* 6:535.

21. GW to John Hancock, 11–13 October 1776, *PWR* 6:534–36.

22. Robert Hanson Harrison to John Hancock, 14–17 October 1776, *PWR* 6:564–66.

23. Council of War, 16 October 1776, *PWR* 6:576–77. A month later, on November 16, Fort Washington surrendered after spirited resistance. Greene had reinforced the garrison to 2,900 troops, of whom 150 were killed or wounded in the battle and the rest captured. More than two-thirds of them died on board prison ships in New York Harbor, quite scandalously supervised by Betsy Loring's husband. See GW to John Hancock, 16 November 1776, *PWR* 7:162–69; NG to Henry Knox, 17 November 1776, *GP* 1:351–52; and editorial note, *GP* 1:354–59.

24. See Charles Lee, *The Lee Papers,* 2 vols. (New York, 1871), 2:255–59; Thomas Fleming, *1776: Year of Illusions* (New York, 1975), 369, for an excellent analysis of Lee's arrival in camp.

25. Henry Steele Commager and Richard Morris, eds., *The Spirit of '76* (Indianapolis, 1958), 487; George Billias, *General John Glover and His Marblehead Mariners* (New York, 1960), 121. It is revealing that Glover thought of Lee rather than Washington for military guidance.

26. For different accounts of the engagement at Pell's Point, see McCullough, *1776,* 231–32; David Hackett Fischer, *Washington's Crossing* (New York, 2004), 110–12; Michael Stephenson, *Patriot Battles: How the War of Independence Was Fought* (New York, 2007), 247.

27. Joseph Plumb Martin, *A Narrative of a Revolutionary Soldier* (New York, 2001), 44–46.

9. POSTSCRIPT: NECESSARY FICTIONS

1. GW to NG, 8 July 1783, in John C. Fitzpatrick et al., eds., *Writings of George Washington,* 39 vols. (Washington, D.C., 1931–39), 26:104.

2. GW to William Gordon, ibid., 27:51–52.

3. E. Wayne Carp, *To Starve the Army at Pleasure: Continental Army Administration and American Political Culture* (Chapel Hill, 1984).

4. Charles Royster, *A Revolutionary People at War: The Continental Army and American Character, 1775–1783* (Chapel Hill, 1979), chap. 8.

5. *Connecticut Courant,* 13 May, 24 June, 29 July 1783; *Boston Gazette,* 29 December 1783; James Morris, "Memoirs of a Connecticut Patriot," *Connecticut Magazine* 11 (1907), 454.

6. Royster, *Revolutionary People at War,* 353–58.

7. Joseph Plumb Martin, *A Narrative of a Revolutionary Soldier* (New York, 2001).

8. Ibid., 249.

9. *DA* 3:184; AA to TJ, 6 June 1785, *AFC* 6:169–73.

10. Howe published his initial speech as *The Narrative of Lieutenant General Sir William Howe in a Committee of the House of Commons* (London, 1780). Ira D. Gruber, *The Howe Brothers and the American Revolution* (New York, 1972), 336–39.

11. *PH* 20:679.

12. *PH* 20:705, 723–24.

13. *PH* 20:748–49.

14. *PH* 20:753, 758–59.

15. *PH* 20:803–4.

16. *PH* 20:805.

17. William B. Willcox, ed., *The American Rebellion: Sir Henry Clinton's Narrative of His Campaigns, 1775–1782* (New Haven, 1954).

18. Ibid., 39, 40–49.

19. Charles Stedman, *The History of the Origin, Progress, and Termination of the American War,* 2 vols. (Dublin, 1794), 1:iii.

20. Ibid., 1:212–26.

21. Ibid., 1:230–49. For those interested in modern analogies, blaming the British defeat on William Howe is eerily similar to blaming the American defeat in Vietnam on William Westmoreland. In both instances, assigning culpability to the military commander obscures the deeper reasons for the defeat and the fatally flawed strategic assessment at the start.

22. I solicited the opinions of four distinguished historians of the American Revolution in response to this question: Would the demise of

the Continental Army and the capture of George Washington in 1776 have changed the outcome of the American Revolution? Edmund Morgan, Gordon Wood, and David Hackett Fischer all said no, though all agreed that the way the war played out would have been different. Ed Lengel, editor of the *Washington Papers,* disagreed on the grounds that Washington was indispensable and irreplaceable.

INDEX

ALSO BY JOSEPH J. ELLIS

AMERICAN SPHINX
The Character of Thomas Jefferson

Thomas Jefferson may be the most important American president; he is certainly the most elusive. He has, at times, been claimed by Southern secessionists and Northern abolitionists, New Deal liberals and neo-conservatives. Now, Ellis restores our most enigmatic national icon to human dimensions, with insight, sympathy, and superb style. Following his subject from the drafting of the Declaration of Independence to his retirement in Monticello, Ellis unravels the contradictions of the Jeffersonian character. He gives us the slaveholding libertarian who was capable of decrying miscegenation while maintaining an intimate relationship with his slave, Sally Hemings; the enemy of government power who exercised it audaciously as president; the visionary who remained curiously blind to the inconsistencies in his nature. *American Sphinx* is a marvel of scholarship, a delight to read, and an essential gloss on the Jeffersonian legacy.

American History/Biography

ALSO AVAILABLE

American Creation
First Family
Founding Brothers
His Excellency

VINTAGE BOOKS
Available wherever books are sold.
www.vintagebooks.com